PHYLLIS FRYE
AND THE FIGHT
FOR TRANSGENDER
RIGHTS

Centennial Series of the Association of Former Students,
Texas A&M University

PHYLLIS FRYE

AND THE FIGHT FOR

TRANSGENDER
RIGHTS

MICHAEL G. LONG AND **SHEA TUTTLE**
FOREWORD BY **SHANNON MINTER**

Texas A&M University Press
College Sation

This paper meets the requirements of ANSI/NISO Z39.48–1992
(Permanence of Paper).
Binding materials have been chosen for durability.
Manufactured in the United States of America

Library of Congress Cataloging-in-Publication Data

Names: Long, Michael G., author. | Tuttle, Shea, 1983– author.
Title: Phyllis Frye and the fight for transgender rights / Michael G. Long
and Shea Tuttle.
Other titles: Centennial series of the Association of Former Students,
Texas A&M University.
Description: First edition. | College Station: Texas A&M University Press,
[2022] | Series: Centennial series of the Association of Former
Students, Texas A&M University | Includes index.
Identifiers: LCCN 2021055983 (print) | LCCN 2021055984 (ebook) | ISBN
9781623499846 (cloth) | ISBN 9781623499853 (ebook)
Subjects: LCSH: Frye, Phyllis Randolph. | Transgender
women—Texas—Biography. | Women political activists—Texas—Biography.
| Women judges—Texas—Houston—Biography. | Transgender people—Legal
status, laws, etc.—History. | Law reform—United States—History. |
LCGFT: Biographies.
Classification: LCC HQ77.8.F79 L56 2022 (print) | LCC HQ77.8.F79 (ebook)
| DDC 306.76/809764—dc23/eng/20211230
LC record available at https://lccn.loc.gov/2021055983
LC ebook record available at https://lccn.loc.gov/2021055984

FOR TRISH

LET ME BE THE PHYLLIS THAT CRIES TO EMERGE.

Phyllis Frye
August 5, 1976

Contents

A gallery of images follows page 78.

Foreword

In June of 2020, when the US Supreme Court issued its landmark ruling in *Bostock v. Clayton County* that transgender people are protected from employment discrimination under Title VII of the 1964 Civil Rights Act, few people could rightfully claim more credit than a Texas-born attorney named Phyllis Randolph Frye. Although her name did not appear on the plaintiffs' briefs, the decision reflected a lifetime of Phyllis's advocacy, scholarship, and movement-building. Without her, there would be no transgender legal rights movement as we know it today. Phyllis's determined, decades-long campaign for legal and employment rights was the driving force behind the emergence of transgender people as one of the most important political constituencies of our time. As the *New York Times* noted in a profile of Phyllis in 2015, she is truly "the grandmother of the transgender legal rights movement."[1]

And what an unlikely person she was to play such a role! Born in San Antonio, Texas, Phyllis's early life gave no indication of the transgender firebrand she would later become. Assigned the male gender at birth, Phyllis was an Eagle Scout and head of the ROTC contingent at her high school. She attended Texas A&M University, one of the most conservative schools in the country. She married, had a son, and joined the US Army. By all outward accounts, Phyllis was on track to lead a life of mainstream masculine success. In the pages that follow, Phyllis shares the riveting story of what happened next—how this apparent paragon of conventional Texan manhood became one of the most influential transgender leaders in our nation's history.

But, to me, Phyllis will always be first and foremost the loving mentor who gave me the courage to be myself. When I first met Phyllis in 1994, I was just out of law school and newly employed by a lesbian rights organization. To put it politely, I was a mess. As Phyllis immediately recognized,

I was struggling with my emerging identity as a transgender man. I was deeply insecure and, above all, afraid to assert my identity publicly. I will forever remain grateful for Phyllis's unflagging support, which gave me the strength to not only come out publicly but become an advocate for other LGBTQ people.

From the moment we met, Phyllis recognized and honored my male identity without reservation. To this day, I can still see the look of warm approval in her eyes and hear her lovely booming voice saying, "Hi, guy!" Her confidence in me gave me confidence in myself. To her, I was the man I knew myself to be but had so much trouble showing to others.

Phyllis is a force of nature. She is an incredibly giving and, at the same time, relentlessly demanding mentor. Just being around Phyllis makes a person feel seen, loved, and validated. During those early years of my career, I noticed that Phyllis was especially supportive of transgender men, who then (as now) had considerably less visibility and social recognition than transgender women.

Right away, Phyllis pulled me into the orbit of her visionary advocacy to—as she put it—"put the T back into LGBT." After Stonewall, where LGBTQ people fought together against police brutality, the mainstream gay rights movement distanced itself from trans people. By the early 1990s, the separation was complete. Not a single mainstream lesbian or gay rights organization considered transgender issues to be part of their core mission. Phyllis was determined to change that, and she did.

In 1995, Phyllis convinced the Human Rights Campaign, the largest and most powerful gay rights organization in the country, to meet with a group of transgender leaders. Under her direction, we made our case to the group's powerful lesbian and gay leadership that trans and gender-nonconforming people were an integral part of their communities and that we should join forces in a united LGBTQ movement. Later that year, at the movement's hallmark annual conference, Creating Change, trans and bisexual people forged a new alliance to advocate for the inclusion of both groups in the larger gay rights movement.

Meanwhile, starting in 1992, Phyllis organized an annual legal conference where transgender lawyers and grassroots advocates from around the country first met and began to coalesce into a transgender rights movement. The mood at those conferences was exhilarating. As a young attorney, I was thrilled to meet both seasoned transgender elders and new advocates. Phyllis's standards were high. The quality of the panels she assembled was astounding, and it was at these conferences that I first heard articulations of the same sophisticated legal arguments that later were adopted by many federal courts and, ultimately, by the US Supreme Court in *Bostock*.

One of the enduring achievements associated with those conferences was the development of an International Bill of Gender Rights (IBGR), which still stands as the most definitive statement of the transgender movement's aspirations. From the outset, Phyllis recognized that the IBGR was critical to the movement's coherence and credibility and threw her full support behind Sharon Stuart, its primary author. And as the name suggests, Phyllis also understood that transgender rights cannot be separated from gender rights more broadly, and that the freedom and equality of transgender people are tied to the freedom and equality of women and all gender-nonconforming people. As its first plank, the International Bill of Gender Rights proclaims: "All human beings have the right to define their own gender identity regardless of chromosomal sex, genitalia, assigned birth sex, or initial gender role."[2]

In everything she did, Phyllis set her sights high and displayed what now seems like astonishing foresight about the future of the transgender and LGBTQ movements. Often at her own expense, Phyllis ensured that every session of the International Conference on Transgender Law and Employment Policy (ICTLEP, as the conferences were called) was recorded and preserved. Even then, she understood that what we were doing was historic and that, one day, future generations would want to document and study the origins of this remarkable legal movement.

Phyllis also understood that the strength of the transgender movement lay in its diversity. In her conference organizing and other advocacy, Phyllis insisted that our movement be truly representative—that it must be multiracial, include people from rural as well as urban areas, and recognize the multiplicity of trans identities. Long before the terms "gender queer" or "nonbinary" became widely used, Phyllis proudly acknowledged and supported people who identify as multiple genders or no gender.

As a result, the ICTLEP conferences were a lifeline for an incredibly diverse group of attorneys and advocates, many of whom built enduring relationships that laid a strong foundation for the transgender rights movement. ICTLEP is where I first met or really got to know many friends and colleagues, from legal giants like Jennifer Levi, Stephen Whittle, Elvia Arriola, Katrina Rose, Alyson Meiselman, and Kylar Broadus to political leaders like Dawn Wilson, Lisa Middleton, Jamison Green, Sharon Stuart, Martine Rothblatt, Jessica Xavier, Melinda Whiteway, and many more. Phyllis fostered an atmosphere that encouraged us to be our best selves and to embrace differences as a source of strength, not division. Like so many other transgender attorneys, I cannot imagine our movement without the relationships forged through ICTLEP.

In between conferences, Phyllis fostered camaraderie and networking through her "Phyllabusters"—email newsletters that kept advocates abreast of the latest legal and political developments. Phyllis also led the charge to persuade the National Lesbian and Gay Bar Association to include transgender attorneys, which the organization—now called the National LGBT Bar Association—voted to do in 1995. In 2001, the organization gave Phyllis its highest honor, the Dan Bradley Award, for her prodigious achievements in helping to forge a unified LGBTQ movement.

As a litigator and legal thinker, Phyllis has made unparalleled contributions to the transgender rights movement. On every major legal issue facing transgender people, Phyllis has broken new ground. She was the first attorney to obtain corrected birth certificates for transgender people who have not undergone gender confirmation surgery. She survived conversion therapy, and she was among the first national LGBTQ leaders to support the movement to ban it. Her classic law review article on transgender people and restrooms, first published in 2000, has helped thousands of employers adopt supportive policies for transgender workers.

In 1999, in a case that reverberated across the country, the Texas Supreme Court voided a thirty-plus-year marriage between Christie Littleton and her husband, simply because Christie was a transgender woman. In response, Phyllis supported transgender attorneys Alyson Meiselman and Katrina Rose in organizing a coalition of transgender lawyers to draft and submit a petition for review to the US Supreme Court. While the Court declined to review the case, many of the arguments developed in the petition proved critical in subsequent cases upholding the validity of such marriages. In 2015, Phyllis herself successfully defended the marriage of another transgender woman in Texas.

Phyllis also successfully challenged laws that criminalize cross-dressing, created questions to weed out jurors who are biased against transgender litigants, and developed many of the legal arguments that attorneys have used to show why antitransgender discrimination is based on sex. She was also the first national trans leader to demand that no trans person should be required to undergo surgery as a condition of legal recognition. To this day, her 1996 manifesto on that topic, "Freedom from the 'Have-To' of the Scalpel," remains a vital foundation of the transgender movement.[3]

In 2010, Phyllis became the first openly transgender person in the country to serve as a judge. On November 17 of that year, Houston mayor Annise Parker appointed Phyllis to Houston's Municipal Court. In recognition of her accomplishments, Phyllis's alma mater, Texas A&M University, has housed her correspondence and other papers, including proceedings from the ICTLEP conferences, in the Phyllis R. Frye Collection at Cushing Memorial Library and Archives.

In her personal life, Phyllis is living proof that a transgender person can have a stable, loving, long-term relationship. Phyllis married her beloved wife Trish shortly before coming out publicly as transgender. Their forty-seven-year marriage, ended only by Trish's death in 2020, countered the stereotype that trans people are unworthy of love or unable to form lasting bonds. Like Phyllis, Trish never failed to lift up those around her. Like so many others who had a chance to know Trish, I will never forget her gentle smile or the love and pride in her eyes any time she looked at Phyllis. In addition to her friendship, that is the gift Trish gave us: the assurance that a trans person can be so dearly loved.[4]

Phyllis Frye is a legal trailblazer, a leader, a friend, and most of all, a person who has dedicated her life to uniting the LGBTQ movement and ensuring that transgender people have a chance to be ourselves. These pages document her leadership and courage at a time when we all could use much more of both.

—*Shannon Minter*

Acknowledgments

Our immediate thanks go to Phyllis, whose generosity in sharing her story is as remarkable as the force of her personality, the courage of her heart, and the strength of her intellect.

Many thanks also to the staff at the Cushing Memorial Library and Archives at Texas A&M University, especially archivists Rebecca Hankins and Michael Jackson, who have done stellar work in securing, cataloguing, and granting access to the Phyllis R. Frye Collection, 1948–2016. Special thanks also to library specialist Vaprrenon "Vappy" Severs. We're also deeply grateful to J. D. Doyle, whose impressive archives at HoustonLGBT History.org have made our research much easier than it otherwise would have been, and to K. J. Rawson and his team at the Digital Transgender Archive, the world's top online source for transgender-related research. Librarians at Elizabethtown College in Pennsylvania also provided first-rate services, and reporters Lisa Gray of the *Houston Chronicle* and Deborah Sontag of the *New York Times* wrote excellent profiles of Phyllis that we relied on heavily. We also found a helpful source in Cristan Williams's work at TransAdvocate.com.

We're happily indebted to the many individuals who spoke with us about Phyllis, including Trish Frye, Ray Hill, Sharon Stuart, Martine Rothblatt, Riki Wilchins, Jessica Xavier, Susan Stryker, Michael Bronski, Gerald Sharp, Fred Biery, Jane Ellen Fairfax, Tricia Lynn, Jackie Thorne, and Cynthia Phillips. We're deeply grateful to Shannon Minter for writing a foreword that is both incisive and affectionate; his voice makes this book better, and we're grateful.

Jay Dew and Emily Seyl of Texas A&M University Press deserve our thanks for their early support, and we're grateful to the entire Press team for their work in turning our manuscript into a book. We offer special thanks to the sharp external reviewers whose critical comments helped us strengthen the content of the manuscript. Sharon Herr, a proofreader of proofreaders, graciously red-penned errors that escaped our best efforts. Sincere thanks to sensitivity reader Guthrie Blechman, whose incisive suggestions made this manuscript—and these authors—more thoughtful and aware.

Finally, Shea thanks Angela Tuttle and Drew Willson for editorial insight and thoughtful conversation, and Michael thanks Karin, Jackson, and Nate for all their love and support, and especially for their curiosity about Phyllis, gender orientation, and transgender history.

PHYLLIS FRYE
AND THE FIGHT
FOR TRANSGENDER
RIGHTS

Introduction

When the music teacher handed six-year-old Phyllis Frye a pair of sticks to play in the rhythm band, something deep inside Phyllis said *no*. She wasn't the kind of kid who should play the boring parts. She was a kid made for the tambourine or the maracas, something colorful that got attention.

When her second-grade teacher split the students into reading groups, Phyllis was assigned to the sparrows. On one level, she knew that was where she belonged—she was not a strong reader—but on another level, she knew it wasn't right. She looked across the room at the cardinals, the strongest readers in the class, and envisioned herself among them, reading fluently about Dick and Jane and their adventures.

Phyllis had a strong self-image from a very young age. She suspects this came, in part, from being the only child at home for many of her earliest years. Her brother Donald Jr., five years older, was almost ready to start school when she was born, and by the time her sister LaNell came along, five years after Phyllis, she was nearly ready to head off to school herself. She was a creative, imaginative child, and she was smart, but most importantly, she was loved. Her earliest years taught her that she was special, and she believed it.

When third grade rolled around, her classmates' favorite playground game was to throw a rubber ball against the school's brick wall. Whoever caught the ball on its rebound made the next throw, and the children jockeyed for that coveted catch. Phyllis wasn't very good at the game, but she longed to be. So she worked at it, playing every day with the other kids, pushing herself until she became one of the best at the game. Stumbling and flubbing didn't fit her self-image; being the best did.

When she started playing softball, she wasn't great at that either, so she was placed in right field. She worked hard. She persuaded her neighbor to play catch with her across the fence. Sometimes her brother would play catch with her too. Over two or three seasons, she improved enough to move from right field to center, and then to left field.

Throughout her childhood and adolescence, whenever she felt a discrepancy between her external and internal realities, she set about making a change. Sometimes the discrepancy could be resolved with hard work, like on the playground or softball field and in the reading groups. But sometimes it required her to argue for herself. Outside of home and close family, Phyllis was shy, but she pushed through that too, like the time her class had a spell-off to determine which two students would advance to the school spelling bee. Phyllis did not win, but she knew she belonged at the bee, so she approached her teacher to argue her case. She persisted until her teacher agreed that she could join the two winning students to compete at the school level.

By the end of elementary school, thanks to her hard work, other people were starting to see Phyllis as she saw herself: as smart, as a leader. By age thirteen, she was voted senior patrol leader of her scout troop by her peers. Finally, they saw what she saw: a determined, tenacious, intelligent person who deserved their respect and attention.

Phyllis never could sit quietly when the world saw her in a way she knew to be untrue. She had to fight it—to work harder, to practice more, to argue in her own defense. Her integrity—her honor—depended on it. Over time, Phyllis discovered one other way her internal truth didn't match how she was perceived by those around her, and that was in her gender identity. She worked to address this discrepancy too, but it was more complex, with greater disincentives and less social reward, and thus took twenty years to fully resolve. Still, eventually, through much struggle, her honor would lead her there—not only to the integration of the internal and external self, but eventually to the same kind of assertiveness, prestige, and leadership she'd been clawing out since her earliest years.

This is her story.

PART I
EMERGING

Chapter One

Confessions

Four-year-old Phyllis Frye was playing with the neighborhood kids when she spotted a teenage girl painting her nails. "Will you paint mine, too?" she asked as she approached the teenager's front porch. The teenager smiled, and for the next few minutes, Phyllis watched the girl brighten her little fingernails and toenails. It was breathtaking, and she felt giggly. But after bursting through the door back home, Phyllis quickly discovered that her parents disapproved. "Boys don't do that," they said with a sharp edge to their voice. Phyllis was dumbstruck—she had no idea why something so pretty could make her parents so upset.[1]

When Phyllis was born to Donald and Alto Frye in 1948, she was assigned male gender and named Phil. Two years before she entered elementary school, Phyllis realized that she didn't always want to act like the boy her parents expected her to be. She really wanted to play with other girls, especially her beautiful cousin, Margaret, who wore her blond hair in pigtails. A year younger than Phyllis, Margaret loved playing with dolls—their hair and bows, dresses and underclothes, socks and shoes—and with her pretend oven and cookware. Whenever Phyllis could manage, she slipped away from the gang of boys she was expected to play with and helped Margaret dress her dolls, host tea parties, and play house.[2] But danger always lurked nearby, and it was usually her mother who found Phyllis playing with Margaret's toys. Her mother would scold Phyllis time and again: "Boys do not play like that."

As she grew older, Phyllis also longed to dress like Margaret. She wanted to grow her hair long, wear Christmas and Easter dresses, and walk around in black patent leather shoes. Stiff suits, stiffer shoes, and slicked-back short hair held no appeal. "If only I could be Margaret," she thought.[3]

There was another girl Phyllis admired, and she even developed a crush on her in the first grade. She constantly dreamed of being just like her friend. But Phyllis still wore her hair short in elementary school, and at the insistence of her gender-conscious parents, she also made sure that the top of her "butchies," her white boys' underwear with the elastic band, was below her navel. According to her parents, only girls wore underpants above the belly button.

At the age of eight, Phyllis thought she had the perfect opportunity when she heard another cousin talking about neighborhood boys who had dressed in drag on Halloween night. Perhaps next Halloween, Phyllis would be able to wear a dress and patent leather shoes without her parents harassing and haranguing her.[4]

But Phyllis's urge to dress in feminine clothing was all-consuming at that point in her young life, and with Halloween so far away, she came up with a more immediate plan that entailed dressing in her mother's clothes while she went grocery shopping and while her father and older brother were away at work and school.

Phyllis's mother went to the grocery store often, sometimes every day or two. She spent most of her days at home with Phyllis and her younger sister LaNell, and going to the store gave all of them a chance to get out of the house. So Phyllis had plenty of opportunities to time the excursion: backing out of the driveway, heading down their street, turning right onto Barbet and then left onto Freiling, driving past Phyllis's elementary school, and then pulling into the H-E-B grocery store. Then they would head inside, shop for a few minutes, and go through the checkout line before driving back home. Satisfied that she had accurately mapped and timed the frequent outing, Phyllis announced to her mother that she was no longer interested in grocery shopping. Though surprised, her mother didn't put up a fight—probably because she was relieved to shop with only one child instead of two riding on the cart, bickering, and asking to purchase every snack in sight.[5]

One day, finally, when Phyllis was about nine years old, she stood next to the dining room window, watched her mother drive off, dashed to her parents' room, cast off her boys' clothes, and rummaged through her mother's closet and dresser for bras, panties, and shoes. The textures, the patterns, the scents, the garments themselves delighted and exhilarated her as she tried on one after another. She eyed her mother's makeup, longing to try it on too, but she knew it would take too long to apply and remove.

Soon enough, when she realized her time was running out, Phyllis took off her mother's clothes, tucked them carefully back into drawers and closet, and hurried into her own clothes. As she returned to her room, she heard the telltale sound of her mother's car coming up the hill to the house, the Chevrolet engine grinding as her mother downshifted. She had made it.[6]

Phyllis began to try on her mother's clothes every time her mother went out for groceries. Meanwhile, when she spent time with her fellow Cub Scouts and their den mothers, she would watch carefully for when the mothers might take off their shoes. Phyllis would try to find a moment to slip her feet into them without anyone noticing.

Phyllis continued to try on her mother's clothing and shoes regularly for about two years. She was well-practiced at it, but one day, when she was eleven, she somehow lost track of time. When she heard the Chevrolet climbing the hill, Phyllis tore off the clothes she was wearing, kicked off her mother's shoes, and scrambled into her own clothes. She heard her mother enter the house and walk down the hall, and as she entered the room with a questioning look on her face, she spotted the clothing strewn across the floor. Phyllis knew her burning, guilty face betrayed her. She held her breath and waited for her mother's reaction.

But Phyllis's mother, Alto, didn't react. She stood there, silent, not offering any comment on the chaotic scene or on Phyllis, shame-faced and flustered.

Alto was a homemaker with dreams of using her artistic talents in the professional world, and Phyllis's father, Donald, was an engineer who considered it his God-ordained duty to be the head of the house in their middle-class neighborhood in San Antonio.

Donald was an active Freemason and volunteered too much for Phyllis's liking, but he was otherwise quite involved in her life. He kissed Phyllis every morning before driving off in the family's red station wagon, and sometimes he took Phyllis to work and let her play in the laboratory. He encouraged Phyllis to join the Boy Scouts, and he faithfully attended pack meetings and pinewood derbies. He taught her how to ride a bike, fish and hunt, work on cars and make concrete, pray at the dinner table and pledge allegiance to the flag. He was a conservative Republican and a US Navy veteran, a Seabee, who educated her about the US military and its role in safeguarding freedom. He even made sure to take Phyllis to Gene Autry's rodeo when it came to town and, even better, to get the star's autograph. Phyllis saw her father as trustworthy and helpful, cheerful and kind, patriotic and reverent.[7]

But Donald was also unbending, particularly in his belief that he alone should be the head of the family and that he alone should be the bread-winner. Traditional gender roles were fixed in the Frye household, and Donald excelled at being the patriarch, especially since Alto did not resist his leadership. "They were just like Tarzan and Jane," Phyllis says, reflecting back.[8]

Alto was creatively inclined, and her passion, other than raising her three children, was for the arts, a love she passed on to young Phyllis. But unlike her mother, who preferred painting, Phyllis loved music and spent hours singing along to records by artists ranging from Bing Crosby to Ernest Tubbs.

When Phyllis was eight years old, Donald and Alto gave her a sec-ond-hand acoustic guitar and paid for lessons that included instruction in singing. "It did not work very well because the instructor kept giving me songs recorded by baritone men and my voice had not yet dropped, so I had to sing falsetto," Phyllis recalls. Phyllis loved using falsetto when singing high notes used by the groups and artists popular on the AM radio she often played in her room. "But my dad and brother were always giving me grief about it," she remembers.[9]

Alto's creativity attracted the admiration of her brother-in-law, who offered her a chance to use her artistic skills in his small factory, which manufactured Venetian blinds and shutters. He hoped to open a show-room to highlight his best products, and he offered his sister a part-time job overseeing the showroom. The tentative plan was for her to arrive at work after she sent the kids to school and to leave work in time to welcome them home.

Alto was thrilled at the prospect, but Donald refused. If she were to work outside the home, he reasoned, it would be a sign that he was unable to provide for his family. He also believed, as many others did in the 1950s, that a woman's place was at home, taking care of the children, while men labored in the workplace. He delivered a firm "no" when Alto told him about the opportunity. She quietly accepted his decision.

Donald and Alto were not regular churchgoers, but they made sure their children attended weekly services at nearby St. Mark's Methodist

Church. Phyllis looked forward to going, and she enjoyed singing soprano in the youth choir and later attending the youth group. She was also fond of the ministers who itinerated in and out of the church. Typical of Methodist ministers of that era, they convinced Phyllis, through their teaching and preaching, that homosexuality was sinful, and that gays, lesbians, and other deviants were destined for the everlasting flames of hell.

More often than not, the church seemed to reinforce the prejudices Phyllis was learning at home, where her parents, no fans of Martin Luther King Jr. and the Black civil rights movement, were intolerant of Black Americans, Hispanics, Asians, Jews, Catholics, and gays and lesbians. As Phyllis puts it, "I was taught racism. I was taught sexism. I was taught all of those things. I was taught that blacks were inferior and that there were only a few good Mexican Americans in San Antonio. I was taught the n-word, the s-word, and I was taught the pejorative phrase for Asian Americans. I was taught 'faggot' and 'queer.'"[10]

Before long, Phyllis joined her friends in hurling "faggot" at any boy they thought was gay, "sissified," or just plain weird. She also emphasized her masculinity in public, acting like the best boy she could be. She played second base in softball, though she wished she could be a cheerleader, and earned numerous Boy Scout badges and awards, though she really wanted to be a Girl Scout. She fished and hunted and was always the first among her friends to tell "queer" jokes. "I was good at being a boy," Phyllis says.[11]

During high school, Phyllis earned the Order of Arrow, became an Eagle Scout, joined the rifle team, and served as ROTC commander—and she dated a lot. In her post-pubescent years, she discovered, with hormones raging, that even as she felt like a girl, she was also sexually attracted to young women. This part of her life pleased her father so much that he offered Phyllis a pack of condoms; it was the manly thing to do. Though Phyllis was grateful for her father's thoughtfulness, she was too embarrassed to accept the gift. She did, however, welcome the opportunity to use the family car on dates. The station wagon, however uncool it was, afforded Phyllis and her date the chance to "go parking," as they called it then, and to engage in some "heavy petting."

With her masculinity on display for all to see, Phyllis made sure that no one would ever call her a "sissy" or any other name suggesting a lack of manhood. "I was so good at being a guy that I should have won an Oscar," Phyllis says.[12] "Her childhood friend Jerry Sharp agrees. "We were geeks, we took the top classes together, we read *Mad* magazine, we went to dances with our dates, and Phil told dirty jokes," Sharp says. "I just thought everything was normal, as in society's norms."[13]

But none of this relieved Phyllis's desire to wear women's clothing. She continued to do so when she could, also using feminine clothing, some of which she stole when visiting friends, to help fuel and fulfill her desires.

Increasingly, Phyllis felt guilt and shame—the church had taught that folks like her were the devil's deviants—and she experienced prolonged periods of feeling "dirty," immoral, and impure. She also developed deep psychological fears, like the fear of castration and the fear that her father would beat her mercilessly.[14] She even experienced pain in her pelvic area as she struggled with her desire to be seen as a girl and then as a young woman.

Phyllis's regular practice of dressing in women's clothing faced a significant hurdle during ninth grade. When she started the school year, Phyllis was 4'8" tall and about 95 pounds, with a size 7 foot. Compared to her peers, Phyllis had been small for much of junior high school, which made her a perfect target for bullies during physical education class. By the end of the year, however, she was 5'5" and about 135 pounds. And that posed a major problem: she could still wear her mother's undergarments, but she could no longer squeeze into her mother's size five shoe. Now a size ten, Phyllis needed to find another way to wear women's shoes. "Oh, it just broke my heart when I was about fifteen years old and I started growing," Phyllis says.[15]

During the second semester of Phyllis's senior year, in the winter of 1966, she returned home one day after school to find her father's car in the driveway. Immediately, she knew something was wrong since he was never home during the workday. When she went inside, her parents' body language told her instantly that *she* was the problem; they looked disapproving and uncomfortable, and this unsettled Phyllis. She held her parents in high esteem and shared the family values of integrity, trust, and honor. Besides, she was the family superstar. While Donald Jr. was struggling with alcohol and flunking out of college, Phyllis was an Eagle Scout and the ROTC commander of her high school. She had always relished her successes, and she wasn't used to experiencing her parents' disapproval.[16]

Phyllis's parents told her that Alto had discovered some of her lingerie in Phyllis's dresser drawer. She had telephoned Donald at work, and he had rushed home. Just as when she was eleven, Phyllis felt her own facial expressions and body language broadcasting the guilt she felt. She didn't know what to say. Finally, as her parents stammered their own uncomfortable questions, one of them asked if this was some kind of teenage experimentation. Phyllis recognized a way out when she saw it.

"Yeah," she said sheepishly.

"It was the answer they wanted," Phyllis recalls. They wanted to believe that her possession of her mother's clothing was anomalous, a passing incident. It was also the answer that Phyllis felt compelled to give as she searched desperately for a way to explain her action. She feared that if she told them the truth about the years she had spent sneaking into her mother's room and going through her things, about her irrepressible urge to wear Alto's lingerie, about her desires to dress like a woman, to be perceived by everyone as a woman, they would kick her out of the house, leaving her without a home, a family, or a future.

"Yes," Phyllis said. "It was just an experimental thing."[17]

Donald and Alto breathed a sigh of relief, and they accepted Phyllis's answer without pressing further. They dropped the matter and didn't speak about it again.

After this confrontation, Phyllis was determined to make a fresh start. Plagued by guilt, she swore off women's clothing for good. But the urge was strong and unrelenting, and within the week she was once again sneaking into her mother's room.

Phyllis felt alone in her struggles, and with good reason. As historian Susan Stryker details in her landmark book, *Transgender History*, cross-dressing came under fierce fire around the 1850s, when cities across the nation passed ordinances that criminalized cross-dressing in public. Stryker notes that while she is uncertain of the impetus for these laws, they might have been an effect of industrialization and the concomitant swelling of urban populations that provided social spaces where individuals felt secure enough to come together and practice gender nonconformity. Another possible factor was male backlash against an emerging women's rights movement that included calls for women to leave behind their oppressive dresses and begin wearing pants and other clothes traditionally designed for men.[18] While banning cross-dressing proved ineffective in many large cities, cross-dressers in Phyllis's world were invisible to her.

Still, she wasn't as alone as she felt. Had she done some research in high school, Phyllis might have come across one of many articles and reports about Christine Jorgensen, an army veteran who had returned from Denmark in 1953 after receiving hormone treatments and undergoing gender confirmation surgery.[19] After graduating from high school in the Bronx, Jorgensen served as a clerk in the US Army and received an honorable discharge a year later. She then traveled to Denmark, the birth country of her parents. Christine had learned that progressive doctors in the country had been using hormone treatments and surgery to help individuals like her, and she wanted the same for herself. (Such procedures were largely unheard of in the United States.)

In 1950, when Jorgensen was twenty-four years old, Danish doctors began to inject hormones into her body. It took two years for her to complete all of the treatment, including surgery. The US media had a feeding frenzy when they learned, perhaps through Jorgensen herself, about her successful transition. "Bronx GI Becomes a Woman!" blared a headline from the front cover of the *New York Daily News*.[20] While the *New York Times* was a bit subtler, tucking an Associated Press story inside, its headline was still a bombshell: "Bronx 'Boy' Is Now a Girl."[21]

Jorgensen loved the limelight, and she told her Danish doctors that she needed "as much good publicity as possible for the sake of all those to whom I am a representation of themselves."[22] Sure enough, thousands of inspired fans wrote to express their gratitude for her courage and to share their own stories of struggle and hope.

The *New York Times* reported on Jorgensen's return to the United States in February 1953: "Wearing a loose fitting nutria coat and carrying a mink cape over one arm, the blond young woman declared: 'I'm happy to be home. What American woman wouldn't be?'"[23] Jorgensen did not return to a quiet life in the Bronx but used her newfound fame to build a successful career as a lecturer and nightclub singer. One of her signature songs was "I Enjoy Being a Girl."[24]

Jorgensen never became a political activist, let alone one who demanded transgender rights, but Stryker argues that her "fame was a watershed event in transgender history," partly because it "helped define the terms that would structure identity politics in the decades ahead."[25] These emerging definitions, advanced at the time by Harry Benjamin, a pioneer in US transgender medical services, sought to distinguish "transsexuals,"[26]

which referred to Jorgensen and others who had undergone gender confirmation surgery, from "transvestites," those who practiced cross-dressing
but were not interested in surgery.[27] Despite Benjamin's best efforts, the
New York Times referred to Jorgensen in 1959 as an army veteran who
"professes to have become a woman in 1952 as a result of a series of
operations and hormone treatments in Denmark."[28]

Jorgensen "brought an unprecedented level of public awareness to
transgender issues," Stryker says.[29] There were other US citizens who had
undergone gender confirmation surgery before Jorgensen, but they had
kept their lives secret, far from the national stage. Jorgensen was the first
in the nation to reveal her transition in public, and the national media,
especially male writers for tabloids, were not only enthralled by her
shocking revelation but also captivated by her stunning looks.

While Jorgensen regularly appeared in the news for many years to
come, Phyllis Frye remained unaware of her and other transgender people
throughout her high school years. "I really thought I was the only one,"
Phyllis remembers.[30]

Though Phyllis utterly failed in her effort to give up wearing women's
clothing following the confrontation with her parents, she continued to
succeed at being boyish and mannish in public. She was certainly not
pretending when she became smitten with a beautiful young woman
during the latter part of her senior year in high school. "Sandy and I really,
really fell in love," Phyllis remembers.[31] The two talked of marriage, and
at least in Phyllis's mind, she and Sandy would enjoy married life while
Phyllis completed her engineering degree at Texas A&M in College Station, about three hours by car from San Antonio. Still, even with marital
intimacy on her mind, Phyllis didn't tell Sandy about wearing women's
clothing; she hoped that her secret urges would disappear when she was
married and enjoying marital sex.

Unsurprisingly, Phyllis's and Sandy's parents intervened and demanded
that the young couple stop such ridiculous talk of marriage. They urged
them to focus on their college educations without the baggage of a
serious relationship weighing them down. Phyllis understands her parents' concerns now. "It would have messed up my college, and it would
have messed up her college," she says.[32] She and Sandy broke up, and the
possibility of Sandy discovering Phyllis's secret didn't matter any longer.[33]

Phyllis enjoyed Texas A&M, where she had won several scholarships, and she wore her Aggie identity with pride. But it proved extremely difficult to wear women's clothes while living in a dorm room—roommates or friends were always coming and going—so Phyllis went home on weekends and found occasions to wear her mother's and sister's clothing.[34]

At Texas A&M, Phyllis continued to date, and by the end of her sophomore year, she proposed to her girlfriend Jeannie.[35] The two married in Phyllis's junior year, on September 1, 1968, despite her parents' earlier protests about the strains of combining marriage and college. Like Sandy, Jeannie did not know of Phyllis's desires to wear women's clothing, and once again Phyllis hoped that her urges would fall away as she started to have sex in a stable marriage.

Phyllis continued to benefit from her ongoing ROTC scholarship and was an active member of the Corps of Cadets, the Singing Cadets, and engineering scholastic fraternities, all while earning an overall grade point average of 3.2. With her focus on both college and marital life, she largely ignored the wider world of politics. She knew a bit about the Black civil rights movement, the assassinations of Martin Luther King Jr. and Robert F. Kennedy, and the increasingly loud peace movement, but she was mostly out of touch with national and international politics—except for the Vietnam War and the possibility that she would end up there as an officer in the US Army.

Phyllis had mixed feelings about Vietnam. Reared in a family full of military veterans, she was committed to serving the country through military service. But the war had frightened her ever since she had attended ROTC camps during high school, where her instructors, noncommissioned officers, shared graphic stories about the maiming and deaths of their fellow soldiers.

Phyllis's military career took a fortuitous turn when her commanders, with a badly mistaken sense that the war was winding down, asked her to stay at A&M and earn a master's degree in engineering. They thought Phyllis would serve the army much more effectively in the long run with a graduate degree that would supply her with tools the army needed for maintaining its infrastructure. Phyllis jumped at the chance, and while she finished graduate school, Jeannie worked at a local telephone company. Meanwhile, Jeannie became pregnant.

Phyllis and Jeannie lived in Bryan, Texas, near the border of Bryan and College Station. Phyllis regularly headed east into College Station for her classes, while Jeannie's job took her west into Bryan. Jeannie's schedule was erratic—since she was new on the job, she was typically given the shifts no one else could or wanted to cover—so the couple tried to find chances to reconnect, and they went out when they could. One day in late 1969 or early 1970, they went to see a movie at the Palace Theater near their home. Before the feature began, a preview played for the film *The Damned*, which followed a prominent family in Nazi Germany. "There was a lot of cross-dressing," Phyllis remembers, "which just freaked me out."[36] She found the experience of seeing people cross-dressing overwhelming, and she blurted out, "That's me!"[37] Jeannie was dumbfounded. In the conversation that followed, Phyllis confessed that she had hidden a stash of women's clothes in their attic and that she wore them in their home while Jeannie was away.

Jeannie did not take the news well. She thought Phyllis was mentally ill and encouraged her to seek professional help. Phyllis did not want to seek help, but she promised to swear off the practice for the sake of Jeannie and the child she was carrying.

Jeannie gave birth to a baby boy, Randy, in July 1970. Five months later, the family of three moved to San Antonio, renting a house just one block from Jeannie's parents while Phyllis worked to complete her basic officer training at Fort Sam Houston.

On one of many visits with Jeannie's parents, Jeannie and her mother were watching a talk show in the living room. The show's host was interviewing the guest of the day, Christine Jorgensen.

"I wasn't in the room, but I was listening," Phyllis recalls, "and I thought, 'Ahhh, so this is not unique to me.'"[38] For the first time in her life, at the age of twenty-three, Phyllis became aware of the wider world of transgender women. At last, she no longer felt utterly alone.

Phyllis's relief and exhilaration were subsumed almost immediately by what happened next: out in the living room, Jeannie and her mother began excoriating Jorgensen. "I was in the bedroom tending to Randy, my son. And I heard all the ugly, vile things that they were saying," Phyllis remembers. Phyllis knew that Jeannie was aware that she had sometimes worn women's clothing, which made Jeannie's reaction to the talk show all the more painful. The experience warned her of what would come if Jeannie and others discovered just how like Christine Jorgensen she was. In that room with Randy, alone, Phyllis vowed again to keep her desires in check.[39]

Phyllis's fear of rejection was so strong that she did nothing with the information she now possessed. Jorgensen had published her autobiography by this point, and she continued to appear frequently in print and on television, but Phyllis ignored it all. She blocked the star from her conscious thoughts and went back to feeling alone.

Meanwhile, Phyllis was offered an opportunity in her military career. After she moved from officer training to a specialty school for Medical Service Corps officers—she was now commissioned as a Regular (not reserve) first lieutenant—Phyllis's commanders noticed her degrees and asked whether she would be interested in a special position related to occupational safety. "Well, I had orders to go to Vietnam by then, so I said, 'Yeah, I'd be very interested in that. Where can I go other than Vietnam?'"[40] Jeannie was wary, given the ongoing tensions in their relationship, but the two discussed the opportunity and decided to put in a bid for West Germany. Jeannie had extended family near Luxembourg, and she and Phyllis thought it would be the perfect opportunity to visit them and travel throughout the area.

The family of three arrived in West Germany in late May 1971, and Phyllis began working for a sanitary engineering group that ensured US-related defense factories operated according to standards set by the Occupational Safety and Health Administration (or OSHA). She enjoyed the work a great deal, but the marriage wasn't going so well. Jeannie had noticed Phyllis wearing a pair of pantyhose under her pants one day. Soon after, Phyllis pressed her for permission to wear women's clothes while at home with her and Randy. For Jeannie, the thought of her husband dressing like a woman in front of their son was repulsive.

When it became clear to Jeannie that Phyllis's desires to wear women's clothing were not merely a passing phase, she insisted that Phyllis get psychological help. Phyllis went to see the army psychologist—it was all the couple could afford—and Jeannie attended the first appointment with her. By the end of the appointment, Jeannie had decided to leave Phyllis.[41] In the words of a US Civil Service Commission investigator who interviewed her several years later, Jeannie "stated that the final incident in her decision was when she and subject went to see the psychiatrist, and [Phyllis] told the doctor that [Jeannie] was to blame for his condition and unhappiness because she would not let him wear women's clothing around the house."[42]

In February 1972, Jeannie took Randy back to San Antonio, and the two lived with her parents while she sought employment. Phyllis agreed to continue receiving psychiatric care, and Jeannie and Phyllis hoped to get back together should the help prove successful. Phyllis followed through on her commitment and met with a psychologist who, to her surprise, suggested that since she was only wearing women's clothing in private, she posed no real harm to the military.

Nevertheless, given the marital crisis, as well as Phyllis's own hopes, the psychologist arranged for her to undergo drug therapy designed to rid her of her urges. Phyllis took the drugs faithfully, but rather than reducing her sex drive, as they were supposed to do, they made her sleep sixteen hours a day and left her vision so blurry that she had to get prescription glasses. As Phyllis recalled in a 1976 lecture, "I was a walking zombie—really, that's what I was."[43]

The psychologist then mentioned the possibility of administering electric shocks to Phyllis's genitals. This never happened, but Phyllis agreed to submit to hypnosis and an aversion therapy that employed repeated vomiting to eliminate or at least reduce her urge to wear women's clothing. "I went through aversion therapy," she said in the same lecture. "I went through hypnosis. . . . You go through this whole thing where you go home, you put on a pair of panties, you throw up. You masturbate, you throw up again. And you do this every day for three or four months. It's not really good for you."[44]

Soon, Jeannie filed for divorce, and Phyllis returned to wearing women's clothing on a regular basis. Jeannie also consulted with a doctor because of her concern about any lasting negative effects of Phyllis's cross-dressing on their son. According to a US Civil Service investigator's report, "the doctor told her that the problem was not hereditary, and that it possibly was brought about by a domineering mother and a passive father."[45]

Phyllis's army work was suffering, too, and when she voluntarily told her commanding officers about her marital troubles and habit of wearing women's clothing, they ordered her to undergo a psychiatric evaluation. She was hoping that her problems might lead to a military discharge that would allow her to reunite with Jeannie and Randy back in the United States. She missed them terribly, and she was lonely and depressed.

In March 1972, the army psychiatrist diagnosed Phyllis as having "Transvestism, chronic, treated, unchanged, manifested by the compulsive need to wear female clothing." The doctor added that the diagnosis "represents a character and behavior disorder," according to military codes, but that Phyllis's "depression, anxiety, and emotional liability have been greatly relieved since he made the decision to seek a route back to the United States to join his family." Most important, though, was the psychiatrist's conclusions: "This individual is psychiatrically cleared for administrative action deemed appropriate by command. The condition diagnosed above does not involve homosexuality nor [does] the individual's demonstrating the above patterns represent a sexual danger to others. It is further felt that consideration should be given to the subject's outstanding civilian and military record."[46]

Even with this conclusion supporting her, Phyllis struggled to obtain an honorable discharge. "I was there by myself, and I was fighting with the military because every level of command was recommending that I be given a general discharge," Phyllis recalls.[47] A general discharge would have indicated that her time in the army was merely satisfactory, and under these terms Phyllis would have been unable to receive some of the benefits offered to those with honorable discharges, possibly including the GI Bill. So Phyllis pushed back, arguing that she was no run-of-the-mill soldier—that she had a Regular Army commission, that she had an excellent record of service, and that she had received first-rate scholarships during her undergraduate and graduate years. Phyllis also threatened her commanding officers with the possibility that she would inform the US media that the army had let her go simply because she dressed in women's clothes in the privacy of her own home, far from work and never during work hours.

Phyllis's requests and accompanying threats eventually landed at the top of the chain of command, and the officer there finally gave her permission to resign with an honorable discharge.[48] It was one of the few battles she had won at that point in her adult life.

Before she was processed out, Phyllis had some vacation time left, and despite feeling low, she decided to take a trip for a bit of rest and relaxation. A gay bartender at the officer's club knew about Phyllis's case and suggested that she spend a weekend in Copenhagen, a city friendly to gays, lesbians, cross-dressers, and so many more groups outside the mainstream of society.

"That was a crazy trip," Phyllis remembers. "I got on the train and I immediately cross-dressed, while I was still in Germany."[49] Phyllis sat with a German couple. At first, it seemed like an unlikely pairing—conservatively dressed older folks across from a youthful cross-dresser—but the couple could not have been friendlier or more helpful. When the train conductor inspected and then refused to give back Phyllis's passport, the woman cornered the harasser in the hallway outside their compartment and chewed him out so thoroughly that Phyllis, who couldn't understand the German barrage, soon had her passport back in hand. The older woman and her husband just smiled warmly.

Copenhagen was everything Phyllis had imagined it to be. Dressing in her finest, she headed to the clubs and danced and drank with men who gladly picked her up in the early morning hours. It wasn't her first time having sex with men—she'd had a few encounters dating back to preteen experiences with boys—but it was refreshing to be with people who seemed so sexually free, and it was empowering to be desired for who she really was.

Still, the trip ultimately left Phyllis feeling empty. She missed Randy and Jeannie, and she wasn't eager to climb back into her military uniform on the way back to base. When she did, she discovered that her nail polish remover bottle had broken. There she was, in full men's military uniform, staring at her shiny red fingernails. Rather than appear freakish to other riders on the train, Phyllis decided to wear gloves the whole way back to base, even though it was July and the heat was oppressive.

Although she had told the psychiatrist that her depression was improving, Phyllis's mental health took another dive the following month. "It was the night before I flew out of Germany," Phyllis says. "I was eaten up with all kinds of guilt. I knew I was going to have to deal with my parents." Also looming was the very real possibility of divorce and rejection from numerous quarters. With her future appearing hopeless, Phyllis slashed her left wrist.

As she watched blood pour from the slash, she immediately thought, "This is stupid."

It was "stupid" because, in the deepest recesses of her heart, she really wanted to live, to be a father to Randy, a spouse to Jeannie—and the woman she knew she was. "So I clapped my hand around my wrist, and I walked over to the hospital emergency room. And I said, 'I need y'all to put me back together again.'"[50]

Stitched up, Phyllis walked away from the hospital. Thirty-six hours later, she was on an airplane back to the States.

Chapter Two

Becoming Phyllis

Phyllis returned to Texas in August 1972, just as the presidential election was kicking into high gear. President Nixon's opponent, Democratic Senator George McGovern of South Dakota, was calling for a withdrawal of US troops, faulting Nixon for executing a pointless and endless war. Nixon remained resolute in pursuing "peace with honor," and a landslide of voters backed him in November. While Phyllis was among the Nixon supporters, she still largely ignored the wider political world.

Phyllis left Germany with the promise of a job designing and fabricating artificial prosthetics in the industrial engineering department at Texas A&M. She had been an excellent student in the master's program, and one of her former professors was eager to welcome her back. Although she was excited about the job awaiting her, most of her thoughts during the flight home focused on seeing Randy and Jeannie again.[1]

Jeannie had mailed Phyllis divorce papers while Phyllis was still in Germany, and all signs since indicated that she remained resolute in her decision to end the marriage. But Phyllis was hopeful, and she went to see her wife and son immediately upon her return. Picking up Randy felt as good as she had imagined, and reconciling with Jeannie was as difficult as she had feared. Jeannie rebuffed Phyllis yet again.

With her left wrist still in stitches, Phyllis went to visit her family back in San Antonio. The reunion was tense, and as Phyllis unloaded all that had happened in Germany, her father was disgusted by the intimate details. He immediately stopped talking to her and expected the rest of the family to follow his lead.

Phyllis's brother Donald Jr. stood by his father while her sister LaNell did not immediately stake out any clear position. Alto played the role of the good wife, trying to soothe her husband, but because she also wanted to be a good mother, she spent countless hours at the kitchen table with

Phyllis, listening carefully and trying to figure her out. She encouraged Phyllis to seek additional psychiatric treatment and even offered to pay for it.

Phyllis rented a duplex on Mary Lake Drive in Bryan, Texas, started her new job, and quickly discovered she had quite a bit of free time after work. Spending every evening with her immediate family was no longer an option, and Phyllis looked for constructive ways to fill her hours, eventually settling on the many activities offered at nearby St. Paul's United Methodist Church.

St. Paul's offered Phyllis a safe haven where she could try to address all the guilt and shame she felt, and she threw herself without reserve into parish life, attending all available services, prayer meetings, and social gatherings. "I was a wreck," Phyllis says. "My wrist was still in bandages, and I was dealing with the guilt of my stitches. I was dealing with the guilt of being in the closet about my cross-dressing. I was dealing with the guilt of being a sinner. I was dealing with the guilt of the divorce."[2]

The guilt and shame served as fuel for Phyllis's participation in church activities two or three times a week, sometimes more. They also created the psychological conditions that made her ripe for the church's mission of converting sinners to Jesus—for turning away from her sinful sexual desires, as the church defined them, and toward a life of sexual purity. Desperate for even a bit of relief, Phyllis dedicated her life to Jesus in a conversion experience that left her feeling forgiven and wholly redeemed. Phyllis was now a Christian on fire for the Lord, joining millions of new converts who were part of the "born again" movement of the 1970s.

The enthusiastic Christian soon subjected herself to what Phyllis now calls "the Great Purge," a spiritually intense period that entailed throwing away all of her women's clothes, going "cold turkey," committing herself to a life free of sexual sin, and praying for Jesus's help along the way.[3] The Great Purge was conversion therapy designed to effect amazing grace; once lost, Phyllis would be found.

Around this time, Phyllis met a young woman named Trish through a mutual acquaintance.[4] Five years older than Phyllis, Trish was a music specialist in the public school system who had come from a dairy farm in rural Bryan, where her relatives were practicing Primitive Baptists, members of a socially conservative church that rejected any accommodation to the secular world.

Both Phyllis and Trish were dating others when the two agreed to get together in October. There were no fireworks when they first laid eyes on each other. It did not make for a "love at first sight" moment, nor was it significant enough for them to decide, right then and there, to date each other exclusively. But as both continued to date others, they found themselves spending a lot of time together and building a fun and meaningful friendship. Phyllis could not have been more pleased. Trish was not only smart and professional; she was a real beauty, petite and brunette, with a warm smile. She also complemented Phyllis's personality; while Phyllis was outgoing and brash, Trish was quiet and reserved, a classic introvert.

When she and Trish first met, Phyllis was still in the middle of the Great Purge, but in mid-November, she went to a lingerie store, purchased some of its finest bras and panties, and took them back to her duplex. Even while Phyllis felt conflicted about her desire to wear women's clothing, putting them on again also felt right, and this time she felt the need to share this part of her life with her new best friend.

Breaking the news to Trish proved challenging. Phyllis discovered that she couldn't look Trish in the eyes as she revealed her intimate secret. As for Trish, she was not a typical Primitive Baptist, and she told Phyllis that although she did not quite know what to think of the revelation, she was still her friend.

Meanwhile, Phyllis's inner turmoil continued unabated, and around this time she went to see Burns DuBose, a psychologist with an office in Bryan. After Phyllis explained her complicated situation, focusing on her faith-fueled guilt, the secular psychologist observed that his client believed in forgiveness for everyone except herself; while Phyllis extolled the forgiveness that Jesus offered even to those who killed him, she regarded herself as the unforgivable sinner. This point was powerful for the born-again Christian, but it was not even close to sufficient for the progressive psychiatrist. What DuBose really wanted to instill in Phyllis was an unwavering conviction that there was absolutely no need to be forgiven for wearing women's clothing or wanting to be seen as a woman by others. "There's nothing wrong with you," he told Phyllis.[5]

Phyllis had never heard such words uttered about any part of her identity, let alone the part that longed to be seen as a woman. Yes, dressing in women's clothing and dreaming of living as a woman had long felt natural, as if it really did fit her mental, emotional, and physical self-understanding, but the thought that there was nothing wrong about all this was strange and shocking—even exhilarating and liberating. When Phyllis had overheard the television special about Christine Jorgensen, it had been a relief to know she wasn't alone, but it was something different to hear DuBose say there wasn't anything wrong with her. For Phyllis, who had always been driven to excel and achieve, this came as an enormous relief and a deep affirmation. Hearing those words, grasping them, understanding them, and beginning to believe them gave Phyllis hope for a future she had thought impossible. Now she just needed to figure out what to do next.

Phyllis soon invited Trish to join her on a trip to the Jesse Jones Library at the Texas Medical Center in Houston, where the two spent hours researching and copying every article that *Index Medicus*, a database for journal articles on medical issues, listed on the subjects of cross-dressing and transsexualism. Phyllis identified and retrieved the articles from the library's shelves, and Trish labored over the flashing copier. Phyllis was never a voracious reader, but she consumed the journals for every tasty morsel she could find. Now that she was beginning to believe there was nothing wrong with her, she wanted to discover everything that was right.

Meanwhile, other parts of Phyllis's life still felt beyond her control. Before visiting DuBose, Phyllis wasn't handling her day job very well. She was an excellent engineer, technically able to tackle the projects assigned her, but the chaos of her personal life had spilled over into the professional. Plus, Phyllis was a talker, not inclined to keep quiet about her personal life, even at work and among colleagues who would rather not know about such things.

Phyllis scheduled a meeting with her immediate supervisor, Thomas Krouskop, to clue him in. Krouskop was surprised at the revelation but encouraged Phyllis to keep her personal life out of the workplace and to keep her nose to the grindstone.[6] Paul Newell, the chair of Krouskop's department, was not as understanding, and when he heard rumors that Phyllis was buying women's clothes at stores in Bryan and College Station, he successfully pressured her to resign.[7] It was the second time Phyllis lost full-time employment because of women's clothing, and it wouldn't be the last.

Krouskop was disappointed—he deeply appreciated Phyllis and her work—and he worked his connections to find Phyllis an open engineering position that involved designing roads, sewers, and drains for recreational land development. Phyllis was grateful, and she agreed that a new job in a new place sounded like the type of change she needed. But the job was in Pittsburgh, more than 1,300 miles from Trish, and by this time the best friends were in love. Concerned about living so far away, and wanting her as a life partner, Phyllis asked Trish to marry her.

Trish took a deep breath and asked for a bit of time; she loved this complicated person, but she wasn't crystal-clear about marrying Phyllis just yet. It wasn't quite the answer Phyllis was hoping for, but she understood all too well that her desires to wear women's clothing and to present herself as a woman in public might pose an insurmountable obstacle for the love of her life.

A few days later, Trish gave her answer, saying that if Phyllis's cross-dressing was the main challenge she faced, then the two had a bargain.[8] With the promise of Trish beside her, Phyllis packed her bags and headed to Steel City in March 1973.

In Pittsburgh, in an effort to blend in with her new colleagues, Phyllis decided to grow a full beard, taking on a considerably masculine look, not unlike the thousands of Steelers fans and steelworkers also sporting facial hair. By June, she was back in Bryan, not because she had lost her job, but because she and Trish were getting married. Trish's parents, delighted that their daughter had found a man with a solid job, hosted a joyful country wedding featuring barbecued chicken, a keg of beer, and chocolate cake.[9]

Phyllis's parents were also present for the wedding. They were happy to see Phyllis appearing so normal—so manly and heterosexual—standing next to her pretty Texan wife-to-be. Donald and Alto even opened their country home near Luling, Texas, for the newly married couple's honeymoon.

After a short stay there, the couple loaded a U-Haul with Trish's belongings and moved to a duplex in Pittsburgh. The migration did not go smoothly. Trish found it impossible to secure one of the jobs that the teachers' union handed out, Phyllis was working too many hours, and they both were homesick for the Lone Star State. Complicating matters yet again was Phyllis's difficulty in keeping her private life secret, as well as her colleagues' subsequent discomfort, which they also refused to keep secret. The predictable result was that Phyllis's boss cut her hours dramatically.

Still, the time in Pennsylvania was not without its personal benefits. In August 1974, Phyllis was surprised and excited to learn that Slippery

Rock State College, about an hour from Pittsburgh, was hosting a seminar on transsexuality.[10] Attending the event in a lavender and white dress, Phyllis made a point of meeting national leaders in transgender social services and medical care, including Zelda Suplee and Paul Walker.

A former owner and manager of nudist camps, Suplee directed the Erickson Educational Foundation (EEF), which was funded by the philanthropist Reed Erickson, a transgender man who had made millions in a wide range of businesses.[11] Erickson was assigned female at birth, and not long after his father died in 1962, he sought to transition with the help of Harry Benjamin, arguably the most important pioneer in transgender medicine in US history. A former colleague of the radical German sexologist Magnus Hirschfield, Benjamin had moved to the United States in 1913 and eventually oversaw progressive medical services for individuals seeking to transition from their assigned gender.

In 1963, Benjamin accepted Erickson as a patient and supervised the medical treatments that masculinized the millionaire and made it possible for him to live as a man for the remainder of his colorful life. Grateful for the transition, Erickson established EEF in 1964 and used some of its funds to support Benjamin's medical practice and research, including the publication of *The Transsexual Phenomenon*, a groundbreaking book in which Benjamin argued that gender identity was self-defined, and that the medical community was obliged to provide the services, including surgery, that made it possible for individuals to fully occupy their gender.[12] EEF also funded a variety of other organizations, as well as educational materials and seminars, all having to do with issues of gender and sexuality.

As EEF director, Suplee played a leading role in the seminars, including one at Slippery Rock State College, where she explained EEF's progressive stance on transgender issues and distributed EEF's educational literature. The foundation's self-published titles were impressive: *Guidelines for Transsexuals, Counseling the Transsexual, An Outline of Medical Management of the Transsexual, Religious Aspects of Transsexualism, Legal Aspects of Transsexualism,* and *Information for the Family of the Transsexual,* among others. Phyllis found everything helpful, and she took in as much information as she could.

Suplee also gave Phyllis a bit of direct advice about passing as a woman. Phyllis had dressed for the conference with Trish's help, but she did not find the results overly impressive. "Trish did her best, but God, I looked ugly," Phyllis recalls. Concerned about her appearance, as well as the possibility of ridicule or danger, Phyllis asked Suplee to accompany her to the women's restroom during a break in the seminar. Suplee agreed, and while they were there, Phyllis chatted nonstop, in her deep and loud voice, about "my wife Trish." Suplee saw it as a teaching moment. "If you want to quit drawing attention to yourself in a women's restroom," she whispered, "quit talking so loudly about your wife." The veteran and novice shared a good laugh over that.[13]

Phyllis also met Paul Walker of Johns Hopkins University, one of the EEF-funded schools that were researching and practicing gender confirmation surgeries. Walker was not a physician in the program, but he was a noted researcher and psychologist who offered counseling to individuals seeking to transition. Like Suplee, Walker gave Phyllis a glimmer of hope that one day she might be able to live the life she wanted.

Back home, Phyllis felt as if she had taken another critical step toward her ultimate dream. "I was also just glad to have gotten home, and not to have been arrested," Phyllis says. "Bless her heart, Trish was just scared to death when I went on that trip, but she knew that was something that I had to do." Shortly after walking through the front door, Phyllis sat down in the quiet of her house and penned a letter to Walker. "I'm a transsexual," she wrote. "Can you help me?"[14]

With Trish unable to find employment, and with the reduction in Phyllis's work hours, the couple decided to make plans for a return to Texas. Phyllis telephoned one of her former professors, William Davis, with a request for help, and Davis arranged for Phyllis to do a phone interview with S&B Engineers, which specialized in services for the petrochemical industry. Pleased with Davis's recommendation, as well as Phyllis's grades and experience, the Houston-based company offered her a job, and in November 1974, Phyllis and Trish packed another U-Haul for the long journey back to Texas.[15]

The homecoming was pleasant. Trish found a job as a music specialist in a public school, and the couple purchased a ranch-style house with a backyard perfect for gardening. Phyllis's father and brother drove from San Antonio to help the couple move their furnishings from temporary storage into their new home in the Westbury section of Houston. The American dream was finally becoming really real for Trish and Phyllis and their happy dog, Sugar.

Trish loved her job, and Phyllis enjoyed her work at the new firm. In fact, she appreciated her colleagues so much that she decided to evangelize them, to win their souls for Christ, during breaks and lunch hours. The engineers were not thrilled with Phyllis's relentless and insistent witnessing; nor were they pleased when she began disclosing that she felt most comfortable in women's clothes. That revelation made the conservative engineers squirm, and they were soon chattering among themselves about the quirky—and annoying—Jesus-preaching cross-dresser among them.

In the early summer of 1975, Phyllis also shared her desires with S&B vice-president Wallace Mauer, who replied by saying that it would be detrimental to Phyllis's career should knowledge of her desire to wear women's clothing become more public than it was. A few months later, to no one's surprise, Mauer placed Phyllis on contract assignment far out of the office, with Monsanto Chemicals, a sprawling company with a plant near Alvin, Texas. Phyllis's work there went well enough, but rather than accepting Mauer's advice, she shared information about her faith and clothing preferences with anyone with ears to hear. Although some Monsanto employees were tolerant of Phyllis's eagerness to share, others told their boss that they found Phyllis offensive and did not want to work anywhere near her.

If she detected her colleagues' disgust, Phyllis did not let it affect her actions. She let her hair grow, teasing it before going to work, and she plucked her eyebrows and grew her nails long, all of which made her appear much more feminine than before. To complicate work matters even further, a Monsanto employee had spotted Phyllis wearing women's clothes at a church banquet.[16]

By this time, Phyllis had begun occasionally to wear women's clothing in public. Having identified local universities as possibly welcoming, she put out feelers to see whether their psychology and sociology departments would be interested in having her lecture about transsexuals, transvestites, cross-dressers, and all related matters.[17] Several professors at the University of Houston (UH) and Rice University expressed an interest and invited Phyllis to speak to their classes.

One of Phyllis's main reasons for wanting to lecture centered around her desire to transition in a safe and slow way. She was tired of being "Society's Prisoner," as she signed a 1975 letter to Ann Landers, but she also wanted to be extra careful in the way she came out.[18] "I was not inter-ested in going to the bars," Phyllis says. "I was not interested in having sex outside of marriage. I was not interested in going out at night." Another major motive was to help make sure that "other people won't have to go through all of the garbage I had to go through."[19] Phyllis also believed that the chance to lecture—to tell her story aloud—would be therapeutic, a way to address all the guilt and shame she carried, and empowering, a way to understand herself more deeply. "It made me explain things to myself."[20] And, finally, there was one more motivation: "to tell people to tell their churches"—those that weren't welcoming to people like her—"to take most of their doctrine and to 'stuff it.'"[21]

On days when she lectured, Phyllis left the house with extra caution, hoping that none of the neighbors would see and report her to the police. "It was terrifying," Phyllis says. "The only two times I was really exposed was when I left the house and when I came home, because I would have to lower and raise the garage door. That was why we bought an electric garage door opener."[22]

But it turned out that Phyllis wasn't safe on college campuses, either, or at least at the University of Houston. As she remembers it,

> Some of the students who had come to the lecture said, "Why don't we go over to the university center and have some lunch?" That was fine, but I didn't pass very well back then. We were sitting down, we were eating lunch, and I was talking to the students. Sud-denly, the campus police just surrounded the table, and they took me into custody, to the police station. They were going to arrest me under the cross-dressing ordinance.
>
> The campus police officers who arrested me—you could see it on their faces and in their eyes that they thought they had a degen-erate, and it gave them a sexual high that they were busting a queer.
>
> I was terrified. I was terrified because I knew what would hap-pen. I knew that I would be taken to the city jail. I knew that I would be booked. I knew that I would be stripped down. Because I had heard these stories of drag queens who'd been arrested in the bars. . . . They were taken down and stripped down and made to parade in front of the jailers and in front of other inmates behind the bars, and just humiliated.

Although shaking inside, Phyllis calmly explained that she was on campus to lecture and asked the officers to contact the professor. The officers confirmed her story, and following the professor's request, they released Phyllis. "It was a scary time back then," Phyllis says. "It was a scary time."[23]

What made it even scarier was a conversation she had with Ray Hill. Openly gay, a longtime activist, and a UH student, Ray introduced himself after Phyllis had given a lecture on campus. Hill was curious about Phyllis and wanted to get to know her, and the two hit it off immediately, starting a friendly relationship that allowed the veteran activist to explain the local LGBT terrain and its threats.

In one of these early conversations, Hill told Phyllis that the vice squad officers had asked him, while he was sitting in a bar one night, for the whereabouts of "this Phyllis Frye person." Hill was surprised the officers knew about Phyllis, and that they knew the name she used when dressed in women's clothing, but he just laughed and shook his head. "Phyllis doesn't go to the bars," Hill said. "At night, Phyllis is home, watching television with her wife."[24] While Ray had laughed at the officers, Phyllis responded to this story with even more fear.

There was one other place where Phyllis felt safe while dressed in women's clothing in public—the local Resurrection Metropolitan Community Church (MCC). Founded in Los Angeles in 1968 by Reverend Troy Perry, a gay Protestant minister, the Metropolitan Community Churches has long been a safe haven for the LGBT community and anyone else open to the church's progressive theology and social justice activism.

Phyllis first learned about Resurrection when she told Hill that she had a lot of downtime on days when she lectured in the morning and afternoon, that she didn't know what to do during the gap time, but that she didn't want to get arrested for cross-dressing. Hill knew all the LGBT-friendly spots in the city, and he suggested that Phyllis hang out at Resurrection, whose pastor, Reverend Bob Falls, was Hill's good friend.

Phyllis accepted the advice and headed to Resurrection one day after lecturing in the morning. Reverend Falls, an openly gay man, warmly welcomed Phyllis, and after the two chatted about the church and its ministry, Phyllis walked alone into the church's plain sanctuary. "They had a small organ and a bunch of folding chairs and a makeshift altar, and the cross was made of two by fours that were notched and put together," Phyllis recalls. Standing in that sacred space and looking at the unadorned cross, Phyllis felt a deep sense of peace and belonging. "I felt safe for the first time in a long time, since I had started coming out. I just felt safe."[25]

Back home, Phyllis told Trish of her moving experience, and the two decided to attend Resurrection on a Sunday morning. They enjoyed their visit so much that they decided to attend regularly, join the choir (Phyllis sang falsetto), and go to social events, including the dinner where a Monsanto employee recognized Phyllis, who was dressed in her finest women's clothes.

The Monsanto worker did not keep that revelation to himself but spread it among his coworkers, adding yet more fuel to the gossip about Phyllis. Complaints about Phyllis became so disruptive that Monsanto's management called Mauer back at S&B with a request that he address the matter directly. Mauer dutifully made the trip to Monsanto more than once, strongly urging Phyllis to stop talking about her faith and her preference for women's clothing and to start dressing in a more masculine way.

Those efforts failed, and Monsanto management told Mauer that Phyllis was a "disturbing influence, spending too much time talking and visiting about things other than engineering."[26] Claiming Phyllis was no longer an effective employee at their job site, Monsanto asked S&B to terminate her contract and transfer her back to the main office. S&B agreed to end the contract, and Phyllis knew her job was on the line. "[R]ight now my job is in jeopardy—yes, this very week my job may be taken," she wrote in a letter. "The knowledge of my feminine self may cost me a year and one-half of managing over 50 projects. . . . It's in the hands of the Lord as to whether He has another mission or if my mission is still here."[27]

Back at the main office, Phyllis's two former supervisors told Mauer that they didn't want her back on their projects. In his meeting with Phyllis in June 1976, Mauer said that Monsanto had found her disruptive because of her constant Christian witnessing, that S&B did not have enough work to warrant her return to the main office, and that Phyllis's new appearance would not be acceptable to the company's conservative clients. Phyllis protested: "I've got a great engineering mind. I've got several engineering degrees. I'm a licensed professional engineer. Stick me in an office. I don't have to interact with people who don't want to interact with me. I can take a pay cut. I can do calculations. I can check figures. I don't have to go out to the drafting pool."[28] Mauer shook his head and gave Phyllis her two-week notice.

Trish wasn't surprised when Phyllis arrived home with the bad news. The story of hiring and firing was familiar by now, and she and Phyllis strategized about what to do next. Trish still had her job as a music specialist, but because Texas did not pay its schoolteachers a living wage, the couple needed Phyllis's salary to make regular payments on their mortgage, cars, utilities, and child support, among other things.

As the two sat at the table, racking their brains about their uncertain future, they decided that rather than subjecting herself to the same destructive cycle, Phyllis should be open with anyone who offered an interview. Given the rampant bias against transgender individuals, they fully understood that this strategy might lead to nothing, but with Houston having so many engineering firms, they hoped against hope that a firm somewhere out there would be tolerant and give them the stable future they desired.

When that didn't happen, Trish threw up her hands and encouraged Phyllis to transition, saying they didn't have much to lose and that Phyllis would be miserable until she did. Just hearing that suggestion from the woman she loved was at once exhilarating and frightening for Phyllis. Years of accumulated heartache seemed to disappear, and yet years of uncertainty and danger also appeared on the horizon. With gratitude as well as trepidation, Phyllis agreed with Trish: it was time to transition full-time.[29] Phyllis typed up a new section for her resume, detailing her current self-understanding:

> I am a transgenderist: an effeminate, heterosexual male.
>
> I have never been released for reasons of technical competence; rather I've received pay raises and praise.
>
> I do not seek publicity, but am forced to be very public due to the fact that I've been dismissed 3 times in 6 years because of my private life. I am not trying to embarrass anyone by my appearance as a woman (socially). However, I cannot hide any longer.
>
> Activities throughout my life . . . senior boots from T A&M U and the siring of a child via first marriage and chosen military, should indicate that I've fought all my life to be masculine. My embrace of womanhood in the social role is not a game and is not being treated lightly by me.
>
> By being frank and honest and by walking with dignity and self-assurance, I ask for, simply, a chance to be me.[30]

Before transitioning full-time, Phyllis stayed in touch with her mother about the struggles she confronted. She told her mother about losing her job at Monsanto and S&B, and about her and Trish's new plan that she present herself as a "transgenderist" when seeking employment. Perhaps most significant, Phyllis told her mother about her and Trish's decision that it would be best for her to dress like—to be—a woman full-time. Alto shared the information with Donald, and the two immediately headed for Houston.

When Donald and Alto walked through the front door, they saw Phyllis with long hair and long nails. She was not dressed in women's clothing, but it was clear to them that some sort of physical transition was underway. Phyllis explained that in the following month she would begin to appear publicly as the woman she was. Alto was silent, and Donald was livid. "If you do this," he said, "you'll be dead to me."[31]

Phyllis stayed in touch with her mother in the days and weeks following the conversation and sometimes wrote her painful letters, like this one from August 5, 1976:

> I enjoyed our conversation yesterday. I do know that you read and pray and really try to understand me. I feel you are earnest when you say that you still feel I am wrong. I know equally true when I feel I am not wrong. But before I debate, let us see what the price is to be paid.
>
> Because of disagreements over whether I shall adorn, house, encase, wrap, soothe, clothe, fondle (or whatever other word to decorate, cover, or play with) my penis in panties or in cottons, the following prices have been paid:
>
> 1. From age 8 to approximately 26, I had periods of self-guilt and/or "dirtiness" which would last from 5 minutes to several hours to two days on an occurrence of at least once a week. (That is, then, a minimum of 936 extra times of self-persecution over what is "normal" for a growing child.)
>
> 2. In addition, during those years I always felt different or "peculiar" and knew that I had a habit or a hobby which I could not share with anyone.
>
> 3. During many of those years, I had to sneak your panties and bras, or buy some and hide them while at college, or steal them

from the dirty clothes hamper when visiting friends, or hide them from my first wife. That is a lot of pressure on a person's mind who doesn't want to get caught for fear of punishment or ridicule.

4. I lost my first wife—no, that is wrong. I deliberately chose to give up my first wife when given the choice of wife or cross-dressing.

5. Similarly, I gave up my son for the freedom to cross-dress.

6. I gave up my first career in the army, as you know.

7. Searching for my identity, I prostituted myself to other men.

8. I did not attempt suicide. At least not for self-sympathy. I was mad—unjustly, I will admit, but even so the emotion was real at that time. I wanted to die so that everyone, especially those of #2 above who had never accepted me . . . could feel bad for what they had done to me. In short, I hated.

9. How many jobs now have I lost?

10. How many churches have I been blackballed from or asked not to join?

11. How many years have I been without you and Dad and Don and Lanny? I could fill five more pages but it should be obvious that I am not playing a game. But we have another price yet to pay—

12. Daddy has lost me because he has failed as a father and (as you stated for yourself) doesn't know whether he has a son or daughter. . . .

Well I've gone on and could go more, but all I say is this:
I'm OK.
There is nothing wrong with me.
I am a feminine, male person.
Accept me as a person. Let me be the Phyllis that cries to emerge. Which is better?

1. A son who is confused and who you rarely see.

2. A child who is warm, feminine, happy, and close by?

I love you all.
Please don't trade my balls for my heart.[32]

Phyllis was also hurt by her siblings' ongoing rejection. In response to her transition, Donald Jr. cited his religious beliefs and cut off communication with Phyllis. LaNell expressed grief and anger—"She said she was angry because I had, in effect, killed her brother Phil," Phyllis remembers—and similarly cut off contact.[33]

Phyllis thought it best if she used a letter to inform their neighbors about her plans. In the self-revealing letter, she sketched her plan to transition, invited questions, and issued an unapologetic statement that she and Trish had a mortgage on their home and were planning on staying in the neighborhood.[34] Phyllis then signed the letter with the name she had been using during her lectures and at Resurrection MCC—Phyllis.

At last, Phillip Randolph Frye was now Phyllis Randolph Frye.[35]

Phyllis put the letters in the mailboxes of their neighbors on both sides, as well as those across the street and behind their house. Penning and sharing the letter was not only her way of gently introducing her neighbors to the new woman they would see walking through the neighborhood, working in her garden, or whatever else she wished to do; it was also an attempt to preempt reactions of shock and horror.

In some ways, the plan succeeded. Everyone who received the letter learned helpful information about Phyllis's transition, and some even reached out to her with warmth and understanding. Two families living behind her and Trish could not have been more generous. One of them had two children, boys who were about three and six years old, and the parents made it a point to sit down with them and carefully explain that the man they had known as Phil was now a woman named Phyllis. "Well," Phyllis recalls, "what computed to the younger kid was that I was Momma Daddy, so he called me Momma Daddy. And the older kid, because he liked me before I began to transition, ripped up a bunch of his mother's flowers and handed them to me across the fence. Those kids and their parents were really sweet to us."[36]

The next-door neighbors on one side of Phyllis and Trish, an elderly couple, were a bit standoffish after receiving Phyllis's letter, but they remained civil and friendly as long as they lived there. A neighbor on the other side approached Phyllis outside one day and told her that he, too, had cross-dressed during his childhood. She had a vague sense that he still cross-dressed, but what was crystal-clear was that he understood her and welcomed her as a good neighbor.

News about Phyllis spread throughout the neighborhood, and then serious trouble began. One morning, when walking outside to get the morning newspaper, Trish discovered that someone had spray-painted "FAGGOT" on their driveway. She turned on her heels, retreated into the house, put the newspaper on a nearby table, and grabbed a can of paint and a brush from the storage area. By the time Phyllis asked what was going on, Trish was heading out the door on a mission to paint over the harassing word. The dark block she painted remained on their driveway for at least two years.

Bigoted neighbors also egged their house. "Do you know what eggs do to house paint? They peel it off, and you need to re-paint it. It was awful," Phyllis says. "Another thing was that some neighbors took a soiled baby diaper, put it in a paper bag, dropped it in on our porch, set it on fire, and rang the doorbell, hoping that we would come out and stomp out the fire and get baby shit all over ourselves." The perpetrators, who were most likely watching the scene unfold from nearby bushes, must have been terribly disappointed when Trish and Phyllis extinguished the flames with their garden hose.

One night a neighbor slashed the tires of Phyllis and Trish's truck, and on many nights, the couple received obscene and threatening phone calls. "Faggot, you're going to die" was a typical message. In Phyllis's memory, the calls came especially during the holiest days of the Christian calendar—in the Easter and Christmas seasons. "Of course," she adds.

Trish and Phyllis never caught the culprits; the cowards made their phone calls anonymously, and they painted graffiti, threw eggs, slashed tires, and set fire to soiled diapers in late hours on dark nights. But the harassment left the couple far more than frustrated; it caused them to carry out their lives with an abundance of caution. As Houston-based reporter Lisa Gray writes, "Phyllis and Trish developed survival skills that bordered on paranoia. They stopped giving candy to trick-or-treaters because they were afraid that if a neighborhood kid were poisoned, Phyllis would be automatically blamed."[37] Perhaps even more telling was the time one of their pet dogs died. They agreed, even in that sad moment, that they needed a friendly neighbor to witness the backyard burial just in case a neighborhood child went missing and their fresh mound of dirt became suspicious.

"It makes you angry, and it also makes you sad, and you become bitter,"

Phyllis says of the harassment. "There's just a whole range of emotions." They also worried that Trish, too, would lose her job, which supplied their only income, because some neighbor would inform the school board about a degenerate in their midst.[38]

Their fears were not unfounded. As Phyllis began to appear outside her house, some neighbors commiserated with one another about the disgust they felt when encountering her. Reporting on this in 1977, a US Civil Service investigator who was trying to determine Phyllis's suitability for federal employment wrote (using he/him pronouns to refer to Phyllis) that one neighbor "has been quite disturbed about the subject's open display of transvestism."

> The witness stated that the situation has been particularly disturbing to her because [of its effect on] children and she feels that seeing subject in this attire would be disruptive in their normal growth patterns. The witness reported that she has called numerous officials with the City of Houston and also officials with the police department to try to get something done about this situation, but was told that there was nothing they could do. . . .
>
> The witness reported that she felt that subject [Phyllis] was trying to push his ideas on the neighborhood and she found this particularly revolting. . . .
>
> Source reported that she has never received any of the subject's mail-outs or other items but stated that a neighbor received a tape one day in her mailbox which contained the text of one of subject's lectures at one of the universities in the Houston area. Source reported that she listened to the tape herself and thought it was disgusting. . . .
>
> According to source, the subject is a big joke among small children in the neighborhood and they often holler various slandering remarks at him when they see him. Source reported the subject gets out in the yard occasionally in very short shorts with his feminine attire and witness also finds this particularly disgusting.
>
> The witness stated that she has met the subject's wife, Trish, and really cannot understand why she continues to live with the subject. . . . The witness stated that she has seen subject and his wife both going out in the evening dressed up in feminine attire and cannot understand the situation at all. Source reported that subject wears very brilliant and bright clothes in walking up and down the

street and source feels that he is just trying to make a spectacle of himself and let his presence be known in the neighborhood. . . .

The witness reported that she would have no reason to question the subject's character, reputation, honesty, or integrity. The witness reported that she did question subject's moral standards because she felt the subject of transvestism was morally wrong and she especially resented the subject's use of biblical and religious material to back up his beliefs in the subject of transvestism. The witness considered subject to be healthy physically but she does consider subject to be emotionally unstable because she does not feel that a grown man would dress in feminine clothing if he were stable. . . .

The witness reported that in one of the tapes that she had heard, the subject pointed out that he did use ladies' restrooms and she also found this to be revolting.[39]

Other neighbors, according to the Civil Service reports, also felt discomfort in Phyllis's presence. One man felt that Phyllis was "obsessed with this desire to discuss and talk about the ideas of transvestism," and that she would rather "advocate the rights of sexual freedom" than "accept his responsibilities as head of the household."[40] Another neighbor, who wondered what type of places Trish and Phyllis went to, was concerned that Phyllis would cause a spectacle by visiting her at her place of employment. Yet another neighbor described Phyllis as "a mental case."[41]

Not long after Phyllis had begun to transition, Trish spoke to her parents about the secret she had long kept from them. The conversation did not go well. They expressed shock and horror, and according to Phyllis, the family "did everything they could to get her to break away from me." But Trish resisted her family and the beliefs they drew from their Primitive Baptist faith. Phyllis characterizes Trish's response this way: "She said, 'It's not fair. Phyllis hasn't done anything wrong. All she's doing is trying to find out who she is. And I know the way she's been treated career-wise, and I know the way she's been treated job-wise. And I know the fact that she's been trying to get a job, and that if I left her, she'd be on the street. And that's just not fair. And I'm not the kind of person who would just dump somebody on the street.'"[42]

Phyllis's grandfather, L. R. Dillon Sr., wrote a tortured letter to her in 1977. "You were the finest baby I nearly had ever seen," he typed. "Too, as a young man, you were tops all the way. . . . You started out right by getting a First Lieutenant's commission right out of school. . . . Your mind, abilities, education, family ties, and ability to work, your stature and appearance, would have made you a general in a few short years."

After declaring that he loved Phyllis and Trish very much, Dillon then took a sharp and hurtful turn. "What is wrong with you?" he asked. "Of course we would hope for you and Trish to see us, but as a man (A Man On His Feet) . . . but you will not be welcomed to come see us as a *woman*." Before closing, Dillon stated that he was an ill man, unable to "stand a severe shock," as would be caused by seeing Phyllis as herself.[43]

The cost of her transition was only beginning to mount, but Phyllis resolved to continue being the woman she was. "There was no going back," she says. "I was who I was, and I hadn't done anything wrong. I didn't do anything wrong—except hide it all those years."[44]

True to form, Phyllis's father disagreed, and he never spoke another word to her. As far as he was concerned, his son Phil had died in August 1976. There simply was no Phyllis.

Chapter Three

Sharing Her Story

After coming out to her family and neighbors in August and September of 1976, Phyllis sat at her kitchen table, with Trish by her side, and wrote another personal letter explaining her transition and offering conversations with anyone who wished to talk. She was determined to let people beyond her neighborhood know about the woman she was becoming; there would be no more hiding, no more secrets, no more fear of exposure. She was still afraid—of being arrested, beaten up, humiliated—but she no longer had to live with the fear that mean-spirited people would expose her secret. She had stolen their weapon and was now wielding it on her own behalf, for her own good.

Phyllis made hundreds of copies of her heartfelt letter and sent it to friends and acquaintances far and wide—those from high school, college, the army, and engineering. The great majority of letter recipients did not reply, and Phyllis was disappointed that only a handful took the time to respond.

Among the few who wrote back, two were Mexican American and one was African American. Her friend Jose Merla, one of those who replied, lived openly as a gay man. In her reply to Merla, Phyllis identified herself as a minority suffering from the type of discrimination known to Black Americans, using a jarring racial epithet to make her point: "It's a real bitch being one of the niggers of this society," she wrote.[1]

A close friend from Texas A&M also sent Phyllis a thoughtful reply. "As a friend, I encouraged our camaraderie in the Corps and the Singing Cadets, and know of nothing that can change what was," wrote Mark Satterwhite. "I must note here, however, that I have not seen you since 1970–71, and can only assume you are basically the same 'ol Phil, in light of the shifts and upheavals in your life, and that nothing irreparably traumatic has occurred to alter your basic personality. All of this comes down to one fundamental fact: We are still friends insofar as our common interests are concerned, i.e., our past good times and love for A&M."[2]

Not everyone was as kind, and the director of the Singing Cadets at A&M had a far different reaction. "I am not able to emotionally or intellectually accept you as Phyllis," he wrote. "As you know, at the end of each of our major programs, we invite former Singing Cadets to come on stage to join us in the Benediction. As a former Singing Cadet, Phil (Fish) Frye, the guy we knew, is welcome to join us. However, Phyllis Frye is a stranger to us, and is not a former Singing Cadet, and therefore would not be welcomed on stage."[3]

A number of Phyllis's Christian friends wrote with warnings that her transition was contrary to God's design. Phyllis should revert back to Phil, they counseled, assume the headship of his household, and be the man God had created him to be. Some pointed to the threat of Armageddon and the pending destruction of the unrighteous, including, presumably, an unrepentant Phyllis Frye.[4]

Meanwhile, Phyllis continued to share her story with university students. She had been lecturing since 1975, and by the time of her transition, she had already spoken to more than 2,000 students.[5] Lecturing gave Phyllis a positive outlet, and it offered her the chance to work on presenting herself as the woman she was. In preparation for the talks, she often made appointments at Bill and David's Beauty Salon, or Flair Beauty Salon, and thoroughly enjoyed the luxurious process of getting her hair cut and styled.

Like the letters she penned, her coming-out talks in the summer and fall of 1976 were intense and revealing, offering insight into her deepest feelings. In a lecture she delivered at the University of Houston shortly after her transition, she said: "I put on my skirts five weeks ago, and I have not taken them off except for two occasions. During the past five weeks, I have felt normal for the first time in 28 years."[6] Frank and open, she even offered intimate details about her sexual practices, which some students no doubt found riveting.

Phyllis invited the students to take out a blank piece of paper from their notebooks, write down any question they wanted to ask, and send their anonymous questions to the front of the class, where she would read them aloud and offer her answers. Some of the questions showed nonjudgmental curiosity. One student asked, "Do you wear women's clothes when making love to your wife?" Another wondered, "When you have sexual intercourse with a man, how do you achieve orgasm?"[7] Still another gently asked what Phyllis thought about the rights of women who did not want to share a public restroom with her.

Other questions seemed more like statements expressing negative value judgments: "Don't you feel incomplete by not having the real equipment a woman has?" "How much time does this drag trip take up?" "You really don't sound like a woman at all." "Why did (or do) you *tell* your work supervisor that you are a cross-dresser? Is it a need you have to be punished?" "It is obvious you are not a true Christian, so what church is it that accepts you?"[8]

While she was glad to answer questions, Phyllis most relished telling the story of becoming herself. The host professors at Rice University and the University of Houston sent Phyllis warm notes after she lectured in their classes, and one that she especially appreciated came from renowned Rice sociologist William Martin, who described her visit as an "excellent educational experience."[9] Student evaluations of Phyllis's lectures weren't as unqualified in their praise; although they were mostly favorable, they also included accusations that she was seeking publicity and being driven by hatred. "He cracked once and will probably crack again and bounce back into men's clothes," wrote one student. "I think he was nuts," said another.[10]

Looking back on her early talks, Phyllis now shudders at some of the personal revelations. Released from the pressures of secrecy, though, she was letting her entire life pour out.

Phyllis did not like to lose. There had been some past battles that she deemed not worth fighting, but there had also been worthy battles that she simply chose not to fight, at least directly and immediately. The most emotionally wrenching of these battles were about her son, Randy.

In February 1976, about six months before transitioning full-time, Phyllis traveled to San Antonio for a scheduled visit. She had been visiting her son regularly since returning from Germany, and she treasured their times together. But the February visit proved troubling.

When Jeannie answered the door, Phyllis detected a sense of shock on her otherwise kind face. It soon became clear that the reason was Phyllis's evolving appearance; her hair was teased, her nails long, and her eyebrows plucked. To Jeannie's horror, Phyllis appeared overly feminine, altogether unlike the man she had married, the man with whom she had given birth to Randy, the man who not long ago was sporting a full beard, the man employed in the masculine field of civil engineering. Little Randy, just shy of six years old, stood quietly next to his mother, not sure what to make of his father's new look. As Phyllis recalled in 1990, Randy "became puzzled by my appearance and his mother was becoming very nervous when I visited."[11] Jeannie was "nervous" partly because she imagined that Phyllis's feminine appearance would negatively affect their son's development.

Phyllis could not deny the uncertainty in Randy, as well as the concern in Jeannie, and after she left their home, she spent a lot of time thinking and praying about what to do. Should she continue to visit Randy, even though the young boy was confused about Phyllis's evolving appearance? Should she dismiss Jeannie's concerns? Asking for full custody seemed far-fetched, but should she consult an attorney about seeking shared custody, or at least an ensured right to visitation?

The answers to these questions were not immediately evident, but when Phyllis decided on which action to take, she moved forward with as much confidence as she could muster. As Phyllis characterized this in 1990, "I made a decision. I would give my son and his mother all the space they needed to come to terms at their own speed with who I was."[12] Phyllis committed to staying away from her son, not just for a week or two, or a month or two, or a year or two, but indefinitely, until that time when the six-year-old boy could "come to terms" with the woman Phyllis was becoming, whenever that might be.

Phyllis recognized the monumental risk of her decision—the very real possibility that Randy would feel abandoned, leading to irreparable harm to his developing personality. Still, while she could not be sure, she thought the sacrifice best, trusting that by continuing to pay child support, about $150 per month in 1976, and writing Randy once a month, letting him know how much she loved him, Randy would grow to know that Phyllis was always nearby, or at least a phone call or a letter away. Fighting Jeannie did not seem worth the pain it would cause everyone, so Phyllis let them both go, free to decide whether or not to accept her.

Meanwhile, Phyllis prepared for a different set of fights on a much less wrenching front. In the past, she had caved to pressure from employers, running and hiding when she was fired for wearing women's clothing. But those days were now long gone. The Phyllis who emerged in 1976 was a transgender warrior, determined to prevail over anyone who sought to confine her to second-class citizenship.

In early December 1976, after exhausting her options in the job search, Phyllis filed two claims with the Equal Employment Opportunity Commission (EEOC)—one against S&B Engineers and the other against Monsanto Chemical Corporation—stating that she was the victim of sex discrimination under Title VII of the 1964 Civil Rights Act. Predictably, S&B and Monsanto balked at Phyllis's EEOC claim and refused to settle.

Even worse, the EEOC decided not to advance her case, most likely because of a Ninth Circuit Court ruling in *Holloway v. Arthur Andersen & Co.*, which stated that transgender individuals were not protected under Title VII's reference to "sex." The EEOC informed Phyllis that while her employers had indeed discriminated against her, it was not illegal for them to have done so, and that although the Commission was unable to represent her, she now had the opportunity, on her own, to pursue additional legal action against Monsanto and S&B.

In an attempt to choose her battles wisely, Phyllis turned her attention away from the discrimination cases to the more immediate challenges of securing unemployment compensation—and the elusive job. With these on her mind, she regularly showed up at the Texas Employment Commission (TEC), where she had first filed her claim for unemployment compensation just one day after leaving her job with S&B.

"S&B did not fight my unemployment claim," Phyllis recalls. "That was the one decent thing they did." But despite the firm's willingness to pay her unemployment compensation, a TEC referee ruled against her a month later, claiming that she had been fired for misconduct. Phyllis wasn't surprised: "The referee never came out and said, 'You're a goddam faggot.' He was professional enough not to give me anything to use against him. But it was very obvious that he wasn't going to help me in any way because he didn't think I deserved it. I could just tell from his body language."[13]

The denial of compensation meant she could not collect the forty-two dollars a week due her with an approved application, a loss that placed significant stress on the skeletal family budget. Phyllis complained about the decision whenever she moved in and around the expansive network she was building among local Democratic activists and gay and lesbian friends. Her constant chatter paid off when local attorney and friend,

Frankie Washington, a former TEC referee, lobbied his former colleagues and helped Phyllis win her appeal more than a year later. That sweet victory resulted in a barrage of checks in her mailbox, and she and Trish were delighted as forty-two dollar sums arrived here and there, sometimes alone, sometimes in a bundle of three or as many as six checks.

But Phyllis was still unemployed, and she was so desperate for a job that she considered selling cutlery. "I really got pissed because I did an interview to sell cutlery door to door, and the son-of-a-bitch said he'd hire me if I dressed like a man," she remembers. "I told him to 'go fuck yourself.' What else are you gonna do? He was very condescending, and he was making fun of the way I presented myself, and I was doing the best I could."

Phyllis also turned to the federal government for employment, submitting her application through the US Civil Service Commission (CSC). While she was hoping for an engineering job, especially one with the US Army Corps of Engineers, she was willing to accept whatever the government might have offered her. "I didn't care," she says. "I just wanted a job." But the government was not so inclined.

On July 3, 1975, the CSC had announced new rules stating that homosexuals—gays and lesbians—were not to be barred from federal employment because of their sexuality.[14] With this new ruling, gays and lesbians experienced some relief in their efforts to secure employment, although biases against them did not disappear, but one group of people remained unprotected—transgender men and women, including Phyllis R. Frye.

In October 1976, Phyllis submitted applications for federal employment at CSC offices in Oklahoma City and Dallas. Although she applied as "Phillip R. Frye"—she had not yet legally changed her name—she laid herself bare in the forms, revealing that "being a transvestite" had led to firings or resignations from her past places of employment. She also emphasized that the references listed in her applications were all aware of her identity as a "transvestite." "Now, hopefully, I can get about the business of working and trying to make a living without fear of job loss for other reasons than my professional performance," she wrote.[15]

But the federal government did not turn out to be a willing partner. More than a year after Phyllis had submitted her application, Thomas Sandow, chief of CSC's division of adjudication, began his letter with the greeting "Dear Mr. Frye," even though he was well aware that Phyllis had changed her legal name from Phillip Randolph Frye to Phyllis Randolph Frye on May 4, 1977.

Sandow's letter summarized and analyzed investigations that CSC had conducted in response to Phyllis's disclosure of "transvestism" in her application. Since Phyllis had gained access to the investigation files in November, she was familiar with some of the contents of Sandow's letter, but she found his characterizations about her "condition," as he put it, personally painful as she pored over them. Especially cutting were Sandow's words about her neighbors, as well as his evaluative conclusions:

> Investigation in the area of your current residence discloses that you have become a disruptive influence since you began openly cross dressing in public and parading in short shorts, dresses and other female attire. You reportedly use every opportunity to try and influence neighbors and associates to accept you as a lady and have gone so far as to distribute unsolicited tape recordings, of lectures you have given on the subject of transvestism, in neighbors' mailboxes. You also have attempted to persuade neighbors to listen to radio talk shows where you discuss transvestism. You have notified them in person and by telephoning them, even though they have expressed no interest in the subject. Additionally, children in the neighborhood call you slanderous names and make fun of you openly because of your manner of dress and the parents of older children have grave reservations about your presence in the neighborhood and the influence you might have on their children. You reportedly seem to be obsessed with the desire to discuss and talk about the ideas of transvestism, and to force not only your manner of dress, but also your ideas and beliefs about the subject on your neighbors and associates. Many of them resent this and are uncomfortable in your presence.
>
> In addition, at meetings of a society of professional civil engineers, where you have appeared in feminine attire, those around you have reportedly been uncomfortable in your presence and have subsequently made cutting and kidding remarks about you.
>
> Matters mentioned above reflect a pattern of unorthodox practices of your desire to impersonate the opposite sex while maintaining your male identity. The evidence indicates that you have made a public demonstration of such beliefs and desires to the extent that

this has had an adverse effect on your employability in the past, and can reasonably be expected to interfere with your ability to be a satisfactory employee in the future.

Under the provisions of Title 5, Code of Federal Regulations, Section 731.202 (b) (1) and (2), delinquency or misconduct in prior employment and criminal, dishonest, infamous or notoriously disgraceful conduct, individually or collectively, may be considered a basis for disqualification of an applicant for a position in the competitive Federal service.

You are being afforded this opportunity to show cause why the Commission should not rate your October 28, 1976, applications . . . ineligible because of your conduct and actions in your employment and personal life which have adversely affected your reputation among co-workers, neighbors and associates.[16]

Beyond being stung by the biased language of the letter, Phyllis was furious that Sandow omitted all positive findings from the investigation. For example, he did not report that Phyllis's colleagues at the American Cancer Society, where she regularly volunteered, were comfortable working with her and that no one there had complained about her use of the women's restroom or her talk about wearing women's clothing.

The CSC administrator also failed to acknowledge that Professor Krouskop at Texas A&M never felt any discomfort in her presence, even when he knew details about her cross-dressing, and that he considered her emotionally stable. Nor did Sandow reference Professor Chad Gordon of Rice University, who believed that discrimination against Phyllis was similar to racial discrimination, and that her presence in a work environment "would cause much less disturbance than a female who dressed seductively or a male who tried to behave like a stud and pursue women in the office." In Gordon's assessment, Phyllis "only wanted to be left alone and would do an excellent job for anyone that would hire him."[17]

Sandow also omitted the words of the president of the local society of engineers, who felt "compassion" toward Phyllis and believed she "should be given a chance to perform and see if she could actually do the work." The president also did not find Phyllis to be a "crusader"; when she did talk of her preference for feminine clothing, he said, she "will back off if the person appears to be offended and . . . does not try to push his beliefs on anyone who will not listen to them."[18]

Finally, Sandow's bias showed in his utter failure to acknowledge that Phyllis's ex-wife Jeannie recommended her for federal employment, and that the great majority of individuals interviewed by CSC did the same.

Phyllis was so angered and upset by Sandow's letter that she replied with a nine-page, point-by-point rebuttal that included the following:

> When I returned home and read your letter, I was visibly dismayed. The dismay was not over the seeming refusal of employment. The dismay was then and is still, as I write to you, that you, Thomas Sandow, a person who knows only some things about me, but who doesn't really know me, writes in a disgust-filled manner while exercising an administrative duty. I am not worthy of the extreme dislike which glares out at me from your letter. Once again, I have been prejudged and therefore misjudged. . . .
>
> Your salutation began as "Dear Mr. Frye." Why? Is to call me Mr., and add to those many people who already have and often do remind me that I am a freak in this society, a nice thing to do? Yes, it did hurt my feelings. Why did you do that? . . .
>
> Yes, I read the S&B investigation. . . . Knowledge of transvestism did not affect my effectiveness. Coworkers' bigotry affected their effectiveness to allow my presence, just as surely as in days past when being black affected the effectiveness of the work atmosphere. . . .
>
> The ladies' restroom [issue that you identified] has been over-exaggerated. To begin with, I have to use *a* restroom. As a male-woman, I tried using the men's and could feel the tension, hostility and insecurity of these men. So I began using the women's, where—as a woman—I belong. It is a very complicated process, which involves walking in, moving to a private stall, closing the stall door, performing a biological function, washing my hands at the sink, checking my hair and makeup and walking out. I've done it consistently now since 13 Sep 1976, when I made the social-gender change to woman, without incident. . . .
>
> Paragraph 5 [of your letter] is the neighborhood, more aptly named "Harper Valley" after the pop song of several years ago. In the first place, I don't parade in short shorts. I don't own any short shorts. Whereas my neighbor wears his jeans so low in the spring and summer while puttering around his yard that my spouse and I can see the cleavage of his buttocks. We thought it nice for the neighbors to not accuse us of smoking pot since some of them do. One even smuggled laetrile while it was illegal. . . .

I'm uncertain as to why some parents of older children have grave reservations about us. We have not instigated, but instead have been on the receiving end of the burned excrement at our front porch, the unburned excrement, the eggs (which have ruined the painting on the house which I did last summer while I was supposedly "parading") . . . the broken light bulbs in our driveway, the slanderous telephone calls, and the nice (?) kids who drive onto our yard at night and spin their tires to "plow" our yard. I ask you—who is really sick?

There are many reasons for what you call influencing the neighbors. Many of the Houston television stations have conducted slanted campaigns to portray homosexuality incorrectly. I am not homosexual, but face the same ignorance and stereotyping. Also, shortly before I became Phyllis, there was an outbreak of child molesting (by heterosexuals). I feared a possible witch-hunt syndrome if I had not been totally open. . . .

I have been neither delinquent nor guilty of misconduct. I am not a criminal, my honesty is what many complain of, I'm not validly infamous nor do I seek notoriously disgraceful conduct. . . .

I am open to and welcome further investigation. I've nothing to hide and am eager to end my ostracism. Hopefully, as you read this, the double standards by which I've been evaluated and the open bigotry by those who do not *really* know me will be more visible. If nothing else, I pray that you hate me no more and that you not use a letter from your office to browbeat another person.[19]

The CSC did not offer Phyllis a job. She applied to NASA's astronaut training program but was not offered a position there either. Had NASA accepted her, and had she successfully completed the program, Phyllis would have been the first transgender astronaut in US history.[20] "Why not?" she says today. But making history was nowhere in her thoughts at the time. "There was nothing lofty in anything I did back then," she recalls. "I was just trying to get a job. You know, unemployment will eat on a person like you just wouldn't believe. You can cope with just about anything if you have the dignity of a job and a paycheck."

Trish and Phyllis's household budget was in awful shape, with much more money going out than coming in. "Things were just overall shitty," Phyllis says. In December 1976, they held a big garage sale for extra income so they might buy small Christmas gifts for each other. "We were also doing everything we could to save money," Phyllis recalls. "We turned off the air conditioning in the summer of 1977 . . . and we turned off lights everywhere. And somehow I'd gotten hold of a sewing machine, and I started making my clothes, and I made some of Trish's, too, because it was cheaper than buying them. Another thing we did was buy powdered milk. It was cheaper to buy a box of powdered milk that made ten quarts when you added water to it."[21]

When Christmas 1977 rolled around, Phyllis had been unemployed for nineteen months, the savings account was empty, and there were no supportive family members to help out. "Christmas was going to be meager," Phyllis later wrote. "We had shoes, but they were not winter shoes. We had some warm clothes, but they were a bit tattered. It was depressing as hell."

But there was a small ray of hope. "Our church family helped to keep the loneliness and the isolation at bay," Phyllis wrote. Because members at Resurrection MCC knew all about the painful costs of Phyllis's transition, they gave her and Trish the White Christmas offering—a collection of canned and nonperishable goods for the poor. "It was really quite wonderful," Phyllis recalled. "We separated the eight boxes of food into categories and took out 10 percent. We then went to another transgendered person, who had been living on the street because she'd also lost her job, and gave it to her. We three cried a lot. With the money we saved from not having to buy food for several weeks, we each bought some warm shoes and a warmer coat. . . . I shall never forget any of it."[22]

PART II
BREAKING BARRIERS

Chapter Four

Into the Streets

In 1976, when Phyllis saw reports of Ann Mayes's arrests on the news, she froze. Mayes was a well-known trans woman in Houston, and just the sight of her was enough to send shivers through Phyllis's body. "I could be arrested too," she thought.

In the 1960s, Houston's police officers had regularly raided gay and lesbian bars to arrest select patrons for violating a city ordinance that criminalized "wearing clothes of the opposite sex." In the late 1960s, though, the vice squad cut back on these raids because of legal threats posed by lesbian bar owner Rita Wanstrom and her customers, and because of the lobbying efforts of gay activist Ray Hill. Nevertheless, Houston's officers continued to harass and arrest individual citizens who cross-dressed in public settings beyond bars and club. These countercultural individuals included the daring Ann Mayes.

On April 1, 1972, Mayes wore a pink miniskirt for her appearance in a Houston courtroom to pay a fine for violating the ordinance. Before her appearance, she had spent nine harrowing hours in the city jail. "I felt terrible," she said at the time. "I had my wig torn off and there were a lot of remarks I didn't care for."

After this painful shaming, Mayes secured a lawyer to challenge the constitutionality of the code. Meanwhile, on June 1, a judge dismissed the charge against her because he considered the cross-dressing code ambiguous; it was no longer clear what "clothes of the opposite sex" meant, he ruled.

In response to the dismissal, the city remained belligerent and changed the ordinance to read: "It shall be unlawful for any person to appear on any public street, sidewalk, alley, or other public thoroughfare dressed with the desired intent to disguise his or her true sex as that of the opposite sex."

Unfazed, Mayes continued to wear women's clothes in public, and in July she appeared in a miniskirt as she stood before city council and asked for a special identification card that would help her avoid arrest. She explained that she was in the process of becoming a woman full-time and that she hoped she would soon have enough savings to pay for gender confirmation surgery. Referring to the language in the new ordinance, Mayes said, "I don't have to disguise myself, because I am being my true self." The council refused her request.

By August, Mayes had been arrested five times and was losing the money she had earmarked for surgery. With few options before her, she visited the chief of police to ask for a special identification card and a reprieve from arrests. The unsympathetic chief, Herman Short, kicked her out of his office, and he later gave his reason to the Associated Press: "We aren't in the business of issuing ID cards to queers. If 'it' breaks the law, 'it' will be arrested."

Before the end of 1972, Mayes was arrested at least three more times, including one arrest that occurred right after she left a court hearing. In December, Mayes also filed a $200,000 federal suit that charged Houston police officers with harassment and sought an injunction against additional arrests and prosecutions. The suit attracted public attention, and Mayes was not arrested again.

Still, she felt secure from future arrests only when she legally changed her name, as well as documentation of her gender, in March 1974, less than three months after she underwent surgery at the University of Texas Galveston Medical Branch. Shortly after her name change, Rachelle Annette Mayes said that she felt "so unique, so wonderful."

Just one month after her transition, the United States Supreme Court rejected without comment Mayes's earlier challenge to the constitutionality of the ordinance. Houston's ordinance against cross-dressing stood proud and tall.

Phyllis had long worried about the possibility of arrest, but now that she had transitioned full-time, there was a far greater chance that she would land in a jail where Phyllis knew it was not uncommon for trans women to be beaten and sexually assaulted.[1] Intensely afraid, she began to undertake her own personal campaign against the cross-dressing ordinance.

"Trish knew every single day that when she came home from work I might be in jail, and that just scared the hell out of her," Phyllis remembers.

"It really took a toll on her. But it wasn't just Trish. I was terrified, too. I didn't want to get arrested."

Fearing the worst case—being arrested, having to undress before guards and inmates, and suffering psychological and sexual abuse—Phyllis sent letters to the mayor and to every member of city council, explaining her status as a fearful transgender woman and calling for the repeal of the ordinance. Her handwritten letter marked the first time she advocated on behalf of herself and the wider transgender community before elected officials.

To Phyllis's delight, she received one positive response—from councilmember Johnny Goyen, who called her on the phone and asked her to come down to his City Hall office, adding that he had been impressed with her letter and credentials. Phyllis was all too happy to oblige, and she soon undertook her first experience with political lobbying in a one-on-one session.

During their conversation, Goyen stated that he had been upset and angered by the vice squad's treatment of Ann Mayes. He did not quite understand Mayes—her clothing and her desire to live publicly as a woman was puzzling to him—but he had no doubt that the city had mistreated her and that repealing the ordinance would ensure that Mayes and other cross-dressers would not have to experience such humiliation and harassment again. It was a matter of equal justice under law.

Here at last was a person with power who supported a policy change that would eliminate the threat of arrest. The two agreed to stay in close touch, and Goyen soon introduced Phyllis to other councilmembers. Phyllis made it her mission to do everything she could to repeal the ordinance; for her, it was a matter of life and death. In the months immediately ahead, she visited City Hall at least once a week, wrote letters, and made phone calls. She lobbied council members, municipal judges, and anyone else who would listen. But the ordinance seemed unshakable.

Phyllis had not marched with the civil rights movement in the 1960s, nor had she joined in any of the anti–Vietnam War protests of the 1960s and 70s. But in June 1977 Phyllis found a cause that made of her a non-violent street-fighter—an antigay campaign led by Anita Bryant.

Bryant was a B-level celebrity in 1977. She had been second runner-up in the 1959 Miss America Pageant, and in the early 1960s, she had developed a successful career in sacred and popular music. Since 1969, she had also served as spokeswoman for the Florida Citrus Commission, a job that gave her the starring role in popular national commercials advertising Florida orange juice.

In 1977, Bryant, a conservative Christian, made a commitment that negatively affected her career for decades to come: she decided to lead an antigay campaign known as "Save Our Children." At first, Bryant's campaign focused on repealing an ordinance amended by county commissioners in Dade County, Florida, to offer gays and lesbians protection against discrimination in employment, housing, and public accommodations. Bryant's devoted followers, many of them also conservative Christians, distributed thousands of pamphlets depicting homosexuality as a threat to the welfare of children everywhere, especially those in public schools. The fearmongering was successful—the ordinance was repealed by a vote of 69 to 31 percent—and Bryant took on the status of a national antigay activist.

Although Bryant was a polarizing figure, the Texas State Bar Association invited her to sing at their annual convention, to be held in June 1977 at the Hyatt Regency Hotel in downtown Houston. During the run-up to the event, Bryant defended herself and her campaign. "We're not trying to take away anybody's human rights," she said. "I've worked with homosexuals all my life and am willing to live and let live, but they're not willing to do that. Not all homosexuals are the nice, quiet, hairdresser type."[2]

Two of Houston's gay leaders, Ray Hill and Gay Political Caucus president Gary Van Ooteghem, set about organizing a response to Bryant's presence in their city. But it was an uphill battle. Houston's gay and lesbian activists had separated themselves into factions, so it was difficult to mobilize everyone at once. Further, the various groups were inexperienced in the type of direct-action campaigns that gays and lesbians in other major cities had been undertaking since the Stonewall Uprising in 1969.

As Ray Hill comically put it, Houston gays and lesbians "thought that the gay rights movement was having cocktail pity parties where everybody gets drunk and feels sorry for themselves because of their lot in life." By contrast, Hill did not consider himself part of the self-pitying crowd: "I was thinking, 'In the streets! Storm the Bastille!'" So he and Van Ooteghem called together about twenty activists and planned for a protest rally—the first ever for the city's gay and lesbian activists—outside the Hyatt on the night of Bryant's performance at the convention. They were realistic about the numbers that would turn out—"Houston's not a demonstration town," Hill said later—but they were hopeful that several hundred friends, peers, and allies would take to the streets. [3]

The organizers blanketed the city with flyers, sent out press releases, and wrote articles explaining the protest and its purposes. "We are not supporting the rally because we hate or fear Ms. Bryant or her kind," Hill wrote in a press release. "We support this effort because we believe in the dignity and individual integrity of all people."[4]

In the late afternoon of June 16, 1977, hundreds of gays, lesbians, and allies began to assemble in the parking lot of the Depository II bar. Not far away, another group gathered, this one made up of vocal supporters of Bryant and her antigay campaign. About two hundred participants had gathered for the Save Our Cherished Kids (SOCK) rally at City Hall. Some of them held signs reading "Protect Our Children," "Read Your Bible," and "Down with Queers" as they prayed, sang patriotic songs, and listened to fiery comments from local Baptist minister Joe West.

The anti-Bryant rally kicked off around 8:00 p.m. with a number of speakers pumping up the crowd, including David Goodstein, publisher of the *Advocate,* the nation's premier gay magazine, and Liz Torres, an actor who played a Puerto Rican boarder in the home of Archie and Edith Bunker on the hit television series *All in the Family.* Wearing a polka-dot dress, heels, and wide sunglasses, Torres told the growing crowd, "I am here because I had a gay high school teacher who taught me all the beautiful things in life. He gave me movies, poetry, love, and theater. Without him I would probably be a ladies' room attendant. It kills me to think that Anita Bryant would deprive a child of that experience."[5] The crowd adored her.

Phyllis and Trish stood in the middle of the still-growing crowd. Hill had encouraged Phyllis to attend the event, and Trish had come along. "She was terrified that something might happen to me, and so was I," Phyllis recalls.[6]

They weren't the only ones who were frightened. Many in the crowd, and many who had not come, were fearful because of the recent murder of Jose Campos Torres. On May 5, 1977, six white Houston police officers arrested the twenty-three-year-old Vietnam War veteran on charges of disorderly conduct at Club 21, a bar in the East End, a largely Hispanic-American neighborhood. Rather than booking Torres at the jail right away, the officers drove him to "The Hole," a favorite police hangout behind a warehouse next to the river that runs through the city. There, they beat him for hours on end. When they finally took Torres to the city jail, booking officials looked at his extensive injuries and directed the officers to take him to the hospital. Instead of following orders, the officers took the handcuffed Torres back to The Hole, beat him some more, and dumped his body into the river. Torres's body floated in the Buffalo Bayou for three days before someone reported it.

Phyllis and Trish thought about Jose Campos Torres as they weighed the dangers of going to a public protest with heavy police presence. Ultimately, the couple chose to go because they trusted Ray Hill. He was their good friend, and he had explained the historic importance of the protest and the need for Phyllis and Trish to be present. Hill also had emphasized that the march would be peaceful, and he had promised Phyllis an opportunity to speak at the rally.

As they stood in the crowd—which had now grown to thousands of demonstrators—Phyllis and Trish kept firm grips on their umbrellas, even though it wasn't raining. "[I]t was suggested that you bring an umbrella in case [counterdemonstrators] decided to throw bottles and rocks," Phyllis says. "It was very scary. We were braced for the worst, but it had to be done."[7]

Hill introduced Phyllis at the rally, and she climbed onto the makeshift stage just a few feet off the ground. Surrounded by fellow protesters, she spoke on the themes that were so common in her everyday conversations with anyone who took the time to listen.

She explained the ordinance against cross-dressing, the damage it caused to so many lives, the ever-present fear of being targeted under the ordinance, and the need to repeal it. She argued that the fight against the ordinance belonged in the wider movement for gay and lesbian rights. Her speech was brief, only a minute or two, but the crowd responded enthusiastically.

It was a historic moment. It was Phyllis's first effort at a public protest to put the "T" into the gay and lesbian movement, and it was no doubt the first time that many in the crowd had ever heard someone connect transgender issues to the gay and lesbian movement.[8] But the history of the moment is clear only in retrospect; none of the reporters present noted it in the articles they filed.

After the speeches at Depository II, the protesters marched toward the Hyatt Center, where Anita Bryant was serenading the Texas attorneys. As they marched, more supporters jumped out of their parked cars and joined in; others leaned out of windows or stood along the route, cheering the throngs as they passed.

Annise Parker, a twenty-one-year-old Rice University student who years later would become Houston's first lesbian mayor, was marching with her friends. "Yes, I had anxiety about participating," she recalls. "There was the fear of being out of the closet and being at a gay event." But Parker also came to realize the empowerment that accompanies one's presence in a march. "There was a lightness to it," she adds. "As you're marching along, chanting, holding hands, you feel the power of the crowd. The longer we walked, the more we felt uplifted."[9]

Trish and Phyllis, like Parker and her friends, felt the satisfaction of safety in numbers, and the swelling crowd now totaled around six thousand. The marchers stopped outside the Hyatt Center to shout their protest slogans. Inside, ten attorneys wearing black armbands had stood up and quietly walked out in protest when Bryant first appeared on stage. Among them was Aglaia Mauzy, who explained, "As a lawyer, I have a duty to express my dissatisfaction with her views. They are analogous to those Hitler used to persecute the Jews."[10]

After Bryant performed her signature slow and sappy rendition of "The Battle Hymn of the Republic," the remaining lawyers—about a thousand of them—and their families and friends responded with a thunderous standing ovation. But Bryant wasn't the only one to sing the patriotic hymn that evening; the protesters gathered, at the end of the first leg of their march, for a candlelight vigil at the plaza next to the Houston Public Library. With candles held high, they recited the preamble to the US Declaration of Independence and sang "We Shall Overcome"—a staple of the Black civil rights movement. After singing "God Bless America," they offered a less sappy but equally rousing rendition of "The Battle Hymn of the Republic." Finally, they closed with "Jesus Loves Me."

As the protesters marched back to Depository II, which was offering complimentary orange drinks, Phyllis and Trish felt a deep sense of satisfaction for having participated in the march and rally. "This was really the beginning of the organized gay and lesbian movement," Phyllis says today, attributing the success of the occasion to Ray Hill. "This was when the movement left the bars and began to organize itself. This was when I too went into the streets."

Inspired and encouraged, Phyllis continued her lobbying efforts, this time seeking a meeting with Houston's police chief, B. G. "Pappy" Bond. He refused her request, but in a move that took Phyllis by surprise, he directed Fred Bangston, the head of the vice squad, to meet with her. As Phyllis headed to the police station for her meeting with Bangston, she thought again of Jose Campos Torres, and she considered the possibility that the police could murder her with relative impunity. "It was a very notorious place, and it was scary," she says.[11]

Phyllis stopped at the main desk, and the person in charge asked to see her identification. She was uncomfortable showing her ID, because while it showed her new legal name, it still listed her sex as male. Upon examining the document, the official gave her a second look before indicating that she could proceed to her meeting. Next, she remembers, "I got on the elevator, and I don't know if it was coincidence or on purpose, but that entire elevator filled up with police officers," she recalls. "*Intimidation*—I almost wet my pants."

When Phyllis entered his office, Bangston huffed and snorted. "He made it plain to me that he did not want to meet with me but that he was on orders from Chief Bond." Phyllis didn't really care about that, and she launched into her case against the ordinance. She recalls the conversation this way:

> I gave him my spiel about the ordinance, and he said, "We arrest people like you all the time, and I don't understand what you're so upset about, because it's obvious to me that people like you who cross-dress get arrested and thrown in the tank with a bunch of other men so you can have sex with them."
>
> That's what he believed! I said, "You're crazy! I'm married. Would you like to see a picture of my wife?" I showed him the picture and said, "We've been married for such-and-such years."
>
> And I said, "Do you have any idea what I've given up and what I have to deal with because of this ordinance that makes me illegal and subject to arrest? I want to know whether the police can relax their efforts on it."
>
> And he says, "No, we're not going to do that, and after you leave here, whenever we find you, I will make sure we arrest you."
>
> He was a real ass, and I was afraid they'd arrest me right there on the sidewalk after I left the station.

Though frustrated and afraid, Phyllis wasn't giving up the fight. Still, she was battling on several fronts at this point: even as she was beginning her lobbying efforts, she was still seeking employment. She had also decided to apply to the University of Houston, not far from her home, for admission into a master's degree program. "I decided," she recalls, "because I couldn't get work, that I would use the GI Bill—which was money—to go back to school, and I thought, 'Why don't I go to the University of Houston and get a master's in business administration, because it would make me more valuable as an engineer?'" This was a savvy move toward employment for another reason too. "I knew that a lot of young engineering management people would also be taking these classes and would meet me in class over a semester and get the chance to see that I did not meet any of their expectations, and possibly at the end of the semester I might even get a job offer. That's really why I went to do an MBA." Further, the move would help to ease financial strain at home; under the GI Bill, Phyllis would receive a check every month she was in school.[12]

Even beyond the practical goals of returning to school, Phyllis saw emotional value in her new plan. "[The program] would give me something meaningful to do," Phyllis recalls. "One of the diseases of unemployment is loss of self-esteem due to being unable to contribute one's talents and energies." The past several years had bruised and beaten Phyllis's self-esteem, almost beyond recognition.

Phyllis appeared as Phyllis at the registrar's office, and to her delight, she had "zero problems"; the office staff was courteous, helpful, and solicitous. While learning more about the MBA program, Phyllis discovered that the University of Houston was now offering a joint JD/MBA program. Though she hadn't thought of studying law before, she considered the issue pragmatically.

"The joint program would do two things," she explained. "It would keep me in school longer, which meant I would get the GI Bill longer, which meant we would get additional income for two-and-a-half years. . . . And also, just as a kick, I figured that if I became a lawyer, it might scare the hell out of some of the people, mostly our neighbors, and they would finally leave us alone."

Interestingly, Phyllis gave no thought to being hired by a law firm, let alone becoming a fierce advocate for transgender legal rights. "At that time," she says, "my self-esteem had been beaten down so low that I did not even entertain the thought of actually practicing law."

Phyllis was pleased and proud when she won acceptance to both programs. Her first year back in school, starting in the fall of 1977, focused on the MBA program. Most of her classes were in the evening, and she attended them as Phyllis. She was pleasantly surprised to find that no one paid much attention to her trans identity. There was no overt hostility, no open ridicule, no oafish behavior. If her colleagues, most of them adults already in their careers, made fun of her, they must have done so behind her back. Phyllis detected nothing but politeness. "The students were either nice or supportive or not glaringly standoffish," she says.

As the first year of business school came to an uneventful end, Phyllis took a bit of time to write some faith-filled reflections on her life since coming out full-time in September 1976:

> God *does* work at God's own pace. Many specific prayers have been asked for over the 20 months since I first began my change as a trans person.
>
> Family? I had none since they turned away. Now, I have several close cousins who were never close before.
>
> Career? It has also gone down the drain—graduate degrees, scholarships, and professional licenses. Now, though still unemployed, a new career is coming as I'm into school again (this time through the front door) using my veteran's benefits.
>
> Financial security? My spouse and I have watched that spin and waver. Initially, our income was reduced by over 65% and after these nearly two years is still down 40%. But we are still together, we still eat well and we still have our home.
>
> Friends? Many left as my change progressed. (They must not have been *friends* after all.) But my friends now are genuine. My spouse is my friend too: that is why we are still one. Jesus is our friend, the center of our home and daily routine.
>
> Family, career, security, friends: my prayers have been answered—not as I asked, but as God knows best of what I needed.[13]

Chapter Five

Trans Rebel

As 1978 began, Phyllis began a low dose of hormones. It took a while, but she eventually started to notice her face becoming smoother, her muscle mass diminishing, and her breasts developing. "The thing that I remember most about the hormones was not the breasts, because I expected those," she recalls. "But you know how the male buttocks are kind of hollowed and the female buttocks aren't? Well, I began to notice that I had a tushy. That was what I enjoyed the most—my new tushy!"[1]

She was also surprised by a significant drop in her sex drive. In later reflections on this, she wrote: "From about age nine or ten, I was constantly horny—with a demanding libido that required release on a daily and sometimes thrice-daily basis. Sex for me was a need, an appetite: almost a distracting obsession."[2] But hormone therapy changed that, and sex became not so much a need as a pleasure to be chosen when convenient and desired.

The hormones—first Premarin, then Ogen, and later Estinyl—did not alter her strong, husky voice. "So Trish and I agreed that we would hire a voice therapist who helped me learn how to talk in a falsetto, and that helped," Phyllis explains. While she was pleased with the changes in her voice, she still got called "sir" by people who heard her voice without visual cues. "It didn't hurt my feelings," she says. "I just corrected them."[3]

As she began hormone therapy, Phyllis returned to lobbying for the repeal of the ordinance against cross-dressing. It was her way of starting the New Year with a proactive posture, far different from the defensive crouches of earlier years. Once again, she sought one-on-one appointments with council members, and when that didn't work, she resorted to writing more letters, like this one to city councilmember Louis Macey:

You have met me and seen me and talked to me. Surely, as you
sensed my sincerity, you must know that I'm hardly a criminal. Yet
one ordinance in this city which is of questionable purpose and
legality makes me to be subject to arrest daily. . . .

Presently, and with respect to you, the council and the city
ordinances, I have four alternatives. The first is to do nothing which
would have caused me to not write this letter or expose myself
needlessly to the types of harassment, pre-judging and stereotyping that many people already offer me in copious quantities. To do
nothing is unacceptable to me since I must live each day and since
I'm so tired of the extra burden that my spouse must carry. . . .

My second alternative is to do the reverse and go back to yesterday. Some people think that my becoming Phyllis is, in effect,
saying that to be a man is not good. No, to be a man is good if that's
what you are—I'm not. It didn't fit! Others say that I quit or that I
couldn't make it as a man. If being an Eagle Scout and high school
ROTC Commander, DeMolay, Aggie Senior Boots, five scholarships, a regular army commission, and being groomed as a project
engineer in the petrochemical industry doesn't falsify that myth,
nothing will. During the last 24 of my 28 years, I lived in growing
frustration of being woman but living man. I think that 24 years of
trying to be who I was not is enough.

My third choice is to go through surgery. . . . Did you know
that I've been told by several people in engineering that if I'd go
through surgery I'd have a better chance at a job? I know that if I
went through with surgery, I could forget the ordinances and let
others struggle through. But I see this to be a mutilation (with
respect to my body, that is) and am saddened to feel pressured into
it in order to work or live without fear. . . .

My fourth alternative is this: to write you and appeal to you
that there are others like me who have enough problems without
also being illegal and afraid of the police. . . .

My spouse and I are trying really hard to be cheerful. When
you pray, please ask that we escape from bitterness.[4]

With her newly acquired business acumen, Phyllis targeted local businesses as part of her lobbying campaign. Although she didn't call for any
boycotts—that seemed too militant a move at this point—she did appeal
to store owners, in writing, to join her in the fight. "This is 1978!" she
wrote. "We do not need anyone in the government telling us how to wear

our hair, what style of shoes to put on our feet, how much makeup to put on or what clothes we can or cannot wear as long as we are clothed to some degree."[5]

Phyllis also made a public pitch for additional transgender rights during a 1978 grassroots event focusing on the advancement of gay and lesbian rights. Town Hall Meeting I was designed to build on the energy of the Anita Bryant protest. The meeting's organizers, Houston activists Steve Shifflet, Ray Hill, Charles Law, and LaDonna Leake, aimed to move the gay and lesbian community from a defensive posture to an offensive one where they would prioritize goals and plan strategies to advance their causes.

On Sunday, June 25, 1978, about three thousand gays and lesbians, including representatives of over forty groups, gathered together for Town Hall Meeting I. Decked out in a red blouse, a blue and red plaid skirt, and white heels, Phyllis Frye was present and eager to participate. Frances "Sissy" Farenthold, former Democratic gubernatorial candidate in Texas, delivered a rousing keynote address that was interrupted more than a dozen times by the enthusiastic audience. "You have organized," Farenthold said. "You have identified and isolated the social and legal injustices leveled against you. You have overcome the crisis of timidity."[6]

Phyllis loved the speech as much as the others did, but unlike most others, she was attuned to what was absent from it—any mention of transgender issues. Phyllis also noticed that none of the resolutions formally submitted for the meeting's action mentioned trans issues either. When it came time for the chair of the meeting, Ginny Apuzzo, former co-chair of the Gay Rights National Lobby, to receive additional resolutions from the floor, Phyllis strode to the microphone and called for passage of a resolution addressing trans concerns.

Phyllis does not recall the exact details of the resolution, but the gay newspaper *Upfront* reported at the time that at least part of it set forth "a request that the Texas State legislature require organizations to comply with court orders in providing documents for transgenderists and transsexuals"—that is, documents governing name and gender changes.[7] The resolution passed, and Phyllis enjoyed her first success in public advocacy for the legal rights of transgender individuals.

The ordinance against cross-dressing remained in effect in the fall of 1978, when Phyllis entered law school and quickly discovered how different it was from business school. "It was three years of mostly hell," Phyllis remembers, referring not to the professors so much as to many of her fellow students, especially those who self-identified as Bible-believing Christians.[8]

Phyllis had been open about her trans identity, including her non-operative status, in her application for law school, and after the registrar announced her acceptance, she became a topic of vigorous discussion at a faculty meeting just before the start of the semester.[9] Phyllis later learned that someone had raised the question of which bathroom she would use—the most predictable of all questions—and some professors responded by saying they would gladly accompany her until everyone grew accustomed to her using the women's restroom.

Nevertheless, in light of this concern, an administrator had a rather uncomfortable discussion with Phyllis about the history of bathrooms at the law school. When the law school was built, he explained, it was an all-male school with bathrooms just for men. Then, when women were first admitted, the school built one-holers, bathrooms designed for one occupant. As more women arrived, the school converted several men's restrooms into women's. Some of the one-holers became unisex restrooms, open to men and women. After explaining this history, the administrator instructed Phyllis to use the unisex one-holers. She agreed to do so and began referring to her assigned restrooms as "Phyllis's potties." But a problem soon arose: none of the designated restrooms were near her study carrel, the library, or her classroom, the three locations where she spent her time.

"So, after a couple of days of long trips with a full bladder, I just started using the convenient women's restrooms," Phyllis recalls. This made some of her fellow students uncomfortable, and about five weeks later, the dean of students called Phyllis into his office and informed her of the complaints he had received. "How many?" she asked. Only a few, he replied. "So I suggested that, since most of the women were not complaining, he merely inform the sexually insecure ones as to which few restrooms I regularly frequented so that they could take their own full bladders on long walks elsewhere." That seemed reasonable enough to the malleable dean, and "the restroom problem" disappeared, at least for Phyllis.[10]

But the conversation about Phyllis and bathrooms continued, even among prospective law school students. "I was talking to some people, and one said one of his neighbors had just been accepted and she had heard about me and that she was terrified about me," Phyllis remembers. "She was worried about bathrooms and all that other stuff, and my friend said, 'Oh, don't worry about Phyllis. Bathrooms aren't a problem. If she has to go, she just grabs a wastepaper basket and goes out to the hallway and sits on it, does her business, and keeps on going.'"[11]

Phyllis was lonely during her first days of law school. She had no close friends, and only a handful of students were openly courteous. "During the first months, there were fewer than ten students who treated me as anything better than an animal," she says.[12] But she would not roll over this time, and she fought the loneliness in several different ways.

During the second week of school, Phyllis met with each of her professors. "I went to their offices one at a time, and I introduced myself to them. I said, 'I know you know who I am. Do you have any questions or any concerns about me? What can I do to allay any fears or concerns that you may have?'" The direct approach was fruitful, and most professors were courteous. "But I scared the hell out of a couple of them; you could just tell from their body language."[13]

Phyllis also used these meetings to ask professors for copies of their seating charts, explaining that she hoped to build a cordial environment by learning the names of all her peers. "I would say, 'Hello, Susan,' or 'Hello, George,' because most people are friendly, and if you speak to them and call them by their name, most of them aren't going to say, 'Fuck you.' Even those who don't like you aren't going to go out of their way to be ugly in public." Still, Phyllis continued to encounter colleagues who shunned her, ridiculed her behind her back, and belittled her in public, like the male student who wore a kilt—and a big smirk—to class one day.

Phyllis recognized that learning names was one thing, and being part of an intimate group was another, so she was excited to discover that a group of law students, the Christian Legal Society (CLS), had put a "welcome all" flyer in her study carrel during the third week of classes. Still a vocal born-again Christian in love with the Bible, Phyllis was thrilled to think of joining a group of like-minded, love-filled, grace-dispensing Christians. She noted the time, date, and location of the next meeting, and she arrived early, eager to meet her fellow travelers—and to find a place of refuge.

"Oh, my God," Phyllis reflects. "That was just like walking into a buzz saw." Several conservative members of the group pummeled her with questions about the relationship between her Christian and trans identities. "They asked about my faith, and I told them how my journey through my transition had tested it, revealing many truths." But the group members felt more certain of their own truths, and they weren't buying Phyllis's story.

When Phyllis attended a second meeting, some group members publicly denounced her as a sinner who had strayed far from the law of God. "There were some very ugly people there, and they did not want me to be there," Phyllis says. "They told me they didn't want me there. They told me they weren't going to pray with me. They told me I was a sinner. I was told to leave, or I'd be shunned. They were really ugly—not all of them but some of them." But Phyllis did not turn and walk away when the group refused to accept her into the fold. "I kept going back," she says, "and I kept arguing." Her reason was simple: "I was a Christian."

Soon, someone in the group suggested a laying on of hands—a ritual in which Christians gather around a sinful or sick person, lay hands on the person's head and body, and pray for God to transform sin into holiness or disease into health. Phyllis agreed. "I said, 'Hey, if you want to lay hands on me, and if you want to pray and do everything else to cure me, believe me, you'll be doing me the biggest favor in the world, because this has not been an easy cross for me to bear all these years. It isn't fun to lose jobs. It isn't fun to have neighbors be ugly to you. It isn't fun to have your family disown you. It isn't fun to be subject to arrest. So go ahead."

Though Phyllis consented to the ritual, she did not agree with the members who believed she was sinful. As she clarifies now, "I was long past the view I was a sinner because I was trans. By the time they laid hands on me, I was very comfortable with who I was. Even so, if they could change me so I no longer had to take so much shit in my life, that would have been OK with me."[14]

Phyllis sat in a chair in the middle of the room, and the group of concerned Christians surrounded her. They laid their hands on her, and for the next thirty minutes, they prayed that God would deliver her from her sinfulness, cleanse her of all unrighteousness, and heal her of her wretched, miserable, devil-infused condition.

"They were praying and praying and praying up a storm," Phyllis says. "And then it was all over with. I was still who I was." The prayer warriors, and the omnipotent God they sought to harness and channel, had failed to restore Phyllis to Phil. Phyllis was still there, still trans, still a woman.

The CLS members knew exactly who was to blame for the ritual's failure. It wasn't God's fault, nor was it theirs. "They got all bent out of shape, and they told me I wasn't sincere."[15]

"That's when they started having their own secret meetings," Phyllis says. "They had two meetings a week—the public ones I attended and the secret ones attended by people who didn't want me in their presence. That really hurt my feelings. These persons considered me to be an awful person in the eyes of God." Still, Phyllis continued to attend the public meetings even as the CLS members continued to harass her for living as a transgender woman. "They gave me that shit about 'loving the sinner but hating the sin' for months—and for years."

In April of her first year in law school, Phyllis spoke at a Houston rally protesting police brutality. About a thousand protesters, many of them gay and lesbian, showed up for the evening rally at City Hall. The target of their ire was the Houston police force headed by Police Chief Harry Caldwell and Assistant Police Chief R. G. McKeehan. Protesters charged that Chief Caldwell was unresponsive to their complaints about police harassment, police brutality against gays and lesbians, and the need for his department to hire gays and lesbians. The rally called for federal intervention in the city police department.

Phyllis helped lead the charge, and the gay newspaper *Upfront* devoted quite a bit of ink to her and her speech. "There is a member of Houston's gay community who commands a presence everywhere she goes," the article stated. "Her bearing, which has been compared to former Congresswoman Barbara Jordan's, suggests she knows exactly who she is and where she is going. . . . When Phyllis speaks, gay people and feminists have learned to trust her words."[16]

In speaking out against police brutality as a trans woman, Phyllis joined a small but proud lineage. Susan Stryker's *Screaming Queens* documents a 1966 uprising against police that was carried out by transgender women, gay men, and sex workers, many of them poor and people of color, in the Tenderloin district of San Francisco. Even earlier, in 1959, drag queens and their allies spontaneously pitched donuts at police officers trying to arrest them at Cooper Do-nut in Los Angeles; the melee spilled into the streets and became violent before the police could reassert control. Even in Houston, trans women used the court system in the 1970s to resist police brutality against trans women arrested during bar raids. Phyllis had lots of predecessors, but her speech at the rally that night was a first for

Houston, as a trans woman publicly denounced police brutality against transgender people.

In the halls and classrooms of law school, in meetings with policy-makers, in crowds of protestors, Phyllis was strong, confident, and assured. But in the quiet and safety of her home, sometimes she broke down. The harassment she encountered at school, especially from the Christian Legal Society, exacted a heavy toll. Her grades suffered, and she sank into depression in the spring of her first year. "I was so distraught over the way I was treated on a daily basis that I got depressed and went into a crying jag, and I stayed home from school for eight or nine days until I was finally able to regain my composure," she remembers.[17] Being absent from school did not help her grades, and Phyllis finished her first year near the bottom of the class.

On Saturday, June 9, Phyllis sat down and penned her father a brief note in anticipation of Father's Day. She wanted him to know that she and Trish continued to hope for a reconciliation: "You taught us to hold fast to our beliefs—to be strong and persistent in those things we feel in our hearts," she wrote. "As various dies have been cast, or milk been spilt, if you will, there are some things which divide us that cannot be undone. However, for these times, when in transition, our fears led us to strike out and wound you, we apologize. . . . What can we do to bring us together again?"[18]

Phyllis's father did not answer. Two months later, her mother penned Phyllis what she called her "last letter," adding that she would never call again, either. (Alto did not keep her promises to cut off contact; she remained in touch with Phyllis until her dementia made it difficult to do so.) "The only reason I have finally given up is because I had hoped to see a fine lady instead of a very determined woman," Alto wrote. "I am for Patriotism, and against anyone that wastes their time and the time of others by marching and rebelling. I like to see people build up, not tear down. You can build and keep your people busy with a flea market or some kind of creative work instead of wasting their talents by marching, and filling their hearts with bitterness and self-pity and feeling insecure."[19]

Phyllis sent a remarkable reply in which she identified herself as part of a long line of rebels and patriots in US history:

> When I march and rebel and fight, it is only aimed at dogmas and myths and stereotypes which are used to oppress people.

I do not riot. I do not throw bottles, nor do I use guns or knives or explosives.

I am trying to build a better tomorrow. Just like the rebels in Roman society who rebelled against the gladiator system of games, or the American rebels (we call them patriots) who met at the signing of the Declaration of Independence. There were the rebels who ran the Underground Railroad to fight slavery. What about all of our great writers—Socrates, Thomas Paine, Harriet Beecher Stowe—or our great speakers—Abraham Lincoln, Martin Luther King—or our great leaders—George Washington, Susan B. Anthony—who resisted in one way or another the oppression? I would hardly call them hateful. I would hardly call them bitter.

I would call them tired of a bad situation. They may have been so tired of the injustice that they found it easier to resist than to take it quietly on the chin. And we call them heroes. We also call them Patriots. Just because America is the best does not mean we should not work to make it better and to include more people within the freedom circle.

I was born in a privileged class: white, heterosexual, Protestant, upper-middle-class male. I knew no artificial boundaries. You and [my sister] LaNell, though women, grew up in a semi-privileged class. You have not felt oppression because you have nothing to compare to. When I began the change that I resisted from within for over twenty years, I tasted the putrid taste of oppression. Being from both sides, I could see the "closed doors" that you don't see. They have always been closed for you, but they used *not* to be closed to me.

I ask why? Because I am a woman? Why should being a woman close doors? I then looked closely at those people who were not included when Thomas Jefferson—another rebel, lawyer, fighter, and Patriot—penned "all men were created equal." There were *bunches* of people left out, but it was still a step. Some rebels fight to include Blacks as equal. Some rebels fight to include women as equal. Some for Chicanos. Some for Native Americans. Some for sexual minorities. Yes, some of the fighting rebels did in fact riot and throw bottles, some had great hate and bitterness.

But most simply did what they had to do, hoping the oppressors would not be so greedy with the equality and that they could all go back to living again. These fighters and rebels include such Patriots as Samuel Adams, Woodrow Wilson, shall I name more?

We hope you visit. . . .

I do so wish to share with you my dreams as we struggle to make America (which is *very* good for some) good for more people. Certainly we must be about the business of sharing with others the social and political freedom of our great system.[20]

Phyllis, a member of San Antonio's Troop 87, became an Eagle Scout in 1962 (Phyllis Frye personal collection).

Phyllis served as the commander of her high school's Junior ROTC program, 1966 (Phyllis Frye personal collection).

Senior portrait at Texas A&M University, 1970 (Phyllis Frye personal collection).

Phyllis and Trish married in 1973 (Phyllis Frye personal collection).

Speaking for transgender rights at Town Hall Meeting I in Houston, 1978 (JD Doyle Archives).

Denouncing police brutality against trans people at a 1978 Houston rally (JD Doyle Archives).

Leading the Texas contingent at the National March on Washington for Lesbian and Gay Rights, 1979 (JD Doyle Archives).

At a candlelight vigil during Houston Pride, 1979 (JD Doyle Archives).

In her second year of law school, Phyllis presided at a symposium on criminal justice reform in Texas, 1979 (Phyllis Frye personal collection).

To the Honorable City Council of the City of Houston:

In accordance with the provisions of Article VII, Section 7 of the Charter of the City of Houston, I submit and introduce to you the ordinance set out below with the request that it be passed finally on the date of its introduction. There exists a public emergency requiring such action and I accordingly request that you pass the same if it meets with your approval.

Date: *August 12*, 19 80

Mayor of the City of Houston /PROTEM

City of Houston Ordinance No. *80-2536*

AN ORDINANCE REPEALING SECTION 28-42.4 OF CHAPTER 28 OF THE CODE OF ORDINANCES, HOUSTON, TEXAS, WHICH SECTION PROHIBITS A PERSON FROM APPEARING IN PUBLIC DRESSED WITH THE INTENT TO DISGUISE HIS OR HER SEX AS THAT OF THE OPPOSITE SEX; AND DECLARING AN EMERGENCY.

*   *   *   *   *

BE IT ORDAINED BY THE CITY COUNCIL OF THE CITY OF HOUSTON:

Section 1. That the Code of Ordinances, Houston, Texas Section 28-42.4 is hereby repealed in its entirety.

Section 2. There exists a public emergency requiring that this ordinance be passed finally on the date of its introduction, and the Mayor having in writing declared the existence of such emergency and requested such passage, this ordinance shall be passed finally on the date of its introduction, this *12th* day of *August*, A.D., 1980, and shall take effect immediately upon its passage and approval by the Mayor.

PASSED this *12th* day of *August*, A.D., 1980.

APPROVED this *12th* day of *August*, A.D., 1980.

Mayor of the City of Houston /PROTEM

The 1980 Houston ordinance repealing the prohibition of "a person from appearing in public with the intent to disguise his or her sex"
(Phyllis Frye personal collection).

Law school graduation, 1981 (Phyllis Frye personal collection).

Phyllis became a member of the State Bar of Texas on May 18, 1981 (Phyllis Frye personal collection).

Houston's Special Blend softball team. Phyllis, upper right, is standing behind future mayor Annise Parker, 1982 (Phyllis Frye personal collection).

Celebrating Houston Pride in 1983 (Phyllis Frye personal collection).

Sporting her trademark hat and smile, 1987 (Phyllis Frye personal collection).

Leading the Texas contingent at the Second March on Washington for Lesbian and Gay Rights, 1987 (Digital Transgender Archive).

Raising the Texas flag behind the White House at the Second March on Washington for Lesbian and Gay Rights, 1987 (Digital Transgender Archive).

Phyllis discussed estrangement from her family on The Phil Donahue Show *in 1989 (Phyllis Frye personal collection).*

Cooling down with Trish and Blaze at their lake house, 1991 (Phyllis Frye personal collection).

Proceedings

FROM

The First International Conference on Transgender Law and Employment Policy

(Third Edition, ©1992, 1993, & 1994)

AUGUST 1992
HOUSTON, TEXAS, U.S.A.

Published by and available from:
Phyllis Randolph Frye, Attorney
Executive Director, ICTLEP, Inc.
5707 Firenza Street
Houston, Texas, 77035-5515 USA
Answering machine: (713) 723-8368
FAX: (713) 723-1800
  (all calls returned collect)

Prices: **$65 written (1992, 1993, or 1994)**
          $95 VHS video (1993 or 1994 only)
          (outside USA add $10 for shipping)
          Volume purchase discount available

Note: **The Fourth International Conference on Transgender Law and Employment**
          Policy (TRANSGEN '95) will be 14-18 June, 1995 in Houston, Texas USA

The cover page of the Proceedings of the First International Conference on Transgender Law and Employment Policy, *1992 (The Phyllis R. Frye Collection, Cushing Library, Texas A&M University).*

Delivering her historic speech at the 1993 March on Washington for Lesbian, Gay, and Bi Equal Rights and Liberation (Phyllis Frye personal collection).

Enjoying the bounty from the backyard garden, 1993 (Phyllis Frye personal collection).

Sharing a kiss with Trish, 1994 (Phyllis Frye personal collection).

Sharon Stuart, center, and a transgender contingent at the twenty-fifth anniversary of the Stonewall riots, 1994 (Phyllis Frye personal collection).

The wooden ICTLEP sign that Phyllis carried to speaking engagements, 1994 (Phyllis Frye personal collection).

Phyllis and her colleagues at the Human Rights Campaign offices in Washington, DC, 1995. From left to right: Sharon Stuart, Karen Kerin, Jessica Xavier, Terre Prasse, Kit Kling, Phyllis, Sarah DePalma, Gary Bowen, and Riki Wilchins (Phyllis Frye personal collection).

Marching with Sarah DePalma at Houston Pride, 1996 (Phyllis Frye personal collection).

Phyllis and Trish, with dogs Abby and Blaze, visiting with son Randy and his family, 1997 (Phyllis Frye personal collection).

Phyllis customized this T-shirt to read "Transgender Menace," 1998. An earlier version, made by Riki Wilchins, had read, "Transsexual Menace" (Phyllis Frye personal collection).

With Trish, Abby, and Lil Bit, 2003 (Phyllis Frye personal collection).

Performing with friend Lilly Roddy at an open-mic night in Houston, 2005 (Phyllis Frye personal collection).

Phyllis, with neighbors and friends, was sworn in as an associate municipal judge in Houston's City Hall on November 17, 2010 (Phyllis Frye personal collection).

Phyllis walking Charly and Sally through her Houston neighborhood, 2018 (Phyllis Frye personal collection).

Chapter Six

On the March

On June 25, 1978, Harvey Milk, a gay rights activist and member of San Francisco's Board of Supervisors, addressed a quarter-million people at San Francisco's Gay Freedom Day Rally. Gays and lesbians, he urged, should march on Washington, "that very same spot where, over a decade ago, Martin Luther King spoke to a nation of his dreams." The idea for a national march for gay and lesbian rights did not come only from Harvey Milk, but his speech provided the most public push.[1] In November of that year, Milk advanced the idea again, this time in a press release calling for a march on Washington to mark the tenth anniversary of Stonewall. A week later, he was assassinated.

Shortly after his shocking murder, Milk's aides called together gay and lesbian groups in the Bay area to encourage them to fulfill his dream of a march on Washington. Needing to channel their grief and anger, the groups backed the idea enthusiastically; so too did the Coalition for Lesbian and Gay Rights in New York City.

With San Francisco and New York City leading the way, gay and lesbian groups across the nation came aboard, and organizers began to lay plans for an October 1979 march. The run-up to the march included two national planning meetings, one in Philadelphia and the other in Houston. The University of Houston hosted the meeting in Phyllis's hometown, and activists from all over the nation—126 from 31 states—arrived in mid-July to discuss and debate, among other things, the principles and goals of what they had begun to call the National March on Washington for Lesbian and Gay Rights.

Ray Hill, now one of the national organizers of the march, invited Phyllis to welcome the activists at the opening session, and she happily accepted. Phyllis also attended many of the lively meetings and made her first formal attempt to inject transgender issues into the national movement for gay and lesbian rights.

As head of the "Transpeople Caucus"—which was really a caucus of one—Phyllis wrote and offered a resolution that called for changing the name of the march to the "Lesbians, Gay Males and Gay Transpeople's March on Washington"—and for using "Gay Transpeople" in all march literature, including its list of demands.[2] When making her case, Phyllis emphasized the discrimination that gays, lesbians, and trans people shared. "The people who hate you are the same people who hate me," she told her fellow activists.[3]

The historic resolution failed. Defeated but determined, Phyllis refined her resolution to state that "lesbian identified and gay identified transpersons shall have equal opportunity to participate in the March at all levels."[4] This one passed, marking the first time in US history that a national gay and lesbian event formally welcomed transgender folks.

Reflecting on the original resolution, Phyllis recalls: "I made a real strong pitch, and I lost, and I was bitterly upset by that." She turned to Ray Hill in the aftermath, and he told her that she should not be disappointed, that she had made huge inroads by making march leaders aware of transgender issues. He urged Phyllis to continue pushing the national community to connect transgender issues to gay and lesbian ones.

Hill was right: Phyllis's contributions to the meetings raised awareness of transgender issues in the wider community of gays and lesbians. The *Lesbian Tide*, which enjoyed a solid national readership, devoted part of its report on the Houston meeting to Phyllis's work, even adopting her unique language. "Perhaps the most surprising and controversial issue to emerge was that of 'transpeople,'" wrote the *Tide* reporter. "Transpeople, as defined by the highly articulate Houston-based Transpeople Caucus, are 'transsexuals, transgenderists, transvestites, drag queens and female impersonators.' Phyllis Frye, a transgenderist from Houston, in fact opened the welcoming Friday night session."[5] More locally, Houston's *Upfront* also referenced Phyllis's efforts in its report of the meeting: "Emotions ran high on some issues as delegates agonized over the inclusion of 'transperson' in all forthcoming literature."[6]

Phyllis committed herself to following Hill's advice. She was also determined to march on Washington. "I'd never been to DC before, but I just knew I had to go, and Trish knew I had to go." But there was a problem. "We couldn't afford airfare or anything of that sort," let alone hotel accommodations and dinners in DC's pricey restaurants.

In typical fashion, Phyllis soon devised a plan. She asked Resurrection MCC members and friends about the possibility of sponsoring and organizing a bus trip. Meanwhile, she buttonholed Clifford Floeck, a gay commercial bus driver she had met at Resurrection, and he agreed to ask his company about making a bus available. When Floeck secured one of his company's large buffalo buses, Phyllis was ecstatic. "They agreed to take their charter bus for a price," Phyllis says, "and I organized the whole thing—where the bus would stop for breaks, where we would have breakfast, and how much it would cost each person," which turned out to be $110 for a round-trip ticket.

Houston's *Upfront* publicized the march in several issues, ran an advertisement about the bus trip, and printed a full-page article by Phyllis—"The Marcher's Songbook."[7] The article included fourteen songs Phyllis had revised for the march. The songs revealed the creativity she had inherited from her artistic mother, the attention to detail she had learned from her father, and the many connections she drew between gay rights, feminism, Christianity, and patriotism. Phyllis's article highlighted her hope that marchers would appear "wholesome" and "patriotic" to the rest of the United States.[8] If Phyllis was militant, as she considered herself to be at this point, she was a conservative and patriotic militant. Far from being a radical seeking a revolution, she was a mainstream reformist seeking to enter US society through the front door.

On the afternoon of Friday, October 12, Phyllis and her entourage boarded the bus. They planned to meet the rest of the Texas delegation in time for the beginning of the march on October 14. "We all slept on the bus, and we were scared," she says. "We were scared because the route we had to take was through the Deep South, and we knew that if someone found out that a bus of queer folk was going through, the same thing would have happened to us that happened to the Freedom Riders." Making matters worse were two men who had paid for the trip but had no interest in the march. "These two guys were doing drugs on the bus, and we gave them the blues for fear of the bus being impounded and a bunch of queers stuck in the middle of nowhere." The men understood, and they politely but sorrowfully ditched their stash.

As the bus pulled into Alexandria, Virginia, on Sunday morning, a few hours ahead of schedule, fear was giving way to enthusiasm. The group had only one short leg of the journey ahead of them before they would arrive in the nation's capital. "We were a couple of hours early, so we washed up a bit before having breakfast and heading back to the bus," Phyllis recalls. Floeck returned to the bus before the rest of the group and turned the key in the ignition. Nothing happened. He turned the key again. Nothing.

When the riders returned to the bus and discovered that it had broken down, they groaned aloud. But Phyllis was a true believer—in her plans, the march, and divine intervention. She approached two MCC student ministers, or exhorters, as they were called, who had come along for the march. "I looked at both of those exhorters, and I said, 'If you don't organize us to hold hands around the bus and to lay our hands on it and to pray for it to start, I will.'" The compliant student ministers followed Phyllis's suggestion. "So we surrounded the bus, put our hands on it, and they led us in prayer," Phyllis recalls. "And the goddamn bus started!"

All on board were newly energized as Floeck headed across the 14th Street Bridge leading into the city. He found the rendezvous point for the Texas delegation, and everyone disembarked. Someone mentioned to Phyllis that since she had organized the trip, she should help lead the delegation. Phyllis loved the idea, taking her place just behind the Montrose marching band—"Clint Moncrief, cute as a button and sexy as hell, was the drum major"—and just in front of gay and lesbian students from the University of Houston, followed by eight rows of Texas flags.[9]

Dressed in a jacket and skirt and wearing knee-high boots with low heels, Phyllis made sure she had two things to carry on the march—a US flag and a copy of *The Way: The Living Bible*. "I used my Bible as my shield against the bigots, and I carried the American flag to show that the Republicans didn't own the flag," she says. She marched through the city streets, past the White House, and onto the National Mall, where about 75,000 people were gathering for the National March on Washington for Lesbian and Gay Rights. "It was very exciting. Every time we went by the religious protesters, I just glared at them and waved my Bible. . . . I was so sick of the queer haters wrapping themselves up in the flag—I'm a veteran—wrapping themselves up in the flag and thinking God was just for them."[10]

The organizers had issued five demands: a gay and lesbian rights law, an executive order banning the government and federally funded organizations from practicing discrimination based on sexual orientation, the repeal of all antigay and antilesbian laws, the end of discrimination in lesbian and gay custody cases, and the protection of gay youth from laws that discriminated against them. Sometimes referred to as the "Great Coming Out Party," the march was the first large-scale national protest staged by lesbians and gays.

"I considered transgenders as being gay, and so the march meant a lot to me," Phyllis says. "I was very proud of who I was, and I was proud that I had helped to promote it. I was very proud of the fact that I thought I was making an inroad for transgender inclusion, at least within Houston and the Texas region."

Those inroads made by Phyllis and other trans marchers stretched far beyond Texas. Their presence at the march meant that activists in gay and lesbian communities across the nation saw transgender activism up close and personal. In addition, marchers read about trans inclusion in the march's official program, in which Houston resident Jerry Mayes had placed a full-page advertisement for two buttons he had made, one of which read, "I'M STRAIGHT AND I SUPPORT GAY★ RIGHTS." Phyllis had helped Mayes design the buttons, and she had insisted on using the asterisk to represent the inclusion of transgender folks. The advertisement's text, just below the buttons, explained Phyllis's handiwork: "GAY★ is an inclusive term meaning lesbians, gay men and gay transpeople."[11] Mayes's advertisement, with Phyllis's touch, marked the first time that "transpeople" appeared in official literature for a national event advocating for gay and lesbian rights.

After the thrill of the DC trip, the beginning of Phyllis's second year of law school was an abrupt return to a harsher reality. At the start of the new semester, the Christian Legal Society once again plastered the law school campus with their "welcome all" messages. This time, perhaps invigorated by her activism in DC, Phyllis fought fire with fire. "I made a quarter-page flyer, printed a bunch of them, and put them up on every bulletin board at the law school," she remembers. "It said the Christian Legal Society is bigoted, and you don't want to go to their meetings unless you want to get prayed over and shunned."[12]

The members of CLS saw her protest flyers as terribly unchristian, and they began removing her flyers. "Well, let me tell you—they went nuts because after every class I'd put up some more to replace the ones they'd torn down. I did this after every class for four or five weeks, until a friend said, 'Phyllis, I think we got the message.'"

But the year also brought positive developments. Phyllis joined a variety of groups (the Black Lawyers Association, the Mexican-American Lawyers Association, and the Women's Law Association), and she appeared in municipal court to represent a friend, Joan Campbell, who had been arrested for cross-dressing in public. Representing a transgender client for the first time in court was a thrilling experience, and not just because it was another "first" in Phyllis's life. As she recalls the event:

> It was the only time after I went full-time as Phyllis that I put on a man's suit, no makeup, and a guy's shoes. I looked like hell. But I didn't want to get arrested.
>
> To save money, I took the bus downtown. It was about an hour ride with many blocks to walk. And I looked like, well, do you remember Tiny Tim? That's who I looked like.
>
> I knew I was going to have a lot of time on the bus and elsewhere, so I took a briefcase and I put a book and an apple and a sandwich in it.
>
> When Joan's case came up, I stood up and said, "Your Honor, I would like to speak to you and the prosecutor about this. I'm a law student and her counsel." So the judge motioned me up, and I came up to the counsel table, set down my briefcase, and flipped up the top to get my notepad.
>
> Well, the judge immediately dove down behind the bench, and all of a sudden both bailiffs rushed me. "Nothing here, Judge," they said, "just a sandwich, an apple, and a book."
>
> I was baffled.
>
> "We thought you might have had a gun," they told me—and that's because I looked like a crazy person.
>
> But the prosecutor agreed to plead Joan out with one night in jail.[13]

Following her first success in the courtroom, Phyllis founded a law student group for lesbian, gay, and transgender law students—Law Students, Friends of Gay★, with the asterisk denoting inclusivity of all sexual and gender identities and expressions. This new group evolved from another that Phyllis had tried to start the prior school year, a study group titled GIRL (Girls in Real Life). She had based this group at Resurrection MCC, targeted transgender folks and their allies, and emphasized its inclusive approach. "GIRL will be neither asexual, heterosexual, homosexual, bisexual, nor try-sexual; black, brown, green, yellow, white, nor polka-dotted; male, female, masculine, feminine, butch, nor Nellie."[14]

The GIRL brochure stated that the group's purpose was to study a wide variety of subjects that affected the everyday lives of "girls" and their allies, including employment, law, therapy, religion, reassignment surgery, non-operative options, fashion, and the arts. GIRL would be open and friendly to gays, lesbians, and bisexuals, as noted in the group's flyer: "[I]f a feminine heterosexual male in a dress or his spouse is prejudiced to queers, don't come!"[15]

Phyllis had advertised the group on the radio, and when it did not take off immediately, she renamed it "Transpeople."[16] While Transpeople attracted up to fifteen attendees and offered attractive programming—for example, on April 11, 1977, Zelda Suplee shared her experience at the Erickson Foundation, and a medical doctor showed slides of gender confirmation surgery—a lack of sustained interest and energy led to its early demise.[17]

Phyllis then turned her attention to Friends of Gay★, the main purpose of which was "to provide association as well as education for changes in social and legal discriminatory practices."[18] Phyllis also hoped the group would "give LGBT students a place where they could join as straight supporters, thus not outing themselves, and yet be supportive and maybe meet others who were similarly closeted."[19]

Phyllis assumed the leadership role, and a few people joined. But it was risky, Phyllis remembers: "When Friends formed, Houston still had the cross-dressing law, Texas still had the antisodomy statute, and no law firms were hiring openly LGBT attorneys. It was a scary time to come out."[20] Still, Phyllis sought to ensure that Friends would have a loud and lasting impact at the law school. Immediately, she sought recognition of the group—and the funding accorded official student groups—by the university senate, the student governing body for all of campus.

"I became very strident during that year, and our budget request became a university-wide hot topic," Phyllis remembers.[21] The topic was so hot that the Young Americans for Freedom (YAF), a national student group known for its conservative politics and activism, enlisted help from Austin-based attorneys to combat Friends' request for the $250 that the senate regularly granted to student groups.

Appearing before the senate, the outside agitators argued vigorously against the request, but they failed to convince the senators of the dangers that the Friends posed to American freedom. The meeting ended with

YAF and Christian Legal Society students clearly angry and agitated. Phyllis remembers what happened next:

> I stayed after the meeting and visited with a lot of people, and I was late getting home. Well, some of the Young Americans for Freedom students and some of the Christian Legal Society students had my home address, and they went to my house to hassle me.
>
> The only person home was Trish.
>
> This was about nine thirty or ten at night, and they started ringing the doorbell and banging on the door and yelling and screaming about how they were going to rape me and sexually assault me and all this other stuff.
>
> By the time I got home, they'd gone.
>
> Trish had called our next-door neighbors, and they had come over and were guarding the front of the house.
>
> At that time, we had a 30.30 Winchester rifle, and Trish was standing in the house, quivering and crying and holding that rifle by the barrel. She was going to use it as a club to defend herself.
>
> It wasn't long after that that I got rid of our guns.
>
> Trish was freaked out for over a year.[22]

In defiance of the YAF and CLS intimidation tactics, Phyllis refused to disappear. Instead, she upped the ante by arranging for Friends to host and sponsor debates for candidates for mayor and city council in October of 1979. When Phyllis moderated the debates, she questioned candidates about their stances on the ordinance against cross-dressing, as well as on the state's antisodomy statute. Her own positions on these issues were immediately, and unmistakably, clear to anyone within hearing range.

Although she easily caught the audience's attention, one candidate in particular seemed especially interested in her. Ernest McGowan, an African American veteran, a United Methodist minister, and a United States postal worker, was running for city council in a single-member district created after the federal government sued Houston on the basis of the Voting Rights Act of 1965. McGowan had never before taken up the cause of gay and lesbian rights, let alone the rights of transgender men and women, but he was a political liberal who understood firsthand the second-class citizenship to which minorities were often relegated.

"After the debate ended and students started going back to class and candidates began leaving, Ernest stayed," Phyllis recalls. "He had a lot more questions about my wanting the ordinance to be repealed. He was very interested in helping me because he felt that I did not deserve to be treated as I had been treated."[23]

Schooled in industrial science, McGowan was also attracted to Phyllis's engineering credentials, and he rightly observed that her technical abilities, coupled with her law training, could serve him well in his role as a councilmember. The two stayed in touch, and after District B elected him, McGowan and Phyllis made a deal with each other: she would spend two afternoons a week at his office, consulting on projects in need of her expertise, and he would arrange opportunities for her to conduct research in the city's law library, to meet with his colleagues on city council, and to work with him to repeal the ordinance.

"He was such a fox," Phyllis says with a chuckle. "City council was in session one day a week, and he would call and tell his secretary . . . to have me come down and bring something to him while council was in session. It didn't matter what it was. Then he would call me over and whisper something in my ear, something like 'How's everything going?' That way he had an opportunity to parade me every week in front of the mayor and city council so they could get used to seeing me."[24]

Some of McGowan's colleagues needled him about his work with Phyllis, and one dour council member asked him which bathrooms she used. According to Phyllis, Ernest said, "I don't know. Phyllis and I don't go to the bathroom together."[25]

After about eight weeks of Phyllis moving in and out of council chambers, councilmember John Goodner said something vile about her transgender identity. When two other council members told her about Goodner's comments, Phyllis broke down in tears. "I heard about it, and it really hurt my feelings," she says. During lunch break that day, she took a deep breath and headed to Goodner's office. "I was in tears and I was sobbing and I said, 'I didn't deserve what you said about me. Do you want to talk about it? Do you want to talk to me? Or do you want to talk about me?'"[26]

In the afternoon session, Goodner told fellow councilmember Lance Lalor that Phyllis had approached him and that he was feeling some regret about his comments. An avid supporter of Phyllis, Lalor took the occasion to suggest that Goodner make a motion to repeal the ordinance.

If Goodner so moved, Lalor would second the motion, and that double action would force the rest of the council to vote on repeal at a later date. Goodner moved to repeal.

Phyllis wasn't a witness to these surprising and hopeful shifts; she was at home, reeling from the pain caused by Goodner's vicious comments. When Lalor called to tell her the big news, he suggested that she stay away from City Hall for a while so that he and her supporters could finish the job without fellow councilmembers feeling overly pressured by her presence. "He told me to trust his skills now that the repeal motion was in motion," Phyllis recalls.[27]

At the same time, another key piece was coming into place—a case before the US District Court for the Southern District of Texas. In *Doe v. McConn,* seven Jane Doe plaintiffs, all of them women seeking to cross-dress in public, a preoperative requirement for their planned gender confirmation surgeries, charged that the city ordinance against cross-dressing deprived them of their constitutional rights. Federal judge Norman Black agreed with the plaintiffs in his April 3, 1980, ruling: "We find that the Ordinance, as applied to individuals undergoing psychiatric therapy in preparation for sex-reassignment surgery, is unconstitutional."

Black cited *Roe v. Wade,* in which "the Supreme Court has recognized a constitutionally-derived right to control one's body," as well as a key sentence in *Chicago v. Wallace Wilson, et al.*: "The notion that the state can regulate one's personal appearance, nonconfined by any constitutional strictures whatsoever, is fundamentally inconsistent with 'values of privacy, self-identity, autonomy, and personal integrity that . . . the Constitution was designed to protect.'"[28] Although the precedent Black cited would seem to have given him cause for a broader ruling, Black limited his decision to Houston transsexuals seeking reassignment surgery.

City council members were aware of Black's decision when, after a series of delays, the repeal was listed on the agenda for the council's August 12 meeting. Mayor Jim McConn was absent that day, and Phyllis's friend Johnny Goyen acted as mayor *pro tempore.* In a sharp political maneuver, Goyen called for a vote while two opponents of the repeal, Homer Ford and Larry McKaskle, were talking on their phones, inattentive to the call to vote. Ford and McKaskell thus did not vote, and according to council rules, their failure meant that their votes were recorded as "yes." The repeal passed with one dissenting vote.

Phyllis, like all other transgender folks in Houston, was finally free to wear the clothes she wanted without fear of arrest. "It was huge," she recalls. "It was huge."[29]

Chapter Seven

Advocating for Others

As she waged her campaign against the city's anti-cross-dressing ordinance, Phyllis also became increasingly outspoken against injustice in the classroom. "Whenever a professor or a student would make some outlandishly sexist, bigoted, or homophobic [comment] or legal conclusion, my hand would go up and the debate would begin," she recalls.[1] Sidney Buchanan, a professor of constitutional law, particularly attracted Phyllis's ire. To Phyllis, Buchanan seemed to favor restricting rights for sexual minorities, and she took him to task in private and public settings.

Buchanan troubled Phyllis not only because of his conservative legal thought but also because he was a Christian and the faculty adviser to the Christian Legal Society. When CLS members harassed her, Phyllis often headed to Buchanan's office, but instead of helping Phyllis address the unjust treatment, Buchanan steadfastly defended the members' right to act on their religious beliefs.

Between the ongoing harassment she endured and Buchanan's defense of it, Phyllis became depressed again. She experienced another "crying jag" for about ten days near the end of her second year. Rather than seeking professional help, as she had done in the past, she hunkered down. "I just had to cry. I just had to get it out of me. It was hell."[2]

At least one strain eased during the second year of law school. Phyllis found a part-time job that paid decent money for the number of hours she devoted to it—selling Amway products. Amway was a direct-sales company, enlisting people to sell their products to consumers in their communities. In 1980, Phyllis became one of about 750,000 Amway agents across the country.

In addition to providing needed income, the job kept Phyllis busy and gave her purpose. But Amway and Phyllis were not a natural ideological fit. By now, Phyllis was a liberal Democrat, and Amway's founders were bankrollers of the conservative revolution that had propelled Ronald Reagan to the US presidency in 1980. The owners of the company had founded and funded conservative institutes, think tanks, direct-mail campaigns, media outlets, and national advertising that extolled conservative policies, including antigay and antilesbian ones. "I knew they were supporters of big Republican pricks and conservative causes, but that really didn't concern me much," Phyllis recalls. "I was hungry, I was making money, and what I was doing was decent."

Phyllis got a big break in her Amway business during a conversation with Andy Mills, the manager of Mary's Naturally, a popular gay bar that also provided space for the city's lesbian and gay political caucus. Mills had a big heart, and he liked the thought of helping out a struggling transgender law student, so he agreed to buy cleaning and paper products from Phyllis. Even more helpfully, Mills spread the word to managers and owners of other gay bars in the city. Stocking gay bars probably wasn't what Amway's founders had in mind, but Phyllis was not an ordinary foot soldier. To further distance herself from Amway's politics, she used some of her income to support local Democratic politicians who favored gay and lesbian rights. Nevertheless, she remembers that she "got a lot of trash from leaders in the gay community." But she didn't let the trash-talking bother her.[3] "I said, 'Get me a job, and I'll quit.' Well, they didn't get me a job."

In her third year of law school, not long before city council repealed the ordinance, Phyllis accepted an internship at the Harris County district attorney's office. When Jim Hensley, the law school's supervisor of internships, first informed the office that he was intending to place her there, district attorney John Holmes and his staff objected loudly. Hensley replied by telling the district attorney that if he did not accept Phyllis, he would not get another intern from the University of Houston. Holmes relented, but he made clear that if Phyllis showed up in a dress, he would have her arrested.

City council took care of that. "They finally got [the ordinance] revoked a week before I went to the DA's office," Phyllis recalls with a chuckle. "I heard Holmes was really pissed off that the ordinance had been repealed and that they wouldn't be able to keep me out."[4]

Preparing for her first day, Phyllis was gratified to know that she could dress in women's clothes without fear of arrest. But then she discovered that Holmes and his staff had assigned her an office on the tenth floor and granted her access to only one restroom—on the second floor. Phyllis felt banished and humiliated. "Each time nature called, I had to get by a guard, since the second floor was secure, then walk past a long row of secretaries."[5]

Aware that her new colleagues and supervisors could make or break her career, Phyllis accepted the restriction at first, but walking the gauntlet on the second floor, sensing that everyone understood she had been banished to the restroom there, proved too humiliating. "So I did not use it. I would hold it as long as I could. The results were many 'accidents' and ... blood in my urine from a bladder infection."[6]

Phyllis came up with another plan. "I went to the criminal court building next door and found a restroom there. I was already there a lot because part of my internship included working in the courtroom of Judge Joseph Guarino, who had accepted me without any problems." But even that building proved unsafe. "After a while, I got called because some of the people in the criminal court building were complaining about me using the restroom there."[7] The call was from the first assistant to the district attorney, who told Phyllis that if she kept visiting the restroom there, he would have her arrested under the ordinance that made it criminal to use restrooms marked for the opposite gender.

"I was distraught, so I went to Judge Guarino's court, and I went back into the chambers, where I was always welcome," Phyllis recalls. "He was there, and he saw me in tears and knew I was in pain, so he rushed me into his office and closed the door." At the end of their conversation, the judge announced to his staff that Phyllis would have access to the restroom in his chambers.[8]

Meanwhile, on campus, Phyllis continued to fight against her unjust treatment by the Christian Legal Society. Near the end of February 1981, as she recalls it, "I sat down with a legal pad and handwrote a detailed memo outlining all the shit that CLS put me through. I made a couple of copies, and I gave one to the dean of students and the others to friends of mine, and I told them they could share it."[9]

The heavily copied memo landed on all the important desks on campus, even beyond the law school. "I took my memo to the provost of the entire university, and he investigated, and before the end of the semester the Christian Legal Society was put on a campus-wide probation for discrimination."[10]

Phyllis's law colleagues and professors read her account as well. "Within about a week after I handed it out, people who'd never spoken with me before, because they were busy and had other things to deal with, went out of their way to come up and greet me and stop and chat to see if I was OK, and it was wonderful."[11]

While finishing law school, Phyllis felt a deep sense of accomplishment. First, she had been accepted into the school despite the fears of some professors and administrators. And then, during her course of study, she had overcome resistance to her use of women's bathrooms, lobbied city council for the repeal of the anti-cross-dressing ordinance, helped inject transgender issues into the national march for lesbian and gay rights, joined in marches and rallies where she constantly raised the issue of transgender rights, won her first court fight for a transgender woman, battled the bigotry of the district attorney's office, formed friendships with judges and attorneys, silenced the Christian Legal Society, and raised her grades. Perhaps most importantly, she had grown confident in her identity as a transgender woman.

Phyllis graduated at the top of the bottom third of her class. "But the magic of it all is that I passed the bar the first time I took it," she says. Her exam results arrived in her mailbox on Graduation Day. Phyllis and Trish were thrilled. "And Monday morning I went straight down to Judge Guarino's court, and he swore me in," she fondly remembers.[12]

Following the swearing-in ceremony, Phyllis informed her neighbors that she was now an attorney who would not hesitate to sue anyone who dared to harass her. "I figured it would scare the hell out of them, and they would leave us alone," she recalls. "And they did. It scared them. They knew I was going to sue the shit out of them. I didn't, but I was bitter."[13]

For the most part, though, the days immediately following graduation were anticlimactic. "Nothing happened," Phyllis says. She had interviewed with firms during career days at the law school, but no one had offered her a job. Interviews off-campus were few and far between. Phyllis's reputation as a trans woman often preceded her, and most firms refused to answer her queries. "I was really angry," she recalls. "I couldn't get interviews—because of bigotry, or a misunderstanding of who I was, or fear of the unknown, or they just didn't want me in their office because they were afraid they'd lose clients. I was bitter."

With no job opportunities on the horizon, Phyllis strategized with Trish about how she could practice law without the assistance of a firm. "We decided to take one of the bedrooms. That's all we could afford. We converted it into my law office, and that's where I practiced law for the next twenty years."[14]

In the first few years, Phyllis's practice did not even amount to significant part-time work. "I tried to get clients by telling everyone I could that I was now an attorney. I knew people in the local lesbian and gay political caucus and in the Democratic Party and in the women's movement, and every now and then someone would hire me. They would need a divorce, or they would want a will, or someone would need to be probated, but there wasn't very much work, certainly not enough to pay the bills."[15] Phyllis also made some money doing occasional engineering work, but most of her income continued to come from her Amway business.

Phyllis's activism continued unabated in this period, partly because it gave her a sense of self-worth and an opportunity to help others. In the fall following graduation, she offered a workshop titled "A Study of Transpersons" at the ninth annual Texas Gay/Lesbian Conference in Houston; it was yet another example of her ongoing attempts to educate gays and lesbians about transgender identities and to highlight the exclusion of trans issues in their own campaigns for rights.

Some of Phyllis's activism during the early 1980s also focused on issues of feminism. As a transgender woman, she had two targets constantly before her: bigotry against trans individuals and sexism against women. The latter target came to the fore in 1982, when she decided to stage and lead a feminist protest at her own church over its refusal to adopt inclusive language in its recitation of creeds, its reading of scripture, and its hymn-singing.

By this time, she had already experienced deep personal disappointment at Resurrection Metropolitan Community Church. During the Anita Bryant campaign in 1977, MCC founder Troy Perry had visited Resurrection, and Phyllis and Trish had eagerly stood in a long line to greet him. In their brief conversation, Phyllis says, the revered founder told her that she was welcome at MCC, but that transgender issues were not part of the mission of the church.

The battle over inclusive language at Resurrection proved to be even more upsetting. As a self-described radical feminist, Phyllis was fiercely opposed to hymns that referred to God as "Our Father," Jesus as "the Son," or people as "man." When Resurrection began holding congregational discussions about purchasing new hymnals, Phyllis insisted that the church buy hymnals with inclusive language. Church leadership assured her that her request would be met, but then, as she remembers it, "some member of the board pulled a fast one and got hymnals purchased that did not have inclusive language."[16]

Phyllis dug in her heels. "During choir rehearsals and whenever we sang in church, when it came to a non-inclusive word, I would sing the inclusive word while the rest of the choir sang the word that was printed."[17] She also penned and mailed a letter to members of the congregation. "I see God as neither womanly nor manly," she explained. "I see God as our creator—our heavenly Parent, not our heavenly Father. . . . Further, I offer to you Jesus as the Savior, Christ, *Child* of God rather than the Son of God. Yes, Jesus was male, but he was human first and that is the important concept—God as flesh, not as God as flesh with the piece of flesh."[18] Phyllis and her friend Cliff Witt organized a handful of like-minded friends to picket Resurrection every Sunday until it agreed to adopt inclusive language in worship. And she took her protests to the media, receiving coverage in print and on the radio.[19]

Many church members were unhappy with Phyllis's tactics, especially her decision to take her campaign public. The choir director was furious, as she recalls, and told her to leave; she and Trish dropped out of the choir.

Phyllis eventually chose to stop the picketing campaign, but not before expressing her anger in another biting statement that she hand-delivered to the congregation. "I'll stop for now the picket, feeling that inclusivity has a higher priority than when it was set aside during hymnal selection," she wrote. "In the stopping, I leave you a question: Why do some folks have to work so hard and have to wait so long merely to include others and to spiritually expand the recited images of our God and Savior?"[20]

As she handed out her statement, Phyllis saw her friends making a quick exit. "All my friends ducked into the side door, which really hurt my feelings, and that was the moment when Trish and I decided we wouldn't go to church anymore."[21]

Phyllis began to turn her attention to other community activities. In 1982, she and Annise Parker, a leading activist in the Houston Gay and Lesbian Political Caucus, traveled to a conference in Austin. On the drive,

Phyllis was talking pretty much constantly, in typical fashion. Parker had been tuning out some of her chatter, but she perked up when Phyllis mentioned that as a trans woman she really missed playing softball.

"At the time, I was coach of a woman's softball team in what is now known in Montrose as the Houston Women's Softball League," Parker explains. "It is a lesbian softball league. We've been around for more than a decade. The league was formed so that we, as lesbian softball players, would have the chance to compete on our own teams against each other without worrying about being harassed by other people."[22]

Phyllis did not know that Parker was a coach, but she could tell that Parker was interested in her comments about softball. "When she heard me, a light went off, and she started asking me all types of questions about when I played, what position I played, was I a good hitter, and I told her yes, I was a very good hitter, and slow pitch was my game, and my favorite position was catcher and my favorite backup position was pitcher."[23]

"I looked at Phyllis and I saw the power hitter I'd been looking for on my softball team," Parker says.[24]

"She invited me to join her team," Phyllis recalls. "And I said, 'I would love to, but I'm not going to put up with any bullshit with me being trans, so you need to talk to the team first and you need to make sure the league isn't going to give me any garbage.'"[25]

Back in Houston, Parker lobbied the league to make room for Phyllis, but she met considerable resistance. The dissension was not so much about Phyllis's transgender identity or her ability to hit homers as it was about the possibility that she might end up injuring players because of her size. As Parker puts it, "It wasn't about Phyllis Frye, a transgender, or Phyllis Frye, who used to be a man. It was about, is it safe for us to play."[26]

Phyllis laughs at the memory. "Hell, in 1982 I had been on hormones for five years, and even though my skeletal structure had not changed, my muscle mass in my upper arms definitely changed."[27]

Parker remembers how she responded to her league's concerns: "I gave a very impassioned speech about how she has nowhere else to go. And we formed this league to fight against discrimination so that we wouldn't be discriminated against. And how dare we even consider turning around and discriminating against someone else."[28] In response, the league voted to accept Phyllis on a provisional basis.

Phyllis took her place on Parker's team, the Special Blend, and was happy to be back playing catcher and swinging for the fences. "As it turned out, there were other women who were just as big or bigger than I and who could hit just as far or farther," she says.[29]

The team soon learned they didn't have to fear Phyllis. In one memorable game, Phyllis was rounding third and heading for home when a player on the opposing team threw the ball. It got a little too close to Phyllis, and "she jumped up in the air and she squealed," Parker recounts. "I cannot even attempt to squeal that way, but she squealed as she jumped over the ball. The entire bench just broke into hysterical laughter. And after that, she got back to the bench and the discussion centered around, 'Phyllis, we're going to have to teach you. We don't do that sort of thing. We're dykes.'"[30]

After leaving the church in 1982, Phyllis also reactivated her membership with the League of Women Voters. A neighbor had recruited her for the League in 1977, and she stayed active until the demands of law school became overwhelming. Upon her return, she joined the natural resources committee, where she offered her engineering expertise, and the administration of justice committee, where she advocated for women's issues and sexual minority causes. Phyllis soon convinced the Houston League to lobby the statewide Texas League to advocate for the repeal of Texas Penal Code 21.06, the infamous law that criminalized gay sex.

With a taste of success at the local level, Phyllis was excited when she learned of an opportunity to attend the League's state convention and personally lobby for the repeal of 21.06. But that opportunity, like so many others, did not come without pain and suffering. The Houston League had its share of women who did not like Phyllis because of her trans identity, and just before the statewide convention, the president told her that no one wanted to room with her. "That really broke my heart," Phyllis remembers.[31] She knew not everyone liked her, but she thought she had found a safe haven in the League, that she had developed a number of solid friendships, and that it was the perfect place to advocate for causes near and dear to her heart.

In tears, Phyllis called one of her League friends, Betty Jane Baker, and told her what the president had reported. Baker's response was immediate: "Tell the president that I will room with you, and that the others would, too." When Phyllis called the president and told her that Baker and about twenty others would be willing to room with her at the convention, the president stammered, quickly backpedaled, and booked Phyllis's room as an official member of the Houston delegation.

Phyllis was fired up. "At that convention, I challenged the Texas League to lobby for repeal of the Texas homosexual conduct law," she says, adding that she made a few enemies along the way. "Most of the state officers just could not stand me because I was very vocal and pushing for the repeal of 21.06."[32] While Phyllis lost at that convention, she was undeterred, committed to making sure that one day the League would advocate for the repeal of Texas's sodomy law.

During this period, Phyllis was also involved with the Texas Democratic Party. She had first become active in Democratic politics when she voted at the precinct level in 1978. At that point, Sam Flannery, a gay neighbor, helped her get elected to the senatorial district convention, and the two hoped she would be able to caucus with other lesbians and gays and then get elected to the state convention, where she and her colleagues could work together to shape the Democratic platform.

"I went to the district convention and had a sign made up and it said, 'Gay Caucus,'" Phyllis says. "I saw a lot of people I knew there who were gay, but they were closeted and nobody else would sit with me in the caucus section."[33] But someone did approach Phyllis: Billie Carr, the godmother of Texas liberals, was so impressed with Phyllis's fortitude and persistence that she arranged for her to get one of the at-large positions at the state convention.

There, Phyllis met other gays and lesbians, and their caucus made a direct impact at the 1980 convention when they publicly backed candidates who opposed the state's sodomy law. The caucus's politicking paid off when delegates to the 1980 state convention voted to include a call for the repeal of 21.06 in their platform. It was a monumental victory for Phyllis and her colleagues in Democratic politics.

Four years later, on May 29, 1984, Phyllis spoke before the Democratic Party National Platform Committee, becoming the first openly transgender person to do so. After sharing her biographical details, Phyllis warned against "authoritarian fundamentalists and 'born-agains.'" "You will be tempted by gay-baiters to downplay the Democratic Party's commitment to gay rights," she said. "[D]o not be gay-baited. Proclaim lesbian/gay citizenship as being in the mainstream because, in fact, it is in the mainstream."[34]

The platform committee accepted Phyllis's words without rancor, though its final platform only spoke briefly against bigoted violence and stopped short of proactive advancement of gay rights: "Violent acts of bigotry, hatred and extremism aimed at women, racial, ethnic and religious minorities, and gay men and lesbians have become an alarmingly common phenomenon. A Democratic Administration will work vigorously to address, document, and end all such violence."[35]

Phyllis also continued her lobbying in Houston. After the repeal of the cross-dressing ordinance in 1980, Houston politics continued to assume a progressive stance on gay and lesbian issues, and in 1982, city comptroller Kathy Whitmire won her mayoral bid with enthusiastic support from the Houston Gay Political Caucus. During Whitmire's term, the city practiced nondiscrimination on the basis of sexual orientation, at least in its own hiring and firing, and the practice became so accepted that liberal council member Anthony Hall proposed an ordinance in June of 1984 that would have added "sexual orientation" to the classes protected in city policies.

However progressive Houston appeared at this point, this was the age of the Moral Majority and its antigay supporters, and all hell broke loose among the city's antigay activists when they learned of Hall's proposal. Council member John Goodner stoked the flames when he suggested that gays and lesbians in city jobs would be poor role models for children.

However loud they were, the antigay activists lacked sufficient power on council, and when Hall's progressive proposal passed in July, Houston's gays and lesbians, including Phyllis, cheered loudly. But those cheers were soon drowned out when an antigay group named the Committee for Public Awareness (CPA) garnered more than 63,000 signatures on a petition calling for a referendum on Hall's ordinance, as well as one that prohibited keeping records on the hiring of gays and lesbians. The campaign was vicious, with CPA supporters citing the spread of HIV and AIDS as a reason to keep gays out of city jobs.

Phyllis fought hard, successfully lobbying the board of directors of the Houston League of Women Voters to take a public stance in favor of the ordinance. She also organized a public forum featuring both sides of the hotly contested battle. But the well-organized campaign against the ordinance was successful: Houston voters defeated the progressive ordinance by a 4–1 margin on January 19, 1985. Phyllis felt brutalized, especially by the Moral Majority supporters who had invoked their faith to make the case for discriminating against gays and lesbians.

Houston's antigay activists sought to build on their victory by running a group of like-minded candidates in the next election for city council. Billed as the "Straight Slate," the group proposed shuttering "sexually oriented businesses" and requiring food workers to prove they were not infected with HIV. The Straight Slate also supported the mayoral candidacy of Republican conservative Louie Welch, who accidentally announced on live TV that one of his plans for fighting AIDS in Houston was to "shoot the queers." After realizing that his off-the-cuff remark had been broadcast, Welch later said, "I apologize, but I don't think I had the gay vote anyway."[36]

Pro–Straight Slate campaign signs popped up all over Phyllis's and Trish's neighborhood, and to Phyllis, they felt like a slap in the face. She was angry, very angry, and so were the LGBT voters who turned out on Election Day, many of them wearing "Louie, Don't Shoot!" T-shirts.

Phyllis remembers the day well: "When I went to my polling place, there was a young man there with a hammer and Straight Slate signs, and he was hammering the signs into the ground. I just walked up to him, and after he was finished hammering, I ripped the signs out." The man's face turned bright red. "He went nuts and started screaming, and he lifted his hammer like he was going to strike me. I just looked at him and said, 'You gotta do what you gotta do.' He backed off, and I could tell he was angry, but I could also tell I gave him a sense of how much hurt the Straight Slate caused me and others."[37]

With Phyllis and most of the LGBT community behind her, Kathy Whitmire and her supporters on city council ended up defeating Welch and the Straight Slate. Breathing a sigh of relief, some members of Houston's LGBT community then turned their attention to withdrawing their support for businesses that had backed the Straight Slate. They also refocused on the AIDS crisis plaguing the city.

In a short piece she published in the *Montrose Voice,* Phyllis sent out a plea for local AIDS activists to provide their knowledge and expertise to a League of Women Voters–led statewide health care project focused on caring for people with AIDS. "I do not feel qualified," she added, but she would assist in connecting the experts to the League and its statewide plans for addressing the crisis.[38] While the HIV and AIDS crisis was one of the very few LGBT-related causes for which Phyllis did not become a vocal leader, she did assume the role of a foot soldier at various protest rallies.[39]

The year 1985 ended on a positive note when *The Battalion*, Texas A&M's student newspaper, published a glowing profile of Phyllis. "The 5-foot-9-inch, brown-eyed brunette openly says that she is a transgenderous or transperson," wrote D. Ann Beeler. "A transgenderous is a person who has taken hormones in order to take on physical characteristics of the opposite sex. Frye says she keeps in shape by working out to Jane Fonda tapes and running." The profile also recounted Phyllis's transgender journey since her days as an Aggie student, as well as her activism for "gay rights, women's rights and human rights," drawing special attention to her work to defeat the Houston ordinance against cross-dressing.[40]

Beeler's conclusion showed how far Phyllis had traveled since transitioning: "Today, Frye's eyes shine. Her smile is friendly. She is ambitious and lives the life she says she's always wanted to live. She's lived two lives, that of a man and that of a woman. She says that the greatest advantage that a man has over a woman is that people will always listen to what a man has to say. 'Women must be assertive,' Frye says. 'Don't let society, or any man, label you (women) as inferior or submissive.'"[41]

Chapter Eight

The Personal and the Political

Phyllis had skipped her tenth-year high school reunion in 1976. "That was the year I was transitioning, and we were broke, and I didn't look very good, so we didn't go," she explains. But she still made use of the occasion to continue her work of bridge-building. "I sent in ten dollars to get a directory, and I used it to write letters to about a dozen people I was close to. I told them about my transition, what was going on, and one of the persons who responded was Fred Biery. He invited me to come see him in San Antonio, where he was serving as a judge."[1] It was a warm gesture, and not altogether unexpected; she had admired Biery since high school, and the two enjoyed several visits in the years to follow.

Although Phyllis was unaware of it, Biery had a personal connection to a trans woman that motivated him to reach out to Phyllis. "My father was a lawyer, a very compassionate lawyer, and he represented a friend who dressed as a woman," Biery explains. "The man was transgender, though we didn't call it that, a local businessman, well-respected, and he had a family. My father never made a big deal about representing him, but that's who he was. At any rate, the pressure became too much for the man, and he killed himself." The horrific story stuck with Biery, and so he made a point of reaching out to Phyllis. "Dad had taught me to 'live and let live,'" he says.[2]

In the summer of 1985, Biery telephoned Phyllis and asked her to visit so they could talk about the upcoming twentieth-year reunion. "I knew that I wanted to go," she says. "I had abundant good memories from those days, with only a few bad memories to discard over twenty years."[3] Still, she had grave concerns about her classmates' acceptance of her as Phyllis, and she asked Biery to inform the committee that she would be attending so they wouldn't be surprised.

In the months leading up to the reunion, Phyllis's life was, as she puts it, "filled with the usual—business, volunteer work, home life, League of Women Voters activities, women's softball—plus the deep fears that I succumbed to each time that I let down my mental guard." Phyllis's "deep fears" were not about her identity as a trans woman, but about the transphobia she continued to encounter in others.[4]

Never one to sit back and wait, Phyllis grabbed her pen and began writing letters to members of the reunion committee. "Bless them," she says. "I am sure they became wary of my letters. Yet I wanted so badly for this to work. I gave them facts to replace stereotypes and many months to think and talk."[5]

Childhood friend and classmate Jerry Sharp received one of Phyllis's letters, and though he was sympathetic, he recalls other letter recipients' resistance to Phyllis's overtures. "They were stubborn," Sharp recalls. "They did not want to use the word 'she,' and instead they used 'it' when talking about her."[6]

"May and June were especially tough months for me," she says. "I was not getting any feedback from the committee, and the fears came up more frequently. I slept fitfully during the two final weeks."[7]

Like Phyllis, Trish experienced a lot of trepidation on the trip to Phyllis's hometown. She recalled the cruelties perpetrated on her spouse through the years, and all the times when the psychological toll of transphobia seemed too much for Phyllis to bear. She knew too well what lasting damage was possible if Phyllis's classmates chose to be careless or cruel.

When Phyllis and Trish arrived at the hotel on the Friday of reunion weekend, they unloaded their bags and warily headed to the registration desk. To their enormous relief, they were greeted with hugs and smiles. One of Phyllis's longtime friends escorted her and Trish to the bar and introduced the two to everyone he knew. "One woman would not release my hand," Phyllis recalls. "She beamed with joy at my joy. She said that my inner joy and peace were so very complete, that I was more attractive now as a woman than when she had known me twenty years ago as a guy."[8]

Not everyone was so open to Phyllis, but most of the classmates who were uncomfortable avoided addressing her directly. One man asked Sharp how he could possibly be friends with her. "Because it's in the Bible,"

Sharp explained. "Jesus was not about judgment." The man huffed off, but not before saying, "It's not in *my* Bible!"[9]

Another classmate told Biery that while he was a Ted Kennedy Democrat, he wasn't quite able to handle Phyllis and the wider push for gay and lesbian rights—that it all seemed just plain wrong. Biery wryly replied that perhaps the man had some repressed sexual issues to work through himself.

Sharp noticed that some of the former football players, plied with alcohol, sought to guard the women's restroom. "How can we let this guy into our wives' bathrooms?" they asked loud enough for Sharp to hear. The aging jocks were not aggressive toward Phyllis, but it was clear that they found her threatening. In making the rounds, Sharp also discovered that some of the women Phyllis had dated had a hard time accepting the dramatic changes.

On Saturday, Phyllis and Trish spent a lot of time at the swimming pool, visiting with classmates over beers and snacks. "Phyllis showed up in a bikini," Biery remembers. "You talk about heads turning!"[10] For Phyllis, the bikini announced that she was assured and comfortable in her skin. "I was looking OK by then," she says.[11] But not everyone agreed; some remarked that she looked like Tiny Tim in a bikini, and others were left speechless.

Looking back on the weekend years later, Phyllis says that "nobody went out of their way to be ugly to my face." The body language of some people was reason enough for her to stay away from them. "But I got no overt negative responses. Nobody stuck out their tongue at me, or said anything ugly to me, or glared at me, or threatened me. Some even wanted to tell me of their own experiences of personal discovery and blossoming. They felt that we were kindred in our discoveries and personal growth."[12] Phyllis headed home feeling exhilarated and decided to write about her experience for *This Week in Texas (TWT)*, a popular magazine for the Texas LGBTQ community. "The weekend filled me," she wrote. "I was saturated with positive feelings."[13]

Soon after the reunion, *TWT* published a glowing profile of Phyllis, marking the tenth anniversary of her firing from S&B Engineers. The article traced the trajectory of her journey from being jobless to becoming a lawyer and activist, and it concluded with a bit of advice.

"We are all going to make it," Phyllis said. "God doesn't make trash and

God made us. . . . The road is still long, but we are going to make it. Be kind and be happy. Don't replay bad memories. Pray often. Don't commit suicide—the bastards aren't worth your life. Set goals. Stay free of drugs. Seek permanence in your relationships. Don't take shit from anybody and don't ever give up. Don't ever give up!"[14]

In response to the article, Rose Faulkner, a transgender woman from Dallas, wrote to *TWT* and explained that her experience with the gay and lesbian community of Dallas was far different than Phyllis's relationship with Houston's gays and lesbians. "I don't know why this Phyllis woman chose to associate herself with gays and lesbians, being that she was trans-sexual," Faulkner wrote. "I was a transperson myself (I am a woman now), and the treatment I received from our gay community here in Dallas was prejudiced, degrading, hateful, and shameful."[15]

Faulkner said that before she came out as transgender, she had been an active member of the gay and lesbian community, joining various groups, including the Metropolitan Community Church, and even protesting for the repeal of 21.06. All that changed, however, when she began to transition. "When I finally came out of my closet and admitted that I was not a gay male but a transsexual, I was shunned. The people I worked with on volunteer political and social assignments no longer called me to notify me of how I could help; my help was no longer desired." Faulkner added that she couldn't even get into the gay clubs she used to frequent. "In closing," she wrote, "I would just like to say that Phyllis is far more fortunate than I; the gay people in Houston sound an awful lot nicer."[16]

Phyllis replied to Faulker with encouragement and advice: "Please do not dismiss my success as mostly good fortune," Phyllis wrote. "I *took* much of what I got. During the first years, I had to demand a place in the community from most of the gays and lesbians that I met. Most of them considered me on the fringe. . . . I persisted."[17]

In January 1986, Phyllis was elected president of the Montrose Business Guild, a largely gay and lesbian organization representing businesses in the Montrose area of Houston. One of her immediate goals in her new role was to strengthen the ties between the guild and the political community of gays and lesbians. But these efforts sometimes led to a backlash on the guild's board. "The guild was a funny thing," she explains. "It was formed in the gay community, and almost everybody who was a member was gay or lesbian. But they bent over backwards to keep from having any public association with the gay and lesbian community, because they didn't want to lose customers."[18]

The following January, Phyllis announced her intention to represent the guild at a planned press conference about a conflict between Mayor Kathy Whitmire and the gay and lesbian community. Board members balked at Phyllis's plan and expressed their disapproval. Not one to be refused, Phyllis resigned in a huff on January 15, 1987, less than a year after assuming the presidency, and headed to the meeting hosted by the Houston Gay/Lesbian Forum, where she learned, to her disgust, that there would be no press conference after all.

Phyllis soon grew to regret her resignation from the guild. She knew the guild offered her standing and credibility in the gay and lesbian community and throughout the city, and it provided resources and a public platform she could not access elsewhere. After some consideration, she rescinded her resignation in a letter she sent to the board on January 16.

But when the board met just a few days later, on January 22, they ignored the January 16 letter and voted to accept her resignation from her office and membership. In an interview with the *Montrose Voice* immediately following the vote, Phyllis said: "It is my feeling that the present board feels the Guild is for business only, that speaking out is always a political action, and that the Guild should stay away from issues, especially gay and lesbian issues. I believe . . . in the interest of good business, a business organization should be able to speak out against discrimination of all kinds."[19]

Publicly humiliated, Phyllis filed a $500,000 lawsuit against the guild, the chair of the board, and a member of the board of trustees, claiming libel, tortious interference with business, negligence, and breach of contract. At the same time, because she also felt burned from the gay and lesbian forum's decision not to publicly air its grievance against the mayor, Phyllis announced she was backing out of Houston's gay and lesbian movement.

It was a momentous development, and conservative Houston resident Jerry Nicholson was delighted when he read about Phyllis's decision in the *Montrose Voice*. In a letter to the editor, he wrote: "After years of perpetuating assorted controversy, I am pleased to read that Phyllis Frye has finally decided to pull back from the gay community. Over the years [she] has instigated an unbelievable string of offensive protest. Now Ms.

Frye is making one last stab at the Houston gay community with her half-million-dollar lawsuit. I can only wish her well. . . .Whatever the end result, it's good that the gay community won't have poor Phyllis to kick around anymore. Happy retirement, dear."[20]

Phyllis soon found herself under great pressure. She had alienated more than a few in the Montrose community, the guild had hired a first-rate attorney, and she was feeling down and depressed. Not relishing a protracted, exhausting, and expensive fight, she agreed to drop the lawsuit, acknowledging that she would most likely lose in the courtroom.

This was a particularly tough period for Phyllis. Not only was she battling the guild, but her Amway business was struggling. Her distributor had recently excluded Phyllis from an in-house trade show for prospective clients, and when she and Trish pressed him for his reasons, he explained matter-of-factly that he did not want to present an Amway team of two women working together.

"Well, that went over like a fucking lead balloon," Phyllis recalls. "I was so pissed that I went to Amway corporate, and they backed us as we cut our ties to our distributor. But that fight took the wind out of us, and we never really recovered from that."[21] Meanwhile, Phyllis's customers, the owners and managers of the city's gay and lesbian bars, were still feeling the pinch of the recession that had begun in the early 1980s and were beginning to cut back on their orders.

"It was just one fucking fight after another," Phyllis says when reflecting back on this time, "and because of all the stress, I developed a bad case of the shingles."[22] As a result of the painful viral infection, Phyllis was forced to give up playing softball for the Special Blend. She was heartbroken.

Ray Hill was a good friend to Phyllis, and he often helped her find a way out of no way. Knowing that she was feeling awful, that her Amway business was crashing, and that her modest advertising was not generating sustainable numbers of law clients, Hill suggested that Phyllis focus on strengthening her financial health by asking criminal court judges to appoint her to indigent criminal cases.

Hill had already proven himself to be a valuable resource to Phyllis's law career. A few months earlier, in the fall of 1986, he had referred to her a gay US Air Force sergeant who was in a full-blown panic about a recent arrest. As Phyllis remembers the call, the sergeant said: "I'm gay, and I'm in criminal court for a DWI [driving while intoxicated], and I'm afraid it'll get out in the media. Can you plead me guilty and keep me out of the media?" The call excited Phyllis because it presented her first chance to appear in the courtroom as a full-fledged lawyer. As the sergeant continued his story, Phyllis thought to herself, "How in the hell can I fuck up a guilty plea?"[23]

For reasons she cannot explain, she was uncertain about her abilities in the courtroom. "I was hesitant, but I couldn't think of a way I could fuck it up, so I said, 'Sure.'" When the sergeant asked about her fee, Phyllis paused; she had never charged anybody for a case like this because she had never had a case like this. "I ended up saying, 'Four hundred dollars, and you're going to have to bring cash.'" He agreed to the terms, and Phyllis instructed him to meet her in the hallway outside the courtroom just before the time scheduled for his case.

After speaking with the client, Phyllis immediately called Hill, imploring him to help out with the case. "Ray, I have no problem going into court and talking to prosecutors," she explained. "But I want to make sure that when I get this guilty plea, they are making me a reasonable plea and not just blowing wind up my skirt or giving me a shitty plea because I'm trans or because I don't have a lot of experience in court. So if you would show up and tell me whether it's a good offer or not, I'll pay you fifty dollars."[24] As an ex-convict who often helped gay men in trouble, Ray was familiar with plea agreements, and he readily agreed to offer his expertise.

Phyllis was nervous when she arrived at the courthouse. She had interned with a lot of the criminal judges there, and she knew her way around the building as well as any of the veteran attorneys, but she was still jittery as she retrieved her client's file and listened to the prosecutor suggest the possibility of probation. Rather than responding right away, Phyllis retreated to the hallway outside the courtroom and ran the details by Ray. He said it was a standard plea and advised her to accept it. Relieved, Phyllis returned to the courtroom and accepted the terms, and she and her client left without a sign of the media anywhere.

It was not the case of the century. It was not a stunning victory against all odds. No more than a handful of people took any notice of the case at all. But it was Phyllis's first courtroom appearance, a groundbreaking and confidence-building experience for her, and all had gone well enough for her to earn the $400 she had charged. After paying Ray his $50, Phyllis headed to the offices of *TWT* and used her $350 to buy her first print advertisement.[25]

But the advertisement did not generate any significant traffic in her makeshift home office, and when her Amway distributorship began to tank, she began to consider Hill's advice that she ask judges to refer indigent clients to her. "I was still kind of gun shy, but I needed the money," Phyllis recalls. "And one day I just kind of woke up and thought, 'I know these judges, I worked with them during my internship, and I know I can ask them.'"[26] So Phyllis donned her best lawyerly attire, headed to criminal court, and started asking judges she knew if they would appoint her to indigent cases. The effort was fruitful, and Phyllis built on her initial success by approaching judges she didn't know. Within a year, she was getting steady work in about six misdemeanor courts and about seven felony courts.

"I had clients every day for a couple of years after I started that process," Phyllis recalls, adding that some of the clients were transgender women. "When I spotted trans women in the docket, I would go the judge and say, 'Your Honor, I would like to represent that person.' They were usually arrested for hustling, and bless their hearts, they were in jail clothes, and all night long they had been peeling the polish off their nails, and their hair was long and ragged. Bless their hearts—they were just targets"—targets for abuse from other prisoners, for harassment from guards and jailers, and for poor representation in the criminal justice system. Phyllis is proud of having represented so many marginalized trans women through the years. "And I was good," she says. "I was so good because I had empathy for people who were down and out."[27]

The extra income from her law work came in handy as Phyllis considered making the trip to the next gay and lesbian march on Washington. The march focused on two major problems: the Reagan administration's lack of attention to HIV and AIDS, and the 1986 Supreme Court ruling on the sexual practices of a young man in Atlanta named Michael Hardwick.

Back on August 2, 1982, one of the most remarkable days in gay rights history, twenty-nine-year-old Michael Hardwick was in his home when a city police officer knocked on his front door. A houseguest directed the officer to Hardwick's bedroom, and when the officer opened the door, he witnessed a sexual encounter between Hardwick and another man. The officer stated that he was there to serve Hardwick a warrant related to public intoxication. After Hardwick protested, saying he had already settled the matter in court, the officer proceeded to arrest him and his sexual partner on grounds that they had violated the state's sodomy law.

With encouragement from the American Civil Liberties Union, Hardwick challenged Georgia's sodomy law in a suit he brought against Michael Bowers, the state's attorney general. *Hardwick v. Bowers* eventually ended up at the US Supreme Court, where Hardwick and the entire LGBT community were delivered a significant blow. Writing for the majority, Justice Byron White argued that homosexuals did not have a "fundamental right . . . to engage in acts of consensual sodomy."[28]

The ruling, delivered on June 30, 1986, rocked LGBT individuals across the nation. "I was really pissed," Phyllis recalls. "I was pissed because it was hypocritical; straight people could give blow jobs, but gay people couldn't."[29] In addition to angering the LGBT community, the decision also propelled gay and lesbian leaders to hasten plans for another march on Washington, scheduled for October 11, 1987.

Phyllis was elected to the national steering committee for the march. Once again, she advocated for the use of "transgender" in the name and the inclusion of trans issues in the list of demands, but once again, she lost. She considered boycotting the event, but Ray Hill changed her mind, saying that while no one would miss her if she wasn't there, a lot of people would notice a transgender presence if she did participate in the highly publicized event.

"By then I had the money for airfare, and I didn't have to put together another bus trip," she recalls, so she booked a flight and a hotel room for several days.[30] She and Jack Valinski, another prominent leader in Houston's LGBT politics, stayed in Baltimore and commuted by bus to the protest events in Washington. A self-described introvert, Valinski remembers Phyllis chatting up bus drivers and anyone else within listening range about the march and her reasons for being there.

One of the more memorable moments for Valinski occurred when he and Phyllis were deep inside the Metro, Washington's subway system, with a crowd of LGBT-friendly individuals heading to the march. "Phyllis pulls out this big Texas flag—and this was before people hated [Texans] because of Bush—and puts that flag up in the middle of the Metro station, and people were just screaming, and the stations are all concrete, so it just vibrated."[31] Phyllis, too, remembers the moment as electric. "The crowd was 100% queer. I raised my Texas flag, and the crowd went nuts. They were crazy. It just energized them, and I don't think any of them were Texans."[32]

Phyllis and Valinski joined the Texas delegation for the march itself, and Phyllis took her place, along with two others, at the head of the group. Wearing a pair of Nike running shoes and a wool cap, she waved the Texas flag as she and her fellow delegates walked past the Reagan White House, demonstrating pride in themselves and disgust with a president who largely ignored LGBT folks and people with HIV and AIDS.[33]

The following morning, Phyllis traveled back to Washington for a protest at the Supreme Court. Around 8:00 a.m., at least two thousand people gathered in front of the Court. An hour later, groups of fifteen to thirty protesters walked past the police barriers and sat in circles on the Court's plaza, where they were handcuffed and led away. Some of the protesters made their way to the Court's front steps, chanting such things as "We have AIDS, and we have rights!" When the police put on latex gloves before arresting the protesters, apparently to protect themselves from HIV, people in the crowd shouted, "Shame, shame!" and "Your gloves don't match your shoes!"[34]

Phyllis watched with pride as Hardwick and about six hundred other protesters offered themselves for arrest. "I thought about it, about getting arrested, but I decided—and Trish was really worried about it—that I just wasn't interested in getting arrested," she says. "I just wasn't excited about it. I was still dealing with all those years of fearing arrest for cross-dressing. But I was there, and I carried my protest sign."[35]

The next day, Phyllis joined a group of protesters who lobbied Congress for the repeal of sodomy laws, for additional funding for AIDS research, and many other LGBT-friendly policies. As she remembers it, she and others from the Texas delegation trekked to the various offices of Texas representatives simply to "let them know that we were queer and we were here."[36]

Like so much of her volunteer work in recent years, there was nothing about her lobbying that was specific to her identity as a transgender woman. But all that would change in the coming months, and Phyllis would make sure that the change would be for the betterment of trans men and women in Houston—and across the nation.

PART III
FROM PROTEST TO POLITICS

Chapter Nine

Radicalized

Phyllis continued to hope that one day she and her parents would be reconciled. She had not talked to her father for about twelve years, and while she maintained a tenuous connection to her mother through occasional phone calls and letters, she longed to have both of her parents in her life. "I just kept holding out this hope that finally, because I was their kid, they would come around," she says.[1]

By this point, Phyllis had developed a range of skills for effecting social and political change—lobbying, marching, boycotting—but she found herself utterly unable to transform the hearts of her parents. She felt helpless, but one afternoon in 1987, she experienced a flash of hope while watching *The Phil Donahue Show*. The silver-haired, blue-eyed Donahue was an expert facilitator of difficult and controversial conversations, and Phyllis admired his intellectual boldness and curiosity, as well as his left-leaning politics.

Phyllis wrote *Donahue* with a programming suggestion. "I told them I was trans, and I said, 'I know you've all done shows on trans, and that's not what this is about. This pitch is about people who have been disowned by their families.'"[2]

The producers jumped on the creative suggestion. They called Phyllis to see whether she would appear on the show, and she was shocked and thrilled. They offered to fly her up the night before the taping, but she said, "No, no, no. I've never been to New York City, so put me on the earliest flight the day before. And can I bring a guest?"[3] The producers agreed, and because Trish had teaching responsibilities, Phyllis invited her good friend Brian Keever to join her.

On the day of the taping, Phyllis was more excited than nervous as she put on her red blouse and gray skirt and applied her makeup. She finished her look with a gold necklace and red heels. Onstage at the studio, the staff sat her between a young Jewish woman in disguise and an older couple from the South. A therapist, an expert on family conflicts, shared the stage with the guests, and Phil Donahue stood in the audience, microphone in hand.

The Jewish woman was the focus of the show's first segment. Her family had disowned her because she had married a Gentile. Shortly after her marriage, her parents had published her obituary, saying that she was "lost to her loved ones" and requesting that no one send them condolences. The older couple, who were the loving parents of a young gay man, would close the show. Right in the middle of the lineup was the large woman with a Texan drawl.

"Guess what?" Donahue began, by way of introduction. "Phyllis Randolph grew up as a boy. She had the sex-change operation, and guess what her parents did to her? They did disown her."[4] Although the producers had clearly misinformed Donahue, Phyllis decided not to correct him on the surgery point, especially since she had to share broadcast minutes with the other guests.

Donahue's introduction included photos of Phyllis from years prior—one in her student military uniform, another during her first marriage, and another from 1976, just after she had transitioned full-time. When the producers showed the last photo, at least one audience member said "ugh" loud enough for everyone to hear, prompting others to laugh out loud. Phyllis did not show any visible discomfort in the moment, but later in the program, she sarcastically referred to "the picture that some of you politely said 'ugh' to."

With encouragement from Donahue, Phyllis explained her reason for being on the show. "I don't have any relationship with my parents," she said, though she noted that she had seen her mother twice in the last twelve years and that the two occasionally spoke on the phone. "I'm a nice person, and I don't know why they don't like me," she continued.

An older gentleman asked Phyllis whether she was happy—and if she was, what was the point of bringing up her estranged parents? Phyllis replied by asserting that she was "extremely happy." She had already noted that she was in a "monogamous, loyal, loving relationship," and now she emphasized that appearing on *Donahue* was a way of asserting her dignity.

"I'm an extroverted person, I have a lot of intelligence, I have a lot of education," she said. "People don't say 'ugh' about me anymore, so I think

I'm relatively attractive. . . . And so I'm hoping that being on television my family will finally get to see . . . who Phyllis Randolph is. . . . They'll finally get to see me, and they'll finally get to say, 'Hey, maybe she isn't who I thought she was.'"

Donahue asked Phyllis whether she missed her parents. "Oh, god," she replied. "You can't believe how much I cry and I cry and I cry. And yes, I miss them. I miss them desperately."

Of course, Phyllis felt many things in addition to sadness about her relationship with her parents, and those feelings were apparent on the show, especially in interactions with the audience members. When a Jewish father said he would disown his daughters should they marry outside the faith, Phyllis pointed her finger at the man and said: "The burden that families put on the child is for *life*, and *damn it, it's not fair!* *You're* not there when I'm crying, and *you're* not there when I'm hurting. *You* start carrying the pain, baby! I'm tired of carrying the pain. *You* start carrying the pain! *You* deal with it! *You* take it!"

A young woman in the audience asserted that, according to the Bible, "homosexuals will receive the full recompense for their sins—and you are." In reply, Phyllis declared herself a proud Christian whose exegesis of scripture had revealed that so-called biblical condemnations of homosexuality were really judgments on fertility rites and pederasty. "Jesus Christ never said anything about homosexuality," she added.

During parts of Phyllis's segments, the chyron read, "Phyllis Randolph, transsexual disowned by parents." "I went on the show as Phyllis Randolph," she explains. "My hope was that my parents or someone in the family, some neighbor, some friend would see the show, and it would cause my family to rethink me. But I didn't want to put my last name out there in case . . . they got outed as having this tranny relative, and it would push them back."

Phyllis returned home. Days and then weeks passed. "Absolutely nothing happened with respect to my family," she says. Her father didn't show up at her door; her mother didn't call with news of a family conversion; her brother and sister didn't write. Phyllis had no indication that anyone in the family had even watched her on *Donahue*. "It wasn't what I wanted. It did nothing that I wanted it to do." But not all was lost. "I got a real nice picture of me and Donahue," Phyllis says. "He's just like what you see on television; he's a really nice, caring person."[5]

Phyllis was excited when she learned that two statewide organizations, the Lesbian/Gay Rights Lobby (LGRL) and the Texas Human Rights Foundation (THRF), were calling for a massive march on Austin in 1989. Activists like Phyllis had been hoping for a statewide march as a way of building on the momentum of the 1987 March on Washington for Lesbian and Gay Rights. She was also pleased when she read in *TWT* that the conveners were issuing an open call for individuals and groups to attend organizational meetings. "It is important from the beginning that this be an inclusive and broad-based organization, if the march is to be successful," said Glen Maxey, an informal spokesman for the two groups. "We must have men and women, all ethnicities, all socioeconomic levels and all types of groups ranging from political to religious to social if we expect to bring thousands of persons to Austin in 1989."[6]

Reading those words, Phyllis hoped that this march, unlike the two national ones, would make transgender individuals equal partners in the formation of the march's title and goals. She had additional reason to hope when Annise Parker, Phyllis's former softball coach, was elected one of the co-chairs of the Houston Committee for the March on Austin. Phyllis hoped Parker might be prepared to argue for her inclusion once again. Phyllis's good friend Ray Hill was also active on the committee.

Phyllis attended Houston's organizational meetings, and she once again argued that "transgender" be included in the name of the march. Phyllis was frustrated to find that her allies, including Parker and Hill, tended to go quiet when she advocated for inclusion. She felt as if she was speaking into an echo chamber, and she ultimately lost the battle over the march's name when organizers settled on "The March on Austin for Lesbian and Gay Equal Rights."

Nevertheless, Phyllis continued to insist that transgender issues be included in the goals of the march, and the organizing committee budged, if only a bit, by agreeing to add the word "transgenderal" to one of the eleven goals ("An end to all social, economic, judicial and legal oppression of lesbians and gays, and people of every race, gender, ability, class, ethnicity, ideology, transgenderal orientation and sexual orientation").[7]

The inclusion of "transgenderal" marked a historic moment for Phyllis.

She had been fighting for inclusion for more than a decade, and this was the first protest, at least of those she participated in, that explicitly mentioned transgender in its goals. Deeply gratified, she attended the march and related events with the gay and lesbian contingent from Houston.

Phyllis followed up her victory in the 1989 Austin march with another success, this one in the courtroom, where she won a judgment of $20,000 for Erika Yvonne Erinwulf, a homeless transgender woman whose few belongings had been unlawfully confiscated by the owners of a storage business. The victory was especially sweet for Erinwulf because one of the owners had shown himself to be transphobic. "I know it was a homophobic action because he screamed profanities and 'faggot'-type descriptions at me as he stormed away from the Dispute Resolution Center," Erinwulf said. In an interview with *TWT*, Phyllis echoed Erinwulf's conviction and expressed dismay that the owners had dragged the case out for two years. "My experience is that people don't react that irrationally over such a long period of time unless they have deeply held beliefs," she said. "You know what I mean—gay men, lesbians, transgenderals—we're all the same kind of unworthy trash to them."[8]

Phyllis's victories—in activist communities and in the courtroom—had complex and powerful effects on her: even as the battles heightened her sense of marginalization, the victories made her hungry for more success. Together, these feelings helped to create a major turning point in Phyllis's activism. Though full inclusion of the transgender community had always been one of her priorities when working with gays and lesbians, the beginning of the new decade saw her acting with greater focus, urgency, and forcefulness to this end.

In January of 1990, at a meeting of the Houston Gay and Lesbian Political Caucus, Phyllis interrupted a discussion about nondiscrimination policies for local businesses, insisting that any proposed policy include trans folks as a protected class. Then, in March, she started a highly publicized campaign to add the word "transgenderal" to the name of the caucus. She began her push at the caucus's March 7th meeting, where she moved to amend the bylaws to reflect a name change.

The debate following her motion focused on the practical effects of the change, with many members arguing that if other "subgroups" would ask for similar inclusion, the name would become too long and unwieldy. The addition of "lesbian" to the name—a change that Phyllis had advocated for—was sufficient for the purpose of informing everyone that the caucus was inclusive, they argued.

Hoping to find some common ground, caucus member Cicely Wynne proposed keeping the existing name and adding the names of subgroups to stationery and other items, but the caucus defeated that motion, too, prompting another member to move to table Phyllis's motion, perhaps for consideration at a later time. When the caucus quickly agreed, Phyllis conceded, if only temporarily. She left the meeting feeling determined. As she saw it, she now had time to educate and lobby her colleagues before future meetings.

She took her campaign to the media, and in a major article on the push for inclusion, *Montrose Voice* reporter Sheri Cohen Darbonne explained Phyllis's rationale: "Frye cites two major reasons for the name change. First, she said, it is 'philosophically correct' for a group like the caucus to include a smaller oppressed group which may be left out. Second, without the word 'transgenderal' in the name as a constant reminder, Frye claimed the caucus itself, as well as the Austin lobby, would 'routinely leave me out of each demand.'"[9]

Darbonne's article also reported on one of Phyllis's opponents, caucus vice-president Larry Lingle, who argued that a name change would "only confuse issues both within and outside of our community." He also shared his belief that the inclusion of transgender folks was not even an issue. "I don't know of any exclusion within the organization—and this is not an issue in any gay and lesbian organization anywhere else in the country," he said. "The term she is using [transgenderal] is not even an accepted term anywhere in the country."[10]

Lingle also claimed that the addition of "transgenderal" would make the group even more of a target than it was. "The point is, the bylaws are already broad enough to be inclusive, [and] if we complicate the caucus name, we only give more fuel to those who want to shoot us down. Those who want to criticize us can zero in on that terminology." Phyllis was "overstating her case," Lingle said. "The term 'sexual orientation' is what is usually used [in legislative proposals]."[11]

Phyllis spoke to *TWT* just before the vote. "It is correct to include another oppressed group which is smaller than your group, which may be left out," she reiterated. She also suggested that the support of the gay and lesbian community would be fair repayment for her own activism on their behalf. "In every fight that I have fought since 1975 for my individual rights and for the rights of other transgenderals, I have always carried your [gay and lesbian] cause with me and fought for your rights as well. It's time for you to overtly carry my cause with you!"[12]

The May 2 vote on the name change was lopsided—and not in Phyllis's favor. Facing widespread opposition, she switched tactics, proposing that the caucus use an asterisk at the end of its name to indicate the inclusion of all other so-called subgroups, just as she had done with the student organization she formed in law school. When that was voted down, she tried one more tactic, insisting on the use of "the inclusive gay and lesbian community" on stationery and in advertisements and caucus discussions. She lost on that point, too.[13]

As the nay votes tallied up at the May 2nd meeting, Phyllis led her supporters in an abrupt walkout. In a later conversation with *TWT,* Phyllis said that she was "carrying a lot of pain" and that she was "totally surprised not only by the lopsided vote, but more importantly by how mean some people got."[14]

Phyllis's defeat in the caucus came right on the heels of another that occurred in the spring of 1990, this one surrounding the boycott of Randalls, a popular grocery chain.

In 1985, rumors began to circulate that a Randalls meat cutter named Steven Little had AIDS and was also caring for a friend who had AIDS. Little's supervisor Ken Fleming confronted him and expressed his concern that a meat cutter with AIDS would pose a health hazard to Randalls customers. Little could either resign or be fired, Fleming said. Little resigned, hired an attorney, and sued Randalls for defamation of character.

The Houston Gay and Lesbian Political Caucus followed the case as it made its way through the courts for three years. Meanwhile, they lobbied Randalls to add sexual orientation and AIDS to its policy on nondiscrimination. In 1989, when Randalls declined to make that policy change, the caucus passed a resolution encouraging "all supporters of human and civil rights and those supportive of compassionate care for PWAs [People With AIDS] and others to join us in shopping elsewhere." Commenting on the resolution, Ray Hill said that Randalls "repeatedly stood up for their right to discriminate against gay and lesbian people and people with AIDS."[15]

Phyllis backed the boycott without hesitation, and her support grew even stronger when trans women told her that the store had asked them to leave after they had sought to use the restroom. Phyllis also supported the activists who regularly picketed a new Randalls store in the Montrose section of Houston, though she did not join them.

With Randalls still not budging, various gay and lesbian groups aligned in the spring of 1990 to create a five-member committee to lobby the chain. The committee met with Robert and Randall Olmstead, the father-son duo who owned the chain, on April 5, and to the committee's surprise, the Olmsteads arrived at the meeting with a letter expressly stating that the company's nondiscrimination policy included gays, lesbians, and people with AIDS.

Pleased with the letter, caucus leaders planned to call a halt to the boycott, and at the April 18 meeting, a caucus member formally moved to end the protest. Phyllis rose to her feet in protest and passionately argued against the motion, stating that Randalls continued to discriminate against trans women and that the company's letter did not mention trans people as a protected class.[16]

"Several folks that I thought were friends openly mocked me, others said the caucus was not trans-inclusive, and others stated that the community at large was not inclusive of transgender folks," she recalls. "I was told in no uncertain terms that they didn't give a shit about the transgender community, that they were more than glad to have me there helping to carry gay and lesbian water, but they weren't going to carry transgender water."[17]

The caucus was unmoved. "All these folks I worked with all that time," she says. "I was pissed. I was really angry."[18] Still, Phyllis decided to stick with the caucus through most of the upcoming election season so she could ensure that they backed her preferred candidates.

Phyllis enjoyed a professional highpoint in July when she was elected to the board of directors of the Harris County Criminal Lawyers Association. In its report on the honor, *TWT* noted that "[t]he significance of this is that Frye practices law totally out of the closet and was elected to this position by her professional peers, a membership exceeding 300 practicing criminal trial attorneys."[19]

Phyllis herself commented on her election to the board by highlighting her push for inclusivity in the gay and lesbian movement. "I am an activist for more than just gays and lesbians," she said. "I believe in activism for an inclusive community—a community inclusive of lesbians and gays and transgenderals and bisexuals and our heterosexual supporters." This statement marked the first time Phyllis publicly included bisexuals in her vision of the inclusive community, a clear sign that she was turning to a new group for allies in her fight.

When Phyllis finished her last order of business with the caucus—lobbying for her candidates—she submitted her letter of resignation at the September 5 meeting:

> Dear Friends at GLPC:
>
> Tonight, after the endorsement votes are complete and the judicial candidates that I believe in are endorsed, I shall give president Dennis Spencer my letter of resignation from the caucus. You are my friends; therefore I want you to know why.
>
> The best explanation is an analogy, and the analogy to use is that of a spurned lover or the rejected child. For so very long I carried the caucus and the movement with me everywhere I went and in everything I did. And many times, beginning with the original Town Meeting and the organization for the first March on Washington, I spoke for inclusion and was [assured] that inclusion was in our movement.
>
> The Randalls thing exposed it all: the message to me was "inclusion *if* convenient."
>
> Maybe my skin is thin; maybe I've just fought so intensely for so many years that my scars remain tender. Anyway, as with the spurned lover or the rejected child, "the feeling is gone." And now, four months later, when I think of it all, I still grieve.
>
> I heard yesterday that a move was afoot to have some nondiscrimination statement drafted. I'm glad—it's long overdue. I hope that it will be enough to bring in others. But it won't be for me, at least for now.[20]

Even as Phyllis left the caucus behind, a steady stream of gay and lesbian clients continued to seek her legal services. Not long after her resignation, Phyllis represented Albert Rivera Jr. in a case of police brutality. According to her defense, Rivera was walking home dressed in shorts and a tank top when a police officer, thinking that he was a gay prostitute, demanded that he stop. The officer did not identify himself, and Rivera started to run away for his own safety. The officer caught Rivera, pounded his head into the concrete, and cuffed him, all before identifying himself. Then he wielded his taser and laughed when the high voltage made Rivera lose control of his bladder. Rivera was charged with resisting arrest.

It took only thirty minutes for the jury to return a not-guilty verdict. "I was proud of the initial jury panel and of the resulting jury," Phyllis told *TWT* at the time. "After the trial was complete, the jury told me up front that they had no problem rendering a not guilty, even though Albert was gay and even though I was a transgenderal." In its report, *TWT* described Phyllis as a "longtime inclusive-community activist."[21]

Phyllis's professional success during this period did not prevent ongoing assaults about her transgender identity. At the end of November 1990, *Houston Post* columnist Paul Harasim attacked her in a column on court-room appearance. This was not Phyllis's first run-in with the columnist; the prior November, she had taken issue with a piece Harasim wrote about the city's ordinance on restrooms. But Harasim's new column attacked Phyllis personally. After ridiculing a man for wearing shorts to jury selection, Harasim wrote that he saw the courtroom as "a place that deserves much the same kind of respect as a church." If judges joined him in that sentiment, he wrote, as some said they did, "then why don't Harris County judges object to a man practicing law in women's clothing? Surely, the courtroom appearance of Phyllis Frye, who is still a man but is taking female hormones and wears women's clothing, gets a few tongues to wagging."[22]

Phyllis was not expecting the column, and she broke down in tears as she read it. Still, she headed to the courtroom for the day as she had planned. When she entered the basement cafeteria, where her colleagues liked to try out their arguments on one another, she still had tears in her eyes. "A lot of people had seen the article, and they felt sorry for me," she recalls. "I was liked down there because I was good, I was very good, and they respected that. Plus, I'm a nice person."[23] The support of her colleagues was fortifying, and when she arrived home later that day, she typed "An Open Letter to the Judges of Harris County":

Some of you do not know me, but most of you do. I have practiced in most of the courtrooms since my 3rd Year Law Student Internship in September 1980 and since passing the bar in May 1981. I continue to strive to be open and honest in my dealings with the court and opposing counsel.

On Wednesday, in a local gossip column, I was "hatchet-ed" in an article dealing with the appearance of jurors. The article, written by Paul Harasim of the POST, is attached.

I will personally tell you that I considered the article to be mean spirited and irrelevant to the theme of the article. Because of what was written, and the meanness conveyed, I did a lot of crying on Wednesday and some still this morning. (I have been Phyllis since September 1976; after 14 years, I continue to wonder if the meanness will ever stop.)

I am writing to you because I assume that since the article dealt with juror appearance, you either saw it or heard about it. I am also writing to you in a continuing effort to be open and honest. Therefore, please know that if any of you have any question about who I am or who I was, please feel free to ask. If any of you wish to chat with me about me or about anything else, please contact me. I do not know how I could have been any more open than I have been, but it seems that Mr. Harasim just felt compelled to take a shot at me.

Finally, I know that Mr. Harasim asked several of you about me in search of a "sensational" story. Those of you who were asked obviously respect me enough not to give him anything. (Actually, I don't know that there is anything.) For this, I wish to say thank you.[24]

Phyllis made numerous copies of her letter. She stapled Harasim's column to each copy, asked the clerks to put the collated material in the mailbox of their assigned judges, and handed out the rest to friends wherever she saw them. "I heard that a lot of judges shared the letter with their staff, and I heard that quite a few judges told their bailiffs to chase Harasim away if he ever appeared near their courtroom." According to Phyllis, the results were astounding. "None of the staff would let him in to see the judges, and I think he never wrote another article on the courthouse after my response."[25]

That positive experience was typical of Phyllis's time in the courthouse.

No matter what might have happened behind her back, she usually encountered professional and personal cordiality from those she worked with in the court. As an active member of the Harris County Criminal Lawyers Association, Phyllis returned the cordiality, even sharing her professional insight and expertise by writing for *Docket Call*, the association's bimonthly publication.

As 1990 came to a close, she published an article in which she argued that Texas Penal Code 21.06, which criminalized gay sex, was unconstitutional because it deprived consenting adults of their right to privacy and equal treatment. On the same day that *Docket Call* published her article, Phyllis learned that an Austin judge had indeed just ruled the statute unconstitutional. "I'm glad for the court's ruling, but the fight is not over," Phyllis wrote a few weeks later. "That there will be appeals is not news; but, that the homophobes in the Legislature will try to push through another law, must be prepared for *now*."[26]

In early January 1991, Phyllis learned that plans were underway for yet another march on Austin. She was in no mood for more rejection from the gay and lesbian community, so hoping to preempt another fight, she mailed *TWT* a forceful letter about inclusion:

> In the spring of 1990, I had a very rude and painful awakening. I had assumed that the 15 years I had spent working for the civil and human rights of my lesbian sisters and gay brothers was an extension and part and parcel of my work for the transgender community (transvestites, female impersonators, transgenderists and transsexuals), for bisexuals, and for heterosexual supporters.
>
> I had assumed that we were all in this together. Gays and lesbians have a huge fight that anyone reading this magazine is already aware of. Heterosexual transgenderals carry the same stereotyping and prejudice plus a bit more. Even if all the legal homosexual barriers are removed, the homosexual transgenderals will still have the fight that heterosexual transgenderals currently fight. Bisexuals in a same-sex relationship are in the same boat. Bisexuals in an opposite-sex relationship carry the fear of the closet door opening with them and the prejudice when it does.
>
> As to heterosexual supporters, just ask Ann Richards or Nikki Van Hightower or the Democratic Party at large. They are constantly being smeared with innuendos and gay bashing.

I remember the history of the pink triangle. The Nazis imposed the pink triangle on them.

We were certainly all in the same boat back then. I also remember the Stonewall riots, which began the modern movement to freedom.

The first March on Washington was heady stuff. But during the planning meeting held at the University of Houston in the late 70s, I had to make a really tough stand to even get the words dealing with transgenderals into the printed material. It was an uphill fight, but the language was inserted. Then it was neatly tucked away and we all marched under the overt title and banner of only gay and lesbian rights.

The second March on Washington was the same. Overtly, we all marched only for gay and lesbian rights.

The March on Austin in 1989 was the same way. I even bought the entire back page of the program to demonstrate financial support. But overtly, we marched only for gay and lesbian rights.

At the time of the last legislature, at least one bill was drafted to allow discrimination on the basis of gender identification (that means transgenderals) in housing. And if you read the federal handicap law, you will see that there are many categories of transgenderals specifically named and targeted for discrimination.

I asked the Houston Gay and Lesbian Political Caucus to overtly inclusify its name by adding an asterisk to the end of both its name and its initials and to include transgenderals, bisexuals and heterosexual supporters in its bylaws. Not only was the "★" soundly voted down, the bylaws change wasn't even debated.

I was told that night and I have been told since that the goal of the caucus is to gain the rights of only gays and lesbians. I have even been called "heterosexual" with the same sneer and hatred that our enemies muster up to call us queer or faggot.

Now the March on Austin is being planned for 1991. Will it put an "★" in its name to signify the community's inclusivity? Will the planners overtly explain in each of the march's releases and all of its literature the need for and desire to have an "inclusive community" of gays, lesbians, transgenderals, bisexuals, and heterosexual supporters?

Will it be the March on Austin for Lesbian and Gay Rights★? Or will it be the March on Austin for the Rights of the Inclusive

Community? Or will it be the March on Austin to Resist Sexual and Genderal Bigotry? Or will it be some other overt name that includes us all?

If not, count me out![27]

The organizers chose the name "the March on Austin for Lesbian/Gay Equal Rights," and though they adopted the 1989 goal that reflected Phyllis's handiwork—"An end to all social, economic, judicial and legal oppression of lesbian and gay people, and people of every race, gender, ability, class, ethnicity, ideology, transgenderal orientation and sexual orientation"—no other goals focused on transgender issues. Phyllis refused to attend the march.

But when Houston Gay/Lesbian Pride Week arrived that summer, she did not absent herself. The organizers excluded transgender from the name of the celebratory event, but they invited Phyllis to submit an article to *Pride Guide 1991*. Phyllis accepted the invitation and used the article to educate her readers, directly and indirectly, about the need to address transgender issues when discussing gay and lesbian rights, including the issue of unity in the movement.

While emphatic in tone, the article did not convey the intensity of Phyllis's anger at a movement that refused to include trans individuals as equal partners. She was still livid with the caucus, and national organizations of gays and lesbians were doing nothing to assuage her hurt. "By that time, I'd get in the mail stuff from Lambda Legal and from the National Center for Lesbian Rights and HRC [the Human Rights Campaign Fund] and a lot of other national organizations that were not doing anything dealing with transgender." Phyllis was also disturbed at the many members of the trans community who seemed more interested in passing as cis men and women than in securing their legal rights. "I was just pissed," she says. "I had just finally had a crawful of it, the local and the national. So I said, 'Fuck you! I'll do it myself.'"[28]

Chapter Ten

Shaping Transgender Law

Phyllis's fury and hurt over the dismissal of trans issues by local, state, and national activist groups could have driven her to give up her social activism, but instead the rejections drew her into a creative and fruitful response. Drawing on her legal work on behalf of those facing discrimination, she came up with the idea of holding an annual meeting that would focus on changing and shaping laws—local, state, and national—for the advancement of transgender rights.

Though she was tempted to go it alone, Phyllis knew she couldn't undertake all the work by herself, so she approached Merissa Sherill Lynn, founder and executive director of the International Foundation for Gender Education (IFGE), at a Houston fundraiser in the summer of 1991. Lynn had founded IFGE in 1987 to promote educational resources for transgender individuals and their allies. By the time Phyllis approached her four years later, she had created a worldwide network through an annual convention, a research library, publishing services, a speakers' bureau, educational documents, and contact information for national and international transgender groups.

Lynn's most popular contribution to the trans community was *Transgender Tapestry,* a quarterly publication that eventually found its way into mailboxes across the world as well as into major US bookstores. In the late 1970s, Lynn had begun *Tapestry* as a newsletter with just a few pages, but by the 1980s she had transformed it into an attractive magazine featuring pieces about fashion, makeup, coming out, and interpersonal relations, as well as articles on transgender law and civil rights.

Phyllis was impressed by Lynn's work and approached her hopefully. "I told her of my idea to have an annual meeting devoted solely to developing strategies for progressive social change as it affected transgenders," Phyllis recalls. "I also offered to work as a committee under the

IFGE umbrella." Phyllis wanted the credibility and resources that IFGE could provide, and in turn she was giving the established organization an opportunity to expand its influence and work in the legal sphere. But Lynn wasn't interested. "I got the impression she thought I was a flash in the pan," says Phyllis. "She wasn't very impressed with me. But maybe she also didn't like my ideas."[1]

Phyllis switched tactics and targets, as she had done so many times before, now setting her sights on the Gulf Coast Transgender Community (GCTC). Based in Houston, GCTC fashioned itself as a social and educational group open to all members of the transgender community, including spouses.[2] According to Tricia Lynn, GCTC president during the mid-1980s, the organization usually held its monthly meetings in a Houston hotel room where members, some of whom waited to dress until they arrived, socialized over drinks and snacks. They shared stories, discussed common struggles, and exchanged tips on fashion, makeup, and hair.[3]

In search of a political base, Phyllis decided to run for vice-president of GCTC with a clear agenda. "I said, 'Don't vote for me unless you know what I'm going to do as vice-president, and what I'm going to do is to use GCTC to fund and sponsor a national transgender law conference.'"[4]

GCTC members, including president Jackie Thorne, reacted positively to this forceful personality in their midst. "I admired her 'guts' and the ration of crap she was handed by not only straights but by some gays for her TG advocacy, particularly in the Houston (Gay) Political Caucus," Thorne recalls.[5] "They thought my idea was fantastic," Phyllis says, "so I was elected, and I immediately formed a committee."

The committee included Thorne, Cynthia Lee, Dee McKellar, Vivian McKenzie, and Cynthia Davis. "They listened to me and let me do whatever the hell I wanted and offered their help. None were lawyers, none knew anything about the law, but they knew what my vision was, and they were very excited about it and supported it as they could. It worked out really well."[6]

Under Phyllis's guidance, the committee soon settled on a name—the Conference on Transgender Law and Employment Policy. Some preferred an earlier version, the Conference on Transgender Law, but Phyllis insisted on the longer name. She knew from experience the many painful costs of job discrimination against trans men and women, and she knew how pervasive it was. Plus, Phyllis believed that employment was key: "In my opinion and experience," she said, "it had to focus on employment, because it didn't matter if your family didn't like you or your church didn't like you—all the different shit a trans person goes through. If they could keep or get a job so that they could experience the dignity and income that come with a job, they could survive their transition."[7]

The name of the conference became even longer when Phyllis received a query from Stephen Whittle, a budding trans activist from England. "Stephen said he'd like to come but couldn't get his law school's support unless the conference was an international one, so I said, 'Fuck! I can put 'International' in the title. I don't care.'"[8] From August 1991 on, the conference became known as the International Conference on Transgender Law and Employment Policy (ICTLEP). As for Whittle, he missed the first conference, attended the second, and went on to become the leading activist for transgender rights in the United Kingdom.

Phyllis learned the nuts and bolts of conference planning from Cynthia and Linda Phillips, members of the Boulton & Park Society (B&P) in San Antonio. B&P was a transgender support group known especially for starting the Texas T-Party, an annual trans-themed conference that attracted individuals from around the world for a week filled with shopping, seminars, discussion groups, wine and cheese receptions, formal dinners, fashion shows, and vendor sales. Under the leadership of the Phillipses, the T-Party had become the largest trans-themed convention in the nation. Cynthia's extensive event-planning experience helped her reach a wide audience through creative marketing in the days before email and social media. She also worked hard to make sure the conference was proactively welcoming—especially to trans people who, like Phyllis, carried painful memories of transphobia and might find the conference attractive but frightening.

Phyllis was impressed with all of it—the T-Party, its attendance, its welcome, and Cynthia's organizing skills—and she asked for advice. "Phyllis and I talked a lot about the law conference before it happened," Cynthia says. "She was interested in the T-Party and picked my brain about it. I gave her a lot of information. I helped her with figuring out prices, how to do registration, how to run a conference."[9] The two also talked about the need for a brochure that Phyllis could mail to trans groups across the country.

Although Phyllis did not have a computer in 1991, Dee McKellar, a resourceful GCTC committee member, had a Hewlett-Packard, and she and Phyllis designed and printed a two-sided, tri-folded brochure featuring the scales of justice on the front cover. Phyllis penned the text, and in spite of space limitations, she included a wealth of information—not just the conference's logistics, but also its target audience, topics, rationale, and purpose.

"This Conference," Phyllis wrote, "is for attorneys and other legal professionals; for employment, personnel, and other human resource professionals; and for members of the transgender community, all of whom have an interest in the current status of and in strategies for progressive changes in either the law and/or employment policy as they pertain to the transgender community." In addition, the conference would address "military law, housing law, insurance law, probate law, criminal law, health law, family law, antidiscrimination law, and employment law and policy," the key areas where she and her trans friends had encountered obstacles.[10]

Phyllis also made clear in the brochure that, unlike some trans groups, the conference would be inclusive of the entire trans community. "Transgendered persons include transsexuals, transgenderists, and other cross-dressers of both sexes, transitioning in either direction (male to female or female to male), of any sexual orientation, and of all races, creeds, religions, ages, and degrees of physical impediment."[11]

Phyllis also emphasized that the need for the law conference was rooted not in the ignorance of trans individuals but in a society that viciously discriminated against their core identity. "This is a *very* unforgiving society for those persons who were born of one sex, yet have a definite opposite gender identity," she wrote. "This disagreement may range from moderate (occasional cross-dressing) to complete (sex reassignment surgery). The condition is observed over such a vastness and diversity in geography, race, education, religion, income, and profession that to be transgendered is *clearly* not a matter of mere choice. Furthermore, rational people do not take upon themselves the burdens placed by unforgiving societies merely to express an occasional cross-dressing fling."[12]

GCTC was not a wealthy organization, but when Phyllis asked for funds to cover the printing and copying of the brochure, it gave generously. The Texas T-Party organizers also suggested including the brochure in their mailings. "We could afford the postage," Cynthia says, and she couldn't, because we were established by then."[13] Phyllis enthusiastically accepted, knowing that if her brochure went out to the T-Party mailing list, it would end up in about four hundred mailboxes across the world. In addition to tapping into the T-Party list, Phyllis also placed advertisements in major trans publications, including *Transgender Tapestry* and *Chrysalis Quarterly*, and spread the word at two upcoming conferences where she had agreed to give workshops on transgender law—the Texas T-Party in February 1992 and IFGE's annual convention in March. In her workshops, Phyllis announced that she was still looking for speakers for three of the nine areas she wanted the conference to cover. "I knew that I had enough local resources and friends to provide speakers in all of the areas except for military law (no military base within 150 miles), health law (an area that I knew nothing about), and employment law (since LGBT folks had NO protection in Texas)," Phyllis recalls. "Interestingly, those were the first three areas for which volunteers appeared."[14]

With help from the GCTC committee, Phyllis also tended to administrative details, using her and Trish's credit card, funds from GCTC, and a $500 grant from the Winslow Street Fund, an endowment created by IFGE, to pay any up-front costs, including reservations for rooms at the Hilton Houston Southwest. During negotiations with the hotel, she insisted that the marquee would read "Welcome Transgender Law Conference."[15]

As the conference approached, Phyllis worried that no one would attend, that her idea would be a bust, and that there would be a significant financial loss, but when she showed up for the preconference cocktail party, she found a roomful of people. She breathed a sigh of relief and walked inside smiling.

She had decided to hold the party at a private club for attorneys, the Courthouse Club in downtown Houston, right near the courthouse complex. She hoped that this location would allow conference participants to experience the support offered by local attorneys, especially the party's sponsor, the local Bar Association for Human Rights. She also wanted trans attendees to be themselves in a safe and public setting. "I didn't want people to hide in their hotel rooms," she explains. "I wanted them to go downtown as themselves."[16]

On the morning of August 28, 1992, Phyllis stood before a group of about fifty people, most of them trans women. "Welcome to the Conference on International Law and Employment Policy here in Houston,

Texas, the United States of America," she said. "This is the first ever! . . .
In effect, we will be shaping future law. I don't know how many of you
have ever shaped future law, but I don't think too many of you have. So
it should be quite an exciting thing."[17]

Over the next few days, Phyllis explained, participants would work
in committees to prepare written reports in the nine areas she had pin-
pointed. Lawyers, three of them transgender, would chair these various
committees, and the reports would review the current status of pertinent
laws and propose concrete strategies for progressive change. Given their
marching orders, the committees got to work, breaking only for lunches
and dinners, when locally prominent attorneys and judges delivered
morale-building speeches.

Phyllis had designed the conference to not only provide instruction
on legal issues but also to offer inspiration to the weary. Most of the
inspiring messages came from Phyllis herself, who talked about the costs
of transitioning and the rewards of coming out. She delivered one of her
most personal messages during the first luncheon.

"My son is named Randy, and I love him very much," she began. After
recounting the tortured history of separation from Randy, she continued:

> I cried a lot during that time. Each of us sitting here who have chil-
> dren and who are facing this situation, or face this situation, we cry
> a lot. Every month when I wrote Randy, my son, the wound would
> reopen. I was very honest with him about who I was.
>
> Before he met Phyllis, I would sign the letters PH blank L. I
> would not sign them with PHIL, because that was not who I was,
> but I wasn't going to force the Y of Phyllis on him. After he met
> me, I signed them Phyllis. Whenever he would send me a letter,
> which was a couple times a year, or his school picture, or whatever
> it was, it was addressed to Phyllis. As you can imagine, Father's Day
> was hell for me every year because my father would not be close to
> me, and my son had not yet figured out how to.
>
> Then came three days before Christmas in 1991. I was sitting
> in my office and he called. He was visiting his grandmother in
> San Antonio. And he said, "Phyllis?" And I said, "Yes." And he said,
> "This is Randy." Well, I didn't know what his voice sounded like,
> and I said, "Randy who?" And he said, "Randy Frye, your son." And
> I said, "Oh my God." And I started crying, and I came completely
> undone, and I cried a lot.

When we decided that I was going to go to San Antonio the next day, I cried several times that evening. I had to go to Court that morning, and as I was driving to Court I broke into tears. I was on an elevator going up to the Court, and I'd see some of my friends, and I'd say, "Guess where I'm going today?" "Where are you going?" [they'd ask]. And I couldn't even get it out [because] I'd start crying. . . . When I got finished at the courthouse, I was going to the airport—driving to the airport—I was crying. When I got in the airplane I started crying. A lot of tension was going on.

Anyway, that day I saw him and we hugged, and of course, I cried, and he hugged me back. His mother and his grandmother were very gracious and loving, and we all hugged and all that healing was taken care of. . . . As we parted that day in December, he indicated that we would get together again, and we have done so often. . . . That's my son, and as we parted, once again, we stated our love for each other.[18]

Phyllis shared several personal stories at this first conference—stories about lobbying for the repeal of the cross-dressing ordinance, resisting discrimination in employment, cultivating self-respect through volunteering—always ending them with the following message: "If I did this back then, you can certainly do it now." Other conference speakers pointed to Phyllis as an inspiring figure in their lives. Judge Fred Biery, her high school friend, described her as one of the few "peaceful rebels, like Gandhi and Martin Luther King and Desmond Tutu, who have been willing to challenge the establishment, to follow the road less traveled, and to make more real the promise of equality and freedom and to lead us in the uplifting of the human spirit."[19]

On the final day of the three-day conference, the working committees presented their completed work. One of the more thorough reports came out of the committee on military law, which was chaired by Sharon Stuart, a trans attorney from Cooperstown, New York. A quiet woman with a fiery sense of justice, Stuart drew from her experiences in the Marines. Describing present law, she wrote, "It is a crime under military law to cross-dress, to wear clothing that is inappropriate to your sex, to flaunt military regulations concerning uniform attire. Those regulations extend to underwear, believe me." The report also offered advice for transgender soldiers such as, "do not wear outer or under clothing, cosmetics, or jewelry which is inappropriate for your biological sex while off duty or while you're on military property or in the presence of other military personnel." The report's proposed strategies for change included the creation of a "permanent military law committee within the gender community" that would, among other things, monitor cases, disseminate educational pamphlets, work to decriminalize cross-dressing in the military, and compile a record of transgendered individuals who had served honorably.[20] Stuart concluded her report on a realistic and hopeful note:

> The U. S. Army's favorite recruiting slogan reads, "Be all you can be. Join the Army." But the fine print reads, "Don't be gay or lesbian, don't be disabled, and above all, don't be a cross-dresser or a transsexual." Not too long ago, the Army's fine print used to read, "Don't be black or Hispanic or Asian-American, and if you are a woman, don't be assertive."
>
> In spite of the shortcomings, the Army and the military services have at various times in our history and various ways acted as a social laboratory, and as an instrument for social and cultural evolution. We have many examples of that. It's our hope that the military will reform itself and will welcome us into its ranks and that we can continue to serve our country honorably.[21]

The health law committee was chaired by Martine Rothblatt, an uncommonly sharp attorney from Washington, DC. Rothblatt's report included a summary of the current status of trans law—"based on the view that persons of one sex who want to adopt any of the anatomical characteristics of the other sex, or too many of the role-playing behaviors associated by society with the other sex, especially appearance, are potentially medically ill and thus deserving of medical treatment in accordance with medical standards"—as well as a description of an emerging, more affirming paradigm in transgender law, one that recognizes "the desire to have other-sex anatomical characteristics of role-playing behaviors as a lifestyle choice, protected by the 'right of privacy' and 'freedom of expression.'" As Phyllis had directed, this report also included strategies for progressive change: urging health law to recognize trans behavior as a lifestyle choice and to "define sex as a continuum of characteristics, and not a basis for the categorization of people, their rights, or obligations."[22]

Perhaps the most important question that the health law committee addressed was whether to recommend removing "gender dysphoria" from *The Diagnostic and Statistical Manual of Mental Disorders, 3rd Edition* (DSM-III). Although the committee itself recommended its removal, Rothblatt filed a minority report in which she warned of the possibility that doing so would actually increase discrimination against trans people in many parts of the world. "It would for example be relatively easy to dismiss a gender dysphoric from a job for being a cross-dresser if it were not considered by definition a mental disorder." Because of this, Rothblatt argued, "it is absolutely essential that we have legislation that protects gender dysphorics from discrimination before we try to remove gender dysphoria from DSM-III."[23]

Phyllis was delighted with these top-notch reports because they offered exactly what she had hoped for: detailed analyses of the problematic areas of existing law and proposals for creating and shaping new laws. Given her own history of unemployment, she was also very pleased with the work of the employment law committee, which had helped to craft an employer's handbook titled *Why Is S/He Doing This to Us?* The innovative booklet—authored by Dana Joyce Cole, published by IFGE, and approved by ICTLEP—included a section on the most volatile issue raised by employers: restrooms. Before listing four concrete options available to worried employers, Cole laid out the issue as clearly as possible: "While the individual's personal presentation/appearance should determine which facility is appropriate, the reality is that most men won't want 'her' in the men's restroom, and most women won't want 'him' in the women's restroom."[24] Like so many others in the room, Phyllis nodded at the harsh truth of those words.

Not all of the committee reports were as comprehensive as Stuart's, as conceptually rich as Rothblatt's, or as concrete as Cole's handbook, but Phyllis expressed gratitude for all of them, calling them substantive and relevant.

With an eye toward the future, Phyllis had recruited students at a local court reporters' school to create transcripts of speeches and reports delivered at the conference. Assisted by others, especially Tere Frederickson, Phyllis compiled these transcripts into a lengthy document titled *Proceedings from the First International Conference on Transgender Law and Employment Policy.* Phyllis intended this document to be a resource for next year's conference, as well as for lawyers and activists intent on shaping transgender law in the months, years, and decades to follow. She also wanted to help the budding movement for transgender legal rights gain legitimacy and traction among psychiatrists, psychologists, prison specialists, and politicians. With this in mind, she sent the proceedings to psychiatric clinics, jails and prisons, and members of Congress and their staffs, among others.[25]

ICTLEP was not the first legal resource for the transgender community—trans magazines and educational groups had been disseminating legal information to the trans community for decades—but it did represent the first time a national conference convened for the sole purpose of shaping transgender law.

"I was ecstatic," Phyllis recalls. "I was ecstatic because it happened, because Trish and I were able to pay off our credit card, and because we were able to put our work into proceedings."[26] Martine Rothblatt agrees that the conference was a rousing success. "It legitimized us and our work, and it gave us credibility. We became credible to the outside speakers and their colleagues, who had the opportunity to see our work firsthand, and the proceedings, once they landed in law schools and judge's chambers and political offices, gave us a sense of legitimacy that we lacked before then."[27]

But the conference also brought Phyllis deep satisfaction for less tangible reasons. "When the attendees left, you could just see they were all empowered," she says. "They had knowledge that they weren't the only ones. They had knowledge that people around the country were interested in the same things. They had knowledge about how transgenders were treated in different areas of the law, and each of the reports gave them ideas on how to make things better. When they went home, they felt like they'd been part of the creation of future policy."

"I got a lot of hugs," Phyllis recalls.[28]

Chapter Eleven

Breaking the Barrier

Rather than taking a well-deserved sabbatical, Phyllis began traveling to transgender conventions in an effort to increase attendance at future ICTLEPs. Her constant companions on these trips were copies of the proceedings, which she sold for about $50, and in later years, mugs and T-shirts. "Whether it was the T-Party or California Dreamin' or the Colorado Gold Rush or Southern Comfort—every place I went, I was able to get a free vendor booth so I could sell ICTLEP items," she recalls. "No matter where I went, I also gave a workshop on transgender law, so I met lots of people, and they became interested."[1]

As Phyllis's reputation grew—she was now one of the few nationally recognized trans activists—so too did the fight for inclusion in the gay and lesbian activist community. An epic battle was underway among activists planning for a third march on Washington for gay and lesbian rights.

As Amin Ghaziani details in *The Dividends of Dissent*—an expert analysis of the many roles of conflict in lesbian and gay marches on Washington—the third march had its roots in a conversation among several activists at the Creating Change Conference in November 1990.[2] As a result of this conversation, Urvashi Vaid, then executive director of the National Gay and Lesbian Task Force, issued a national call for interested parties to attend a meeting in Washington, DC, on March 9, 1991. That meeting, and others that followed, resulted in the formation of an organizing structure, including a national steering committee (NSC), and a schedule of national planning conferences.

At the NSC's first planning conference, in Los Angeles in January 1992, a fierce conflict emerged over the first order of business—selecting a title for the march. Conference delegates pitched twenty-one titles, including several that Phyllis, who was not a delegate, would probably have supported—for example, The Gay, Lesbian, Bisexual, Transsexuals,

Transvestites, and Other Gender Persons March on Washington; March on Washington for Lesbian, Gay, Bisexual, Transgenderal Rights 1993; and The Translesbigay March on Washington 1993. One of the more colorful proposals—Dyke Sluts from Hell Take Over D.C., Fags Can Come, Too, Fuck Me Silly in the Nation's Capital—was greeted with enthusiastic cheering.

During the debate, more than a few delegates argued for those titles that reflected the diversity of the movement. According to Ghaziani, "One delegate chided, 'To exclude bisexuals and transsexuals from the title is to exclude them from the march, because the public is not being made aware that bisexuals and transsexuals are out there. In a sense, it's the same kind of exclusion that hets [heterosexuals] do to gays and lesbians.'"[3] Another activist noted that trans people had been at Stonewall and that to exclude them would be to shut out those who were always the first to be beaten up and abused.

After considerable debate, a majority of conference delegates voted to include "transgender" in the name of the march. It was a surprising and historic development. But passage required a two-thirds majority, and after even more debate, some of it tense, the delegates settled on "The 1993 March on Washington for Lesbian, Gay, and Bi Equal Rights and Liberation."

The issue of transgender inclusion reared its head again at a third NSC meeting, this one in Denver two months after the first ICTLEP, when trans activists threatened to boycott the march if delegates excluded their demands from the platform. The executive committee responded, issuing an apology and a conciliatory statement: "It is in the spirit of inclusivity, cooperation, and good faith expressed at the Los Angeles NSC meeting to include 'transgendered people' extensively in March on Washington literature, that we, the Executive Committee, acknowledge our oversight in the platform document and correct this oversight."[4] The revised platform now included explicit reference to the transgender movement, as well as the addition of transgender demands in four of the seven major planks.

The march's transgender caucus responded to these changes by congratulating the lesbian, gay, and bisexual movements for "opening up to the question of transgender oppression." In addition, the caucus stated: "Where once this movement was gender-baited into ignoring or denouncing us, they are beginning to see that our communities have a lot in common. All of us are ridiculed, hated, and humiliated because of who we are. All of us have had to discover our unique identities in a hostile society. All of us can be discriminated against, harassed and attacked. And all of us need each other to fight together for liberation."[5]

Phyllis appreciated the historic inclusion of trans concerns in the march's platform, but "I was ticked once again that we were not in the name," she says.[6] So was Anne Ogborn, cofounder of Transgender Nation (TN), a radical direct-action group based in San Francisco. On November 21, 1992, Ogborn and other TN radicals stormed a March on Washington town meeting in San Francisco, demanding the addition of "transgender" to the name of the march. When the local committee did not respond to their satisfaction, they brought the meeting to a screeching halt by blowing whistles. "Without the inclusion of 'transgender' in the title, it's not my march," Ogborn shouted.[7] She also warned that TN would disrupt the march should the national organizers not meet the group's demand.

Phyllis was not as militant on this point as Ogborn and Transgender Nation. In fact, even as she expressed anger about the exclusion of "transgender" in the title, she argued against a transgender boycott of the march. She made both points in a piece that was published in the march's official newsletter:

> At the planning meeting for the first March on Washington, I had to visibly boycott the meeting to get "transgender" recognized in the brochure. During the second march, I noticed that the transgender community was once again given a short shrift by those in charge. Now I note a third march: the transgender community was omitted one more time from the name, but we are mentioned in the literature.
>
> So, I keep asking myself, why should the transgender community attend and march alongside lesbians, gays, bisexuals, and supportive heterosexuals for equal rights under the Constitution? The answer for us is the same as the answer for supportive heterosexuals: demanding equal rights for anyone is the right thing to do! It is worthwhile to help to open any window to help any oppressed people!
>
> This March on Washington for Lesbian and Gay and Bisexual (and also should be for Transgender) Rights is the place for any freedom-loving person to be—whether recognized or not.

Further, as most prejudice against transgendered people is based on homophobia, any "sexual orientation" gains made in law by lesbians, gays, and bisexuals may assist in attitude—but not necessarily legal—changes regarding transgenderals.

Sexual orientation does not include transgenderals! The [correct] classification term for transgenderals is Gender Identification. When this March is over, and lesbians, gays, and bisexuals are discussing legislative and lobbying strategies, push, push, and push again to ensure that the terms put forth are "sexual orientation" and "gender identification."

Insist that the term "gender identification" is included. Insist that the term "transgender" is included. They used to say gay. Then they learned to say lesbian and gay. Now they are learning to say lesbian, gay and bisexual. Insist that they learn to say lesbian, gay, bisexual and transgender. Insist that they learn to say sexual orientation and gender identification. Insist that the inclusion of others does not stop with the continuing exclusion of the transgender community![8]

The fourth NSC meeting, held in Washington, DC, during the first weekend of February 1993, saw trans activists once again objecting to their exclusion from the title. "I pissed off so many people on the executive committee," recalls protester Jessica Xavier, one of three trans members of the host committee. "But our purposeful exclusion was stupid, hurtful, and insulting."[9]

Xavier told the committee that march organizers were excluding those who had long fought beside gays and lesbians, extending back to the Stonewall Uprising. Other trans activists, including Princess La Rouge, Kaz Suzat, and Rena Swifthawk, emphasized that there was a significant overlap between trans issues and those rooted in sexual orientation, but that because some trans issues were unique to the trans community, the march's emphasis on sexual orientation was discriminatory. Swifthawk, who had been feeling ill, collapsed right after delivering her remarks. Despite that dramatic moment and the arguments of the activists, NSC delegates voted not to reopen the issue.

Meanwhile, there was marked progress in the selection of speakers for the march. As organizers developed a list of possible speakers, they decided to include one representative from each so-called subgroup, including the trans community, and Phyllis Frye emerged as a top contender. After some discussion, the executive committee achieved the consensus required to extend Phyllis an invitation to speak at the march, and she gladly accepted, recognizing the invite as yet another historic step toward full inclusion.

But the promised presence of a trans speaker, and the addition of trans concerns to the march's platform, did little to assuage the anger of Transgender Nation activists, and they were primed for battle when they showed up for the trans caucus meetings a day before the march. TN members Anne Ogborn and Susan Stryker argued for direct action: "We were advocating lying down in front of the lead contingent to make the march have to step over the excluded bodies of trans people," Stryker recalls.[10]

Jessica Xavier opposed the idea on pragmatic grounds. "I just didn't think it was going to work," she says.[11] Phyllis also joined the opposition. "I was fixing to speak, I was personally being honored, and I didn't want to wreck that," she recalls. "So very selfishly—there was a lot of 'Phyllis selfish' at that time—I didn't want to do a big protest and miss out on being able to make the address at the Mall." Still, her argument extended beyond herself. "What I was saying was that our name's still not in the march, but we are getting more and more recognized, and we are getting more and more organized, and the ICTLEP conference is going on . . . and they're giving us a speaking position, and that's never happened."[12]

Listening to Phyllis speak at the caucus, Stryker was struck by the differences between them. "I remember Phyllis in what I call her 'church lady' outfit, a flowery dress and a big sun hat," Stryker recalls. "And I remember thinking that she came from a very different political tradition, one that advocated for persistent incremental change within established institutions, while marching behind a banner about voting, whereas I was coming more out of the ACT UP/Queer Nation style of AIDS-crisis-fueled protest and direct action."[13]

Ogborn and Stryker were not swayed by the voices of moderation and compromise. "After the trans caucus voted not to protest, Anne and I were going to do it anyway, as a Transgender Nation action," says Stryker. "It was actually Leslie Feinberg, one of the people scheduled to carry the banner at the start of the parade, who persuaded Anne that protesting the march would be counter-productive, that things were on the cusp of change re trans-inclusion, that we should build bridges rather than disrupt."[14] Feinberg—the author of *Transgender Liberation: A Movement Whose Time Had Come* (1992)—embraced a Marxist perspective deeply respected by Ogborn and Stryker.

On the night before the march, members of the trans contingent helped to pack the Sylvan Theater on the Mall. The DC host committee, thanks to Xavier and her colleagues, had wrangled money from the executive committee to rent the theater for a blow-out drag show. Xavier suspects that the committee agreed to this expense out of guilt about excluding trans people from the march's name.[15]

The rollicking affair featured some of the best drag performers in the nation, along with speakers still wanting to voice their protest. Xavier was one of those to grab the microphone. "We're with you, and we love you," she said, speaking to gays, lesbians, and bisexuals in the audience. "But it hurts when you don't include us when we are marching and working right beside you."[16]

On the morning of the march, Phyllis awoke to the smell of potato pancakes at the Silver Spring home of her host, Martine Rothblatt, the trans attorney who had spoken on health law at ICTLEP. Despite the historic moment—she would soon be the first openly trans person to speak at a national march on Washington—Phyllis wasn't nervous. She was a veteran speaker, and though the crowd would be larger than any she had addressed before, she felt confident as she and Martine headed to the march's assembly area.

According to trans marcher Davina Anne Gabriel, "The Transgender contingent, though small, reflected the diversity of the march as a whole, including every possible variety of trans person imaginable: pre- and post-operative male-to-female and female-to-male transsexuals, transvestites, transgenderists, drag queens and kings, gender benders, all of every possible sexual orientation from exclusively heterosexual to exclusively homosexual and everything in between, and of course, at least one very supportive non-trans person."[17]

The small but mighty contingent cheered every time speakers, especially Jesse Jackson, mentioned "transgender" in their speeches. Xavier, who was helping with set-ups at the assembly stage, was moved to tears during Jackson's speech, but she was also growing concerned as the various constituencies began their respective marches past the White House and back to the Mall for the afternoon rally at the main stage. As more and more contingents left the assembly area, fewer and fewer people were left for Phyllis to address.

The dwindling numbers turned Xavier's concern to anger, and she lobbied her boss to move Phyllis up in the speaker schedule. Her lobbying didn't work, and by the time Phyllis took the stage around 3:00 p.m., the crowd was thin. "I was pissed," Phyllis remembers. "Maybe ten percent of the people were still there, and that really pissed me off."[18] Phyllis's friend Sharon Stuart, who was in the crowd, remembers that "[w]hen Phyllis got on, the crowd was milling about, not paying much attention, and the sound system was awful."[19]

Phyllis's anger came through as soon as she began her historic speech:

> Listen up! I've got something to tell you! Why is it that the first March and the second March and this the third March does not have transgendered in the name of the March?
>
> The transgendered community includes cross-dressers and transvestites, passing women and female impersonators, drag queens and male impersonators, and pre-, non-, and post-operative trans-sexuals. We definitely include females-to-males as in Joan of Arc, George Sand, Leslie Feinberg, and the transgendered women who fought bravely as soldiers in our colonial and civil wars. Knowing this, why is it that with two rally stages, all day long, there are no female-to-male transgendered speakers? We embrace all races, sexual orientations, creeds, religions, ethnicities, nationalities, ages, and physical impediments. Why is it then, that with two rally stages, all day long, there is only one transgendered political speaker?
>
> This, my friends, is a very unforgiving society for transgendered persons and their loved ones. While we were reared in one gender identity, we have a definite, true-but-opposite gender identity which must express itself. The empirical data show that being transgendered is not a matter of mere choice. No, rational people do not take upon themselves such unrelenting and often hate-filled social pressures for a mere fling! Transphobia is at the heart of queerphobia.
>
> We are here today in the grand effort to change law and social understanding. *The First International Conference on Transgender Law and Employment Policy* revealed that the transgendered have no legal protection and no employment protection. The transgendered require legal protection on the basis of "gender identification."

Together, my sisters and brothers, we must seek legal protection from discrimination on the basis of *both* "sexual orientation" and "gender identification."

Listen to me. One of the ten legal strategies that we will develop at the 2nd Transgender Law Conference this upcoming August in Houston will be to resist those surgeons who demand that heterosexual couples divorce as a condition to transgender surgery, even though both partners wish to remain married. Sex reassignment surgery on one half of an ongoing heterosexual marriage yields a same-sex marriage. Therefore, my lesbian, gay and bisexual sisters and brothers, it will be the transgendered community who leads you into the legalization of same-sex marriage. Why then is transgendered not in the name of this march? Our history reveals that the majority of those people who died at the beginning of the Nazi Holocaust while wearing pink triangles were the transgendered of all sexual orientations. Our history reveals that the real heroes in the Stonewall uprising were the transgendered, the leather cultists, and the street hustlers who stood up to the bully cops and presented in-your-face resistance to being pushed around further. Why then, are the transgendered being omitted and snubbed from the focus of the upcoming Stonewall 25? Sadly, the reward to the transgendered, the leather cultists, and the street hustlers of Stonewall is condescension and stereotyping.

You see, pitting lesbians, gays, and bisexuals against the transgendered is another of the bigots' ploys. It's called division. Many in the lesbian, gay and bisexual community resent being stereotyped as "cross-dressing effeminates" simply because the bigots, the dividers, have successfully cast such with a pejorative label. Others in the transgender community resent being stereotyped as "homosexual/ bisexual" simply because the bigots, the dividers, have successfully cast such with another pejorative label. While we quarrel amongst ourselves over stereotypes and labels, the bigots, the dividers, that fire us, that resist our marriage, that refuse us our citizen's share, those bastards continue to win hands-down.

In order for us to resist this bigots' ploy, this division, we must today embrace each other's stereotypes. We must embrace each other's labels with pride: we must unite. We must go into Congress and into the state houses speaking for lesbian and gay and bisexual and transgender—*and transgender*—say it—*and transgender*—and transgender rights. We must seek legal language that protects us on the basis of both "sexual orientation *and gender identification.*" When you speak to your Member of Congress, tell them House Bill 431 needs to be amended to add "and gender identification"—"sexual orientation and gender identification."

And in conclusion, when you see Sam Nunn, tell him that Phyllis Frye is an honorably discharged army officer.[20]

As she finished, Phyllis then stood even more erect than usual and delivered a military salute to the crowd, a symbolic protest of US Senator Sam Nunn's vocal opposition to gays and lesbians serving openly in the military.

Davina Anne Gabriel depicted the speech as "the most exhilarating moment" of the march. "Much to our surprise and delight, what we had expected to be a gracious thank-you to the queer community for the newfound recognition that it had given us, turned into an admonishment of the community for its continued transphobia and exclusion of trans persons, and a demand for an immediate end to it. . . . We were utterly ecstatic."[21]

Terry M., writing for *Renaissance News*, echoed that feeling. "We finally had a chance to celebrate ourselves and the purpose of the March with our own dynamic speaker on the podium," she wrote. "Wow! It was the thrill of a lifetime!"[22]

"I was knocked out," Xavier says. "Phyllis had so much energy, and stature, and presence. I had never met a trans woman who was so empowered. She was a Texan, and not just a Texan but an Aggie—a Texan times ten. I thought, 'This is somebody I need to learn from.'"[23]

"Her talk was really symbolic," says Sharon Stuart. "It showed we had leaders who had important things to say, that we were more than lone wolves, that we had established organizations."[24]

The significance of the moment was not lost on Phyllis. "It definitely felt historic," she says. "Plus, I didn't get booed."[25]

Around 3:30 p.m., about three-and-a-half hours after the first group had kicked off the march, the trans contingent left the assembly area, and helping to lead the way was the big blue banner that read "TRANSGENDERED & PROUD AND WE VOTE!" A few individuals held other signs proclaiming trans pride, and the contingent as a whole chanted as they marched: "We're here, we're queer, and we won't be excluded!"; "No more exclusion!"; and "We're queer too!"[26]

Even in the midst of the march, Phyllis and many other trans participants had mixed feelings. While Phyllis had been given an opportunity to
speak, she was the only trans speaker in the entire program, and she was
assigned a lowly place in the speakers' lineup. "They didn't give Phyllis
top billing," Stuart says. "We weren't shunned, but we weren't on equal
footing. The big organizations were still wary of us. I felt part of it, and yet
I also felt alienated."[27] Trans marchers also observed that many speakers left
out "transgender" in their remarks, while others spoke of discrimination
against gays and lesbians as the last acceptable discrimination in the United
States.

Phyllis returned home "with a sweet and sour taste." She regretted
discouraging the creative demonstration pitched by Ogborn and Stryker.
"That was one of the biggest political mistakes I made in my life," Phyllis
laments. "We should have lain down in front of the march. If we'd been
laying down, we'd have been two to three years ahead. . . . And I just kick
myself so many times for changing their minds."[28]

Still, the trans community had made modest gains at the march, and
Phyllis and her colleagues in the movement recognized that they had
achieved a new level of acceptance and respect. As Gabriel put it in her
post-march reflections, "we may still be sitting in the back of the queer
bus, but at least it's not still trying to run us over like it sometimes has in
the past."[29]

The second ICTLEP was just four months away, and Phyllis continued
to give workshops around the country to publicize the upcoming event.
In her travels, she began to notice a curious pattern:

> At my workshops, I would tell my story, and I'd make sure ev-
> erybody knew I was pre-op (later on it became non-op). Then I
> would run into transsexual women who would offer to buy me a
> drink so we could chat.
>
> And I learned, whenever we were one-on-one late at night,
> with a couple of drinks in us, that a lot of them weren't all that wild
> about the surgery they had, and that the only reason why they had
> the surgery was because they thought that's what they had to do.
>
> That's what the medical community was telling them. That's
> what the psychological community was telling them. That's what
> the transgender community was telling them—that you gotta go all
> the way.

Some of them were very happy with their surgery, but there was a significant number, and I can't put a percentage on it, who said that if they had known what they knew after hearing me speak, they probably would have stopped at the same place I did.[30]

Phyllis decided to build on those late-night conversations by giving a talk on gender confirmation surgery at the second ICTLEP. "I thought talking about choice was important—the choice of whether to have surgery," she says. "You know, surgery is a big deal. It's expensive, and if you're not happy with it, it's a travesty, and it's life-threatening."[31]

Further inspiration for her talk came from Jamison Green, a trans man who had elected to have metoidioplasty rather than phalloplasty. Less extensive than phalloplasty, metoidioplasty is a surgical procedure that uses one's existing genital tissue—usually a clitoris enlarged by testosterone therapy—to create a new penis, a neophallus. "When I heard Jamison Green talk about metoidioplasty," Phyllis says, "I kept thinking, 'He's a complete guy, and we see him as a complete guy. So how can I help transgender women feel complete if they do everything that stops short of full surgery, or vaginoplasty?'"[32]

Phyllis decided to speak with her endocrinologist, Keith Smith, about how to construct a compelling case for trans women like the one Green was presenting to trans men. A creative thinker, Smith suggested that Phyllis refer to the shrinking of the phallus—the inevitable result of hormone therapy—as clitoral hypertrophy. With this wording, Phyllis could suggest that trans women who took hormones but stopped short of surgery would simply end up with an enlarged clitoris, a sexual organ fundamentally different from their former penis. Hearing their status described this way, they might begin to feel sexually complete as a woman.

Phyllis was delighted with Smith's suggestion, and she wove it into her most important contribution at the second ICTLEP—her talk on gender confirmation surgery:

I want to explore a little bit more of this notion of the hormonal SRS [sexual reassignment surgery] and the surgical SRS.

We are continually evolving in our language and in our definition of ourselves. This is extremely critical because, heretofore, we, of the transgender community—be we cross-dressers or what some people call transgenderists, whatever our frequency of cross-dressing might have been, whether we are preoperative, postoperative, whatever—we've always been defined by people who study us, but not by anybody who *is* us. They don't know what we're going through. And it seems to me that back when this was still experimental and still new that the doctors—and I'm not fussing at them—didn't know who we were and they didn't know what we were going through.

There was even more sexism then than there is now. So they saw someone who appeared to be a man and who had male genitalia and they wanted to make someone who appeared to be a woman and appeared to have a woman's genitalia to fit the stereotype and to keep the sexes polarized. So they came up with the fact that you either go through the surgery or you're not part of the program. You either wear your high heels or you're not part of the program. You really look femme or you're not part of the program.

Of course there's a reverse side. We should not always give it as a "reverse" side and not always as a second comment, but there is the entire other half of our community. It is surfacing. It is the female-to-male community and they still have the same stereotypes to struggle through.

I have been very privileged in that my spouse did not leave, but she stayed with me through my transition. She said that she may leave sometime; she wasn't sure, but she wasn't going to leave now. She gave me time; I didn't have to rush; I began to discover, within myself, that the hormone change was sufficient. And she still tells me that any time I feel that I absolutely have to have the surgical change that I can have it and that she will stay with me.

I don't want this to be misconstrued. I will say several times I don't want this to be misconstrued. I will stand for and I will fight for, I will storm barricades, I will do everything I can, legally, to ensure that the right of someone who wants surgery, who feels that they have to have the surgical intervention, gets it.

I feel that because we were not given the choice of being a nonoperative transsexual that a lot of people have unfortunately rushed into surgery that surgery wasn't right for. This is not to detract from the people who did surgery and the surgery has been right for them.

We are developing, what you've called properly and very efficiently, the hormonal SRS and the surgical SRS or what I'm calling the nonoperative transsexual and the postoperative transsexual, respectively. . . .

Until you decide, you are always preoperative. When you decide that you are going to go for the surgery, you are postoperative once you have that surgery. Or you stop short of surgery and say, "I am nonoperative, and I'm going to stop here."

In my case, I consider myself nonoperative. I've been preoperative since 1976. I've been nonoperative, definitely nonoperative, for a couple of years. I consider myself fully and completely female. . . .

I am not going to allow myself to be forced into surgery, unless I want it, just to be female.

In my deposition, if they ask me about my genitals, my answer—and I've checked it out with a doctor—my answer is, "I have clitoral hypertrophy." In other words, I have an unusually large clitoris. And in deposition or in sworn testimony if they go after the fact that I have, what they might call testicles, I will simply say, "Well I'm sorry, but that was a birth defect. Actually those are ectopic ovaries that were in the wrong place on my body." There are medical cases all through the medical literature of clitoral hypertrophy and ectopic ovaries. And if he says, "But you don't have an opening down there," that's very simple. A lot of females, what they would consider females, are born without an opening. It's called vaginal agenesis.

I'm hoping that this law conference comes up standing for the right of not only someone who wants to have that surgical change, be it female-to-male or male-to-female, to have it—you have our blessing, we will fight for you—but that you could be fully female or fully male, non-operatively, without having to go through expensive and dangerous . . . surgery which may or may not prove satisfactory. In the case of a female-to-male, that person would have an underdeveloped penis, and I'm sure there's a medical term for it. In the case of the male-to-female, she has clitoral hypertrophy, as I do, ectopic ovaries, as I do, and vaginal agenesis, as I do. I think we'll save a lot of people from a lot of suffering.[33]

Phyllis's talk received a wide range of responses from the conference attendees. "Several people came up to me afterwards and thanked me, and several people came up to me afterwards and were really pissed," she says. "They had had surgery and felt that that made them a real woman, and since I hadn't had the surgery, I wasn't a real woman. And they felt challenged by that. Or they felt that they just absolutely had to have surgery and that I was negating their need to have surgery." The confusion led to numerous, painful one-on-one discussions. "So for each one of them, I'd say. 'You misinterpreted what I'm saying. All I'm saying is that you have a choice.'"[34]

Despite the mixed response, Phyllis was determined to share this message, and she continued to emphasize choice in almost all of her talks during this period. "I really feel that I, personally, have given my community the choice of surgery," she states. "Up until then, surgery had not been a choice. If you were trans, everybody expected you to have surgery, even if your family was supportive, even if your wife or husband was supportive. I pissed a lot of people off, but I was just trying to give people a true choice of whether or not they wanted surgery."[35]

Phyllis also had another concern, one she expressed quietly in a 1994 letter to a friend who had questioned her position on surgery. "I do not think that SRS per se is wrong," she wrote. "But I do think that the doctors are butchering the guys right now and will continue to do so until they 'practice' on enough to get it right." Phyllis added that she thought phalloplasty for men in transition was nothing less than "hideous mutilation."[36]

Phyllis's own choice took new shape just a year later, after the death of an elderly gay neighbor for whom she had been providing care. Phyllis remembers a conversation she had with Trish in bed one night, after they had kissed goodnight, with the lights out. "I said to Trish, 'I hope and pray that when we get old, I go first.' And she said, 'Why's that?' She's five years older than I am, and I said, 'Because I went through all this with Sam in the nursing home, and Sam was just a gay man. I know that if I go to a nursing home with my surgical status below my waist, they will have a field day with me. You can imagine all the micro-aggressions that I would go through.'"

Trish remained quiet at that moment, but about three months later, she returned to the topic, telling Phyllis that she had more than fulfilled their early agreement. Phyllis recalls that, not long after she came out in public, "Trish was under a tremendous amount of pressure from her family to leave me, and she knew she could lose her job. She said, 'I only have one thing I want you to do.' I said, 'What's that?' She said, 'If you don't have bottom surgery, I'll see if I can hang on.' Well, gee whiz. She was going to let me be me. She was going to let me change my name. She was going to let me take hormones. She was going to let me do everything that I felt inside that I had to do to be who I was. And at the same time, she wasn't going to leave me. She was going to stay with me. And the only thing I had to do was stop short of full surgery? That's a pretty good deal. So that's what I did."[37]

Now, years later, and three months after Phyllis's comments about their neighbor, Trish revisited their agreement, this time saying that if Phyllis wanted surgery, she shouldn't wait any longer. "That was really a very generous thing for her to say," Phyllis notes. "So I thought about it for a while. I really didn't give a damn whether I had a vagina or not, because I had been Phyllis by then, full-time, for almost twenty years. Because of the hormones, everything had shrunk quite a bit, but I still had those bidoopies [testicles] down there that were kicking out testosterone, and I was trying to suppress it. So I said, 'You know, what I'd really like to have is a bilateral orchiectomy, and that's all I'm really interested in because I'm tired of having to take all this medication to suppress the production. Plus, I don't like those things down there. The other's just a large clitoris—big deal.'"[38]

In December 1995, nearly twenty years after transitioning publicly, Phyllis underwent an orchiectomy, a surgical procedure that removed her testicles. "It was the best thing I ever did in my life—for me," she says. "My need for female hormones went down about 90 percent. I'm always out about that. When clients come in and say, 'I'm going to have my surgery later on,' I say, 'That's fine. You have your surgery, but if you decide somewhere down the line that it's not for you, let me tell you my story, and let me tell you that I've been very happy.'"[39]

The second ICTLEP's most publicly significant product was the initial draft of the International Bill of Gender Rights (IBGR). Leslie Feinberg praised the work in hir groundbreaking history of transgender people. "Documents such as these in history have proved their power. Martin Luther nailed his demands to a church door. French and American revolutionaries proclaimed and fought for a Bill of Rights. A Bill of Rights is a powerful weapon. It will win us allies as it widens understanding of what we're fighting for. And it's a rallying cry in our fights for our rights and ultimately our liberation."[40]

It was Phyllis's friend and mentee, Sharon Stuart, who was also heading the military law project, who had the idea for the IBGR. "I saw Phyllis as the leader I had been looking for—someone who knew the law," Stuart recalls. "Transgender legal theory was a mess at the time. I thought the movement needed lawyers, real lawyers who could fight lawsuits. The gay and lesbian movement had real lawyers; we didn't. The law conferences that Phyllis developed represented the first effort to address transgender legal theory in an organized and significant way."[41]

Stuart's work on the IBGR began long before that meeting, however. During the 1970s, while she was still in the Marines, Stuart researched human rights codes as part of her charge to write a legal memorandum for her superiors. She thought then about drafting a bill of rights or a human rights statement for trans people, but she didn't act on the idea until she attended an IFGE convention in the late 1980s and wrote an article about human rights for the convention newsletter. That article served as the basis for what would become the IBGR.

Stuart was not the only person inspired to work on a bill of rights for trans people. "Unbeknownst to me was that JoAnn Roberts, one of the founders of Renaissance [the Renaissance Education Association Inc.], was expressing the same ideas," says Stuart, who later found Roberts's work in a Renaissance newsletter. "My goal became to flesh out her work and put it into a legal framework." But Roberts was not flattered by the attention. "I tried to collaborate with her, but she refused," says Stuart. "I wanted to carry the project forth, but she was angry. She didn't think she was getting credit."[42]

Stuart moved ahead anyway, making sure to consult a wide variety of experts (including Phyllis, Joanna Clark, Susan Stryker, law professors, and other ICTLEP leaders), human rights documents, and the experiences of other civil rights movements, especially the disability rights movement, in using law to advance rights. Above all, Stuart turned to basic human experience as the most important source. "Human experience precedes the emergence of ideas that justify or do not justify the experience," explains Stuart. "So if things are not right, if we're being treated unfairly, one of the ways we resist is to make claims, to say, 'We have a right to do this!'"[43]

In this sense, the International Bill of Gender Rights is "a basic statement about claims, about what the law should be for [trans people]," Stuart says. "But it's also a basic statement of human rights that anyone would want for themselves, whether they were trans or not. I don't think there's anything in that document that's not pertinent to all human beings. It's really a restatement of basic human rights with a transgender theme."[44]

Phyllis led the second ICTLEP in formally adopting the first draft of the IBGR, and two years later, the conference affirmed the final version of the document. According to Stuart, the IBGR named two fundamental rights: the right to define gender identity and the right to freely express gender identity. Eight other rights built on the foundation of the first two: the right to secure and retain employment and to receive just compensation; the right of access to gendered space and participation in gendered activity; the right to control and change one's body; the right to competent medical and professional care; the right to freedom from psychiatric diagnosis or treatment; the right to sexual expression; the right to form committed, loving relationships and enter into marital contracts; and finally, the right to conceive, bear, or adopt children and to nurture or have custody of children and to exercise parental capacity. These ten rights were not special in any way, as the IGBR stated in its introduction: "All ten parts of the IBGR are universal rights which can be claimed and exercised by every human being."[45]

"If there's a Magna Carta for trans people, this is it," says Stuart, while also adding that the document has its limitations. "When we wrote the articles, there was some question about whether we needed to say more about children [struggling with gender identity], and I decided to let the issue go, saying that the language of the bill included children by implication. What I didn't realize was that the issue of trans children would drive a lot of the public debate about trans rights. If I were to amend the bill, that would be a place where I would start."[46]

Reflecting on the document's legacy, Stuart says, "In my study of other human rights documents—the United Nations has a huge collection—I noticed that many get little attention at the time [of their writing], but they do as history goes on and people live them out. It's impossible to know how much influence the document has had . . . but many people have discovered it for themselves."[47]

Over the years, Stuart has heard from numerous individuals who found the IBGR emboldening and empowering. "Those conversations make me feel as if I did not waste my time," Stuart says. "A transgender lawyer at a leading LGBT organization saw me at a conference and said, 'I'm able to do the work I do now because when I was fifteen I found the IBGR and it gave me the courage to do what I do.'" Stuart tears up remembering her conversation with that lawyer. "I don't need any more than that," she says.[48]

Phyllis had high hopes for the IBGR and circulated it as widely as she could, sending it to judges, attorneys, politicians, and other trans organizations. She hoped that ICTLEP might one day present the IBGR to the United Nations.

Phyllis included two other significant documents in her mailings about the second conference. One was a policy statement on the treatment of trans prisoners, a topic of special interest to Phyllis given her ongoing fear of being arrested as well as her legal work with trans prisoners. The first of its kind in the nation, the policy was authored primarily by gay activist Ray Hill, who was a former convict.

Equally historic, although considerably more controversial, was the other document Phyllis circulated—*Health Law Standards of Care for Transsexualism.* Martine Rothblatt was the primary author of the document and its list of five principles and standards for health care professionals treating transsexualism. In the impressive report, Rothblatt contended that "a quasi-legal regime has evolved over the years that unfairly impedes transsexual endeavors with a mental health label and yoke."[49] Rothblatt added that she and her ICTLEP committee wholly agreed "that transsexualism was not a mental illness even though that is a wide-ranging view in the health law field today. We felt that if there was a mental illness in transsexuals, then it was caused by the tremendous discrimination and unacceptance that transgendered people are faced with by society. In essence, it was society that was ill in their treatment of transsexuals."[50]

Phyllis was very pleased with Rothblatt's work, and she used it in her own critique of the psychiatric treatment of trans people. Not long after the conference, for example, she drew from Rothblatt's argument in a sharply worded letter to an associate of the W. G. Burnham Psychiatric Clinics of Vancouver, British Columbia. "As a transgendered person who has been out for over seventeen years, as ICTLEP Exec Dir over two conferences, and as the sole tg speaker at the April March on Washington, I must ask you to reconsider your use of GDI or 'gender dysphoric individual,'" Phyllis wrote. "Yes, I know that is what the doctors call us, but we resent it. *We do not have gender dysphoria. Society imposes gender dysphoric punishment upon us for simply seeking out who we are.*"[51]

But Rothblatt's report was met with resistance, especially from those who preferred the standards of care first established in 1979 by medical and psychiatric experts affiliated with the Harry Benjamin International Gender Dysphoric Association (HBIGDA). Brenda Thomas, a Tri-Ess member and editor of the *Femme Mirror*, published a lengthy critique in the widely read *TransSisters*. In it, Thomas referred to Rothblatt's work as "distressing," calling it an expression of "total disregard" for HBIGDA's standards of care.[52] She focused on Rothblatt's refusal to define transsexualism as a mental disorder in need of psychiatric care. "PARDON ME!" Thomas wrote. "Would someone please show me ONE person who presents himself or herself for hormonal or surgical procedure who does not require psychological services? . . . What we are seeing here from ICTLEP is hormonal and sexual surgery ON DEMAND!"[53] Thomas also suggested that ICTLEP lacked the expertise required for writing standards of care. "Upon examination of the people on the board of ICTLEP, I see four attorneys and one CPA," she stated. "Where are the doctors, psychologists, social workers, therapists and sex counselors or marriage counselors?"[54]

Rothblatt crafted a response and sent it to Phyllis for comment. "Brenda's article was pure 'self-defeatist' trash," Phyllis replied. "I am getting sick & tired of people claiming that wanting to change your gender is a disease. Also, people better wake up & realize that shrinks were all wrong. Sex is in our mind, not between our legs."[55]

"If this is the Brenda Thomas that I know from Houston, then I am pissed," she added. "She and I recently did a panel presentation; she never said anything about what you wrote. Further she has never bothered to have input of any kind."[56] After confirming that the critic was indeed Brenda Thomas of Houston, Phyllis fired off a letter. "*Your attack article was the first indication that I have received from you on this issue.* Your method was both chicken-shit and cowardly. Your assertions were wrong, were wrong, were wrong! I invite you to register for the 17–21 August [1994] conference and participate in revising our standards—if you can stomach diversity in opinion in a face-to-face format."[57]

Chapter Twelve

Stonewalling

As the twenty-fifth anniversary of the Stonewall Uprising approached, organizers began planning a march, which they titled "Stonewall 25: The International March on the United Nations to Affirm the Human Rights of Lesbian and Gay People." Phyllis and her good friend Jessica Xavier were outraged by yet another omission of trans people. Xavier made plans to sound her protest at a January 1994 meeting of the event's US steering committee, while Phyllis, unwilling to wait, drafted and sent a protest statement to steering committee members, LGBT media outlets, and even trans leaders beyond the United States. "I am angry," she wrote.

> We are angry. Once again, the transgender community is being left out, this time out of the Stonewall 25 event name. We were omitted from names of all three of the Marches on Washington, beginning in 1979, and yet we were active and supportive and attended all three. (I was there for each one.)
>
> NEWS FLASH!! The transgendered made the Stonewall incident happen twenty-five years ago. Drag Queens and Drag Kings of many colors created the Stonewall incident. We were arrested, and we fought back in 1969 at Stonewall. We had better be put into the event name or we will be in New York City in June 1994 to protest the attempt to drag us from our rightful place in history. We will be in-your-face big time, and we will stand against you to be arrested at the Stonewall 25 event.
>
> Yuppie gays and yuppie lesbians, pay close attention!
>
> My people are fixing to do battle with you. THERE IS NO COMPROMISE—NONE AT ALL—TO FULL AND COMPLETE INCLUSIVITY! We, the transgendered, are just as stereotyped by you as you are by the heterosexists. Shame on you! We are in this rights struggle together. Shame on you! Get over yourselves. Shame on you! If "transgender" is not in the name right

beside "gay" and "lesbian," then I will encourage every transgendered person I know, and I am very well known in my community,
to be there and to loudly and publicly embarrass you about your
prejudice. Shame on you!

Yes, shame on you! How dare you try to "drag" us from our
place in history. Shame on you! Your cross-dressed sisters and brothers of many colors, at Stonewall twenty-five years ago, were among
the first to be arrested and the first to fight back. If Stonewall is
anyone's history, it is transgendered history. If you yuppie queers
were there, you probably fled at the first opportunity. Similarly, the
cross-dressed in Nazi Germany were among the first arrested and
sent to the camps. Similarly, most yuppie queers probably hid that
one out, too. So get over yourselves, accept us, put us in the name
and stand beside us to fight the true enemies—the bigots that divide us, that take our jobs, that deny our marriages and that wreck
our self-esteem.[1]

Despite Phyllis's claim, her bold statement did not reflect the views
of the entire trans community. After reading Phyllis's words in *TV/TS
Tapestry Journal*, Laura Masters, founder of TransEqual in Canada, sent
the publication a pointed dissent. "This is no time to attack the gay and
lesbian community," she wrote. "In fact, we would do well to learn from
their example. They have established their own separate group identities,
they have learned to honor their own heritage, and they have formulated
a community pride that is virtually absent in our midst. . . . Ms. Frye
does not speak for me. I want no part of her hollow threats and babyish
tantrums. Our community has enough problems without pissing off yet
another 10% of the population."[2]

Phyllis's letter also infuriated more than a few members of the US
steering committee. Xavier says that the letter had a "chilling effect" on
the organizers, partly because it added to the negative publicity they had
already received for excluding Stonewall veterans from early planning
efforts and for fundraising campaigns that made the march appear overly
commercial. Xavier sensed the tension as soon as she stepped before the
steering committee on January 17. "I was the only transgender present,
and I had walked into a hornets' nest of opposition," she recalls.[3] Still,
Xavier proposed that the powerful US steering committee "demand that
ILGA add 'Transgender' to the Stonewall 25 title."[4]

But Nicole Ramirez-Murray, a drag performer and national co-chair of the steering committee, argued against changing the title, saying that trans concerns were already included in the event's demands and in its call to action. She also went further in her comments, offering an opinion that Xavier and other trans activists found offensive. "There is no transgender, only drag and transsexual," she stated.[5] Xavier's proposal went down in flames by a vote of 51–17.[6]

Xavier decided to reintroduce her proposal at the steering committee's mid-March meeting in New York City. Once again, Phyllis helped prepare the way, this time by issuing an ultimatum:

> Stonewall 25, an international march on the United Nations to affirm the human rights of lesbian and gay people, will be held on the 26th of June, 1994 in New York City. Throughout the organizing of this event, there have been numerous calls to inclusify the title, which remains exclusive of the transgender community.
>
> The International Conference on Transgender Law and Employment Policy (ICTLEP) calls herein a protest of the Stonewall 25 event in the form of transgender, queer and national media information, in the form of loud and visible protests of "Shame, Shame, Shame," and in the form of stopping the marches and being arrested.
>
> The annual ICTLEP Conferences have defined the transgender community to include both homosexual and heterosexual persons who cross-dress to the dress imposed by society as dress relates to gender roles. ICTLEP defines the transgendered to include the homosexual drag community, the heterosexual transvestite or cross-dressing community, the transsexual—pre-operative, non-operative and post-operative—community, and any other person, male-to-female or female-to-male, occasional or part-time or full-time, who challenges by their attire the gender roles of society. ICTLEP's Health Law Project estimates this worldwide population to range from ten million (more than the population of Sweden) to one hundred million (more than the population of France).
>
> To the Stonewall 25 organizing committee: either inclusify the TITLE of this event and we will march with you, or continue to exclude us from the TITLE and we will march against you. To exclude the transgendered from the title of THIS event is absurd.[7]

On the night before the New York meeting, Xavier shared her plans to petition for the event title change with activists Riki Wilchins, Denise Norris, and Leslie Feinberg. Wilchins and Norris were the founders of Transexual Menace, a high-energy, direct-action group that had convinced the organizers of Gay Games IV, which were to be held at Stonewall 25, to allow participants to compete under the gender of their choice.[8] The organizers had previously required documentation proving that transitioning individuals had changed their name and received hormonal therapy for at least two years. The policy change, which Phyllis supported, was a monumental victory for Transexual Menace and for the wider transgender community.[9]

Wilchins, Norris, and Feinberg expressed their enthusiastic support for Xavier's plan, and Xavier and Norris stayed up all night to make flyers for distribution to committee members attending the plenary.[10] The following morning, they handed out their flyers and headed to a meeting of Stonewall 25's women's caucus, where they succeeded in winning support for the inclusion of "transgender" in the title. Then Xavier and other trans activists, including Feinberg and Jeffrey Pendleton, delivered their best pitches to the steering committee.

"Why must the price of your liberation be my continued oppression?" Xavier asked. "I am not your oppressor. . . . [T]he failure to include bisexuals, drag and transgender in Stonewall 25's title leaves the event open to accusations of one minority oppressing other smaller minorities." Xavier added that while inclusion of transgender in the event's demands was important, titular inclusion "speaks much louder to so many others who will not read all of the demands."[11]

Xavier asked the committee to consider the costs of counterprotests led by trans people. "If the threats of boycotts, counterdemonstrations and negative press come true, they will only serve to demean the all-important message of this event: that we are queer, proud, and *united*. The straight media will have a field day with queers fighting each other."[12] Xavier concluded her remarks by saying, "The price of international gay and lesbian empowerment cannot be the continued oppression through marginalization of other sexual minorities. Put bisexual, drag and transgender in the title of Stonewall 25! Please!"[13]

Xavier, Feinberg, and Pendleton lost by a vote of 37–28, with 20 abstentions. "I was disappointed but not bitter," Xavier recalls. "We had fought hard and left with our heads held high. Human liberation movements are always longitudinal struggles, and Stonewall 25's title was only one battle."[14]

Wilchins and Norris turned their attention to lobbying for other types of trans inclusion, and in an April 8 meeting with Stonewall 25's executive committee, the two activists secured promises that organizers would "seek the participation of all people from the Gender community"; "denounce discrimination or exclusion of the gender segment of the queer community"; "increase visibility in the gender community's role in the Stonewall Riots"; and provide "adequate representation of Gender community speakers at the Rally."[15]

Though this victory pleased her, Phyllis was unwilling to leave behind the problem of exclusion from the title, and on April 15 she issued "educational guidelines for nonviolent, civil disobedience."[16] This was her first time leading a civil-disobedience campaign, and she wrote detailed guidelines for protesters.

"Stonewall 25," the international march on the United Nations to affirm the human rights of ONLY lesbian and gay people, will be on the 26th of June 1994 in New York City. Despite numerous pleas, the event organizers refuse to include the words "transgender, drag and bisexual" in the title of the event. Therefore, ICTLEP issues these educational guidelines for non-violent, civil disobedience.

1. Participants in the "Educational Protest of Non-Inclusion" will be three types: (a) those who will carry signs, wear special T-shirts, place themselves (in repeating teams) into the march route and allow themselves to be arrested; (b) those who will carry signs, wear special T-shirts, shout "AND, AND, AND" and observe the arrests from the curbside; and (c) those who will carry signs, wear special T-shirts, shout "AND, AND, AND" and march in the event.

2. All signs and T-shirts will be white with black lettering. Signs are to be of poster board only, either hand carried or on cardboard tubes (not wooden sticks). The signs and T-shirts will emphasize the need to inclusify the lesbian, gay, transgender, drag and bisexual movement: they will be simple and read as follows:

A N D

transgender

and drag and

bisexual and

gay and lesbian

3. Those wishing to participate shall meet at 3:30 PM, Saturday the 25th of June, in the law offices of Margo Diesenhouse . . . for organization and my instruction in non-violent civil disobedience: NO ONE will be in the arrest teams who does not attend. Teams will be organized for repeated stopping of the march, NOT for resisting arrest. Every effort will be made to notify the police. I will be in the first team to be arrested. The observers will follow the arrest teams through the arrest-jail-court-release sequences.[17]

Phyllis again heard from trans activists who disagreed with her plans. "I don't see any connections between Gay and Transgender," Laura Masters replied after reading the flyer. "What does Gender Identity have to do with Sexual Orientation? In my opinion you are seeking inclusion in a 'foreign' minority and creating a situation no less bizarre than connecting black and jew. This can only deepen the public misconception that transgenderists or cross-dressers (Canadian definitions) are homosexual."[18]

Trans activist Kristin W. Holt, writing for *TV/TS Tapestry Journal*, responded similarly, saying that "gender orientation has nothing to do with affectional (sexual) orientation." Because of this, protesting at Stonewall 25 would make trans activists seem "schizophrenic," confused, and confusing. "We want the world, through the efforts of our educational foundations, to understand that our nature is one of gender orientation, *not* sexual orientation," Holt wrote. "Then we try to force our way into a movement whose sole reason for existence is sexual orientation, screaming, 'Me, too!' The dichotomy cannot be lost on the public."[19] Holt concluded her argument by encouraging trans activists to let go of the gay and lesbian movement and to build alliances with a gender-driven group—women's rights activists.

The trans publication *Renaissance News & Views* also published a dissenting voice. Advocating for trans support for Stonewall 25, Terry M.

wrote:"It offers us a unique opportunity to demonstrate our own struggle for dignity and freedom with the whole world watching. We have the real and very significant potential of staging the largest and most publicized transgender human rights march and rally in history!"[20]

Still another critic, Nancy Nangeroni, faulted Phyllis for targeting friends rather than enemies of the transgender movement.[21] Martine Rothblatt assumed a similar position, stating in a letter that she agreed with Phyllis's earlier position, as expressed at the 1993 march, that "in-fighting is the bigot's ploy." Rothblatt also made an intriguing suggestion: "Why doesn't ICTLEP convene a '1995 March on Washington for Queer Rights'? Since we are the first organizer, we call the shots, at least title-wise. It is better to teach by opening a book for someone, rather than by hitting them over the head with the book."[22]

The critics did not sway Phyllis, and she continued to prepare as the march grew near. "We won't be excluded any longer," she said at the time. "[I]f you're not in the name, you're just left out. . . . We've got to get in the official name. No one can say we were not at Stonewall. We were there. To exclude us now is mean-spirited, stupid, and transphobic."

More than ever, Phyllis was determined not to re-live her experience at the 1993 March. "After the '93 March was over, and I realized that we had gotten screwed, that I had gotten screwed when the organizers put me so far down the speakers list, I decided, when Stonewall left transgender out of the name, that this is what I was going to do," she says. "You would have thought that at Stonewall, of all places, we would have been included. It was just too much to take."[23]

Shortly before leaving for the march, Phyllis reiterated the need for protest during an interview with the *Texas Triangle*, a lesbian and gay weekly based in Austin. "We really feel our backs are against the wall politically," she said, "that the term 'Lesbian and Gay' hasn't included us, doesn't include us and we constantly get left out of stuff. It's for our very survival."

The root of the problem, she stressed, was nothing other than transphobia. "The bigot always uses transgender, drag, sissy, whatever to denigrate the gay and lesbian community, and the gay and lesbian community continues to flinch because of it," she explained. "So a lot of the gay and lesbian community is transphobic." But in Phyllis's view, the reverse was also true. "A lot of the transgender [community] is homophobic," Phyllis added, "because they are constantly being denigrated by the bigots for being lesbian and gay. So the bigots are playing the transgender community and the lesbian and gay community against each other, using one to make the other look bad, when there's nothing bad about either one of us. We're both good folks."

The solution was far easier than most people thought, she added. "People keep telling me, 'Oh, but that's more and more words.' It's seven or eight fucking syllables—Drag-Trans-Gen-der-and-Bi-sex-ual. They're too lazy to write seven or eight syllables." Phyllis also mentioned the possibility of using an all-inclusive umbrella term—queer.[24]

Two days before the march, Phyllis and Trish flew to Albany, New York, where they rented a car and drove to Sharon Stuart's home in Cooperstown. While Phyllis felt supported by some trans leaders in her campaign—IFGE and the Congress of Transgender Organizations had passed resolutions condemning titular exclusion, while Transexual Menace backed the anniversary after it had won major concessions—no one stood by her more closely than her mentee Stuart. Despite professional concerns—she was an accomplished archivist and worried that civil disobedience could compromise her professional reputation—the part-time trans woman committed to joining Phyllis in breaking the law and, if need be, going to jail.[25]

Phyllis and Stuart took the train to New York City on the day before the march so that they could speak with their attorney, Margo Diesenhouse, about their plans. Both feared being arrested and jailed. "I didn't want to get arrested, but I was prepared for it," Phyllis says. "I didn't know what [the NYC jailers] would do to me. I knew what they used to do to transgenders in the Houston jails. They used to strip them down and make them walk naked in front of all the jeering inmates. I heard all the horror stories."[26]

Diesenhouse had something else to put on the table. As Phyllis recalls, "She said she had talked to the organizers and that they were taking me very seriously, so seriously that they were planning to make sure I wasn't arrested. They were going to have a group of people follow me, and when I laid down, they would form a human perimeter around me and direct the marchers to split, walk around me, and then re-form and continue marching. That way the march would go on, I would get to make my protest, and at the same time I would not be arrested—which I thought was kind of neat."[27]

But Diesenhouse's main point was that the organizers finally seemed to understand that transgender exclusion in any area—from the title to the demands to speakers to advertising—undermined the strength and unity of Stonewall 25 and the wider movement for LGBT rights. "She was plugged into the lesbian and gay community, and she assured me that they were taking all this very seriously," Phyllis says.[28]

Diesenhouse concluded by giving Phyllis a bit of advice. Phyllis remembers her saying, "You should do what LBJ should have done in the 60s. He should have declared victory and brought everybody home. That's what you should do. You've made your point. Now you should declare victory and go have fun and march."[29]

Phyllis was still upset by the title, but she understood that her demand was virtually impossible to fulfill at this point and, more important, that the organizers had indeed moved toward greater inclusion of trans people in Stonewall 25. "I knew in my heart that the leadership in the community, who had been so slow to include transgenders, were starting to get the message," she recalls.[30]

After Diesenhouse made her case, Phyllis and Stuart looked at each other in silence. "OK," Phyllis said. "We'll march." Stuart beamed her agreement—and relief. Like Phyllis, she had been willing to go to jail, but she also feared it and was grateful for an alternate plan.

"So that was it, and we left the attorney's office," Phyllis recalls.[31] Writing on behalf of ICTLEP, she issued a press release several hours later: "After considering (1) the initial non-inclusion of the transgender community by the Stonewall 25 event; (2) the movement towards inclusion by the Stonewall 25 event since complaints formulated by ICTLEP beginning in January and carrying through until this date: and especially (3) THE SENSE OF DISSATISFACTION WITH BEING EXCLUDED COMBINED WITH THE SENSE OF UNITY THAT THE TRANSGENDER COMMUNITY APPEARS TO NOW POSSESS; therefore, the International Conference on Transgender Law and Employment Policy, Inc., calls for an end to the planned nonviolent civil disobedience that it initiated for the purpose of education."[32]

Less than an hour after issuing the release, Phyllis attended a meeting of Stonewall 25's transgender caucus and announced that she had called off the counterprotest. The caucus erupted with applause. Terry, an activist with the Monmouth Ocean Transgender Group, recalled the moment in a bittersweet way. "Although no one was content with the exclusion of the word 'transgender' from the title we were nonetheless ecstatic that Ms. Frye and her supporters decided to march with us. Thus we were able to present ourselves with great enthusiasm, pride, unity, and dignity."[33]

The day of the march was sunny and warm—perfect for the hundreds of thousands demanding basic human rights for LGBT individuals. Organizers had separated the marchers into distinct contingents, including one for drag kings and queens and another for "transgender specific," as Phyllis later put it.

Phyllis, Stuart, Yvonne Cook-Riley, Aaron Davis, and others carried the blue banner used in the 1993 march—"TRANSGENDERED & PROUD AND WE VOTE"—leading a transgender-specific contingent that extended for blocks. Banners or signs representing other trans groups—Transgender Nation, Transgender Rights, Sally's II, Miss Vera's Finishing School, IFGE, the Monmouth Ocean Transgender Group, and others—were also on full display as the march made its way past the United Nations and into Central Park, where the first speaker for the afternoon rally was trans activist Leslie Feinberg of the Workers World Party. As she made her case for transgender inclusion, trans activists cheered wildly from the front row. The trans community had arrived at center stage, and they were not going away.

Not long after the march, John Gallagher of the *Advocate* interviewed Phyllis and other trans leaders about their efforts at Stonewall 25. "It was our own Stonewall this year," Riki Wilchins said. "For transsexuals, 1994 is 1969." Phyllis seconded the point. "The transgender community is much more activist and more organized as a result of (the Stonewall 25 controversy). Five years ago I was pretty disillusioned. Now so many leaders and activists are coming up, I see nothing but progress ahead."[34] That progress, she stressed, would be marked by "titular recognition in *all* future events."[35]

A path to another type of progress was also becoming clear to Phyllis. "We've been organized for a long time for social and support events, but as far as demanding our rights, it's still in the early stages," she stated. "We need to stress to lawmakers and activists that the phrase sexual orientation does not include transgendered people unless it is specifically defined to include us."[36]

In July, Phyllis traveled to Washington, DC, for a hearing in the US Senate Committee on Labor and Human Resources. Chaired by Democratic Senator Ted Kennedy of Massachusetts, a reliable champion of gay and lesbian rights, the hearing would focus on the Employment Non-Discrimination Act of 1994 (ENDA), a bill that prohibited discrimination in employment on the basis of sexual orientation.

The previous month, Kennedy and Republican Senator John Chafee of Rhode Island had introduced the bill in the Senate, and Democratic Representatives Gerry Studds and Barney Frank of Massachusetts and Connie Morella of Maryland had done the same in the House.

The press conference announcing the introduction of ENDA featured sponsoring politicians as well as prominent supporters in human rights movements. Coretta Scott King, whose presence gave the bill credibility as civil rights legislation, took the occasion to say: "I support the Employment Non-Discrimination Act of 1994 because I believe that freedom and justice cannot be parceled out in pieces to suit political convenience. . . . Like Martin, I don't believe you can stand for freedom of one group of people and deny it to others."[37] But transgender activists soon discovered that some of the people smiling broadly at the press conference had deliberately excluded trans people from the bill for the sake of political expediency.

ENDA was the product of a drafting committee formed a year earlier by the DC-based Leadership Conference on Civil Rights (LCCR), an umbrella organization of civil rights groups, including the Human Rights Campaign Fund (HRCF), which itself was a consortium of gay and lesbian groups. The committee's initial purpose was to draft an omnibus gay civil rights bill, but following the spectacular failure to overturn the gay military ban in the early part of the Clinton presidency, the committee decided in the fall of 1993 to focus on what it thought was a winnable issue—employment discrimination.

The committee also resolved, shortly after its formation, not to include employment discrimination against trans people. Committee member Chai Feldblum, a professor of law at Georgetown University, characterizes the decision this way: "While the group felt such discrimination was wrong, the LCCR mandate had been given to develop legislation that dealt with 'gay and lesbian discrimination' and the group chose to adhere strictly to that mandate."[38] But Feldblum concedes that there were other motivations at play, including the sense that transgender inclusion would ensure the bill's defeat. It was difficult enough to win congressional support for gays and lesbians; adding trans people to the mix would be a disaster. It was a "strategic matter."[39]

Karen Ann Kerin, the first openly transgender delegate at a Republican National Convention (1992) and a candidate for the Vermont House of Representatives, first learned about ENDA when Senator Jim Jeffords wrote to tell her of his support for the bill. With help from Jeffords's staff member Reg Jones, Kerin realized that the bill had excluded trans people and that Senator Kennedy would soon hold a hearing on ENDA. Though the hearing's agenda had already been set, Kerin resolved to attend. She also phoned her dependable ally, Phyllis, and the two promised to go to the hearing together.

On July 22, seven days before the hearing, Phyllis phoned Senator Kennedy's office and offered to testify. She followed up with a letter to Kennedy staffer Mike Iskowitz. "I just talked to your assistant about transgender input to the above-referenced hearings," she wrote. "Essentially, 'sexual orientation' does not protect the transgendered. We, the transgendered, are discriminated against by the *same* people and for the *same* reasons as are gays and lesbians. So give us a chance to put down their stereotypes . . . and allow Sen. Jeffords to call us up."[40]

Phyllis and Kerin met at the Baltimore-Washington International Airport on July 28, and Jessica Xavier hosted the women for their overnight stay. Phyllis and Kerin boarded the Metro the following morning, fully prepared to do what they could to advance trans inclusion in ENDA.

Senator Jeffords welcomed them to his office in the Russell Senate Office Building, right across from the Capitol, and introduced them to his staff before Reg Jones explained there would be virtually no chance for the two to testify since they weren't on the agenda. Phyllis and Kerin were disappointed but determined to make their presence known. To distinguish themselves from the rest of the crowd, Phyllis had made badges that included their names, their home states, and their transgender status. Further, because the trans activists had submitted written testimony for the hearing, they remained hopeful that one of the senators might call on them.

No one did; nor did anyone offer testimony on behalf of trans inclusion. Perhaps the lowest point of the hearing came when a man testifying against ENDA wondered aloud how people would feel if a man came to their office in a sequined dress and high heels. Phyllis, sitting there in her conservative attire, thought, "The fucker doesn't know who we are, and even if he did know us, he wouldn't care."[41]

After the hearing ended, Phyllis and Kerin introduced themselves to as many people as they could, and during the course of these informal conversations, someone—Phyllis cannot remember who—informed them that it wasn't conservative politicians who had excluded trans people from ENDA. Rather, the drafting committee, specifically LCCR and HRCF, was behind the decision. Phyllis and Kerin now had a clear target, and they began to make plans for what would turn out to be a prolonged campaign against HRCF.

Their presence at the hearing also resulted in Jeffords's office asking them to put in writing their suggestions for amending the bill to include trans people. It was a rich opportunity, and back in their respective homes, Phyllis and Kerin faxed each other until the language was just right. Their proposal was simple and straightforward: strike out the phrase "sexual orientation" wherever it appeared in the bill and add "sexual or gender orientation." The two activists then mailed their suggestions to Jefford's office, and they received assurances that the senator would seek to amend the bill.[42]

Phyllis and Kerin shared the troubling news about ENDA at the third ICTLEP, held in Houston in mid-August. In her conference speech, Kerin identified, though not in detail, those responsible for the decision to exclude the trans community. The news that gay and lesbian leaders left them behind yet again registered no surprise on the faces of the attendees.

Phyllis and Kerin then distributed a sample letter for attendees to use when writing to their members of Congress. The letter urged members not only to vote for trans-inclusive legislation but also to vote against a trans-exclusive ENDA.

The activists also shared copies of letters they had already sent to gay, lesbian, and bisexual activists, as well as straight supporters. This letter sharply highlighted the first demand adopted by the 1993 March—"We demand passage of a Lesbian, Gay, Bisexual, and Transgender civil rights bill"—and encouraged recipients to write their own lobby letters and help finance the overall effort. "If transgender does not get included in this law, then we will probably have to *wait another generation* for federal job protection for transgendered citizens."[43]

Kerin also made a bold proposal that ICTLEP give birth to a lobbying organization with paid staff. "We now have a brain trust that sits here and meets once a year, and it grinds exceedingly fine," she said. "And it comes up with some really nice ideas. But dammit, we don't do anything."[44] While noting that ICTLEP's legal status as a 501(c)(3) prevented it from lobbying, Kerin argued that the conference was "facing a time when we got to stand up and be counted." Given past and present trans exclusion, "we have to stick our face in the face of politicians, and we got to tell them, 'Enough is enough, dammit. I'm an American, too, and the Bill of Rights applies to me as much as it does to anyone else.'"[45] Since the introduction of legislation affecting trans people was occasional rather than ongoing, Kerin suggested that the trans community needed a part-time presence in Washington, perhaps four to six weeks a year.

In the comment period following Kerin's talk, Jessica Xavier emphasized the need to engage in constant communication with major gay and lesbian political groups. "If we do not engage in these conversations . . . they will nullify our attempt to lobby the Congress directly," she said. "We just can't go after Congress; we've got to go after the gay and lesbian political group as well."[46]

Xavier made her own call to political action during her talk at ICTLEP. "You professionals of the transgender law conference have succeeded in gathering a powerful knowledge base, upon which we may begin to build a secure future for ourselves," she said. "But without political activism, there will be no new laws created that afford protection from discrimination to those with differing gender identities and expressions. Unfortunately, the gender education and outreach efforts of . . . ICTLEP itself can only go so far in improving the lot of transgendered people."[47] More effective than ICTLEP would be a "national transgender political action committee, or trans pac, if you will."[48]

Xavier envisioned more than an occasional and informal group of trans people committed to lobbying when necessary. "We need transgender political action groups all across America, with state lobbies in every capitol and a permanent national lobby in Washington, DC, to deal with not only the major gay and lesbian political organizations but also with the federal government and the Congress of these United States."[49] She also proposed that the group work in concert with Transgender Nation and Transexual Menace in planning and executing direct-action campaigns.

On the evening of August 19, Kerin, Xavier, Jane Fee, Sarah DePalma, and others interested in forming a national transgender political action group gathered in one of the meeting rooms at the hotel and founded an organization they called "It's Time, America!" (ITA). The name came from Fee, who had played a key role in "It's Time, Minnesota!," a grassroots group that had successfully lobbied for the first-in-the-nation nondiscrimination statute that explicitly protected transgendered people. The group also elected Kerin and Xavier to be ITA's formal leaders and began conversations about its core principles and goals.

Phyllis introduced ITA to the rest of the conference the next day. "There's a lot of energy here, and we've given birth to another organization," she said in her opening comments. "ICTLEP will remain, ICTLEP will continue with its purpose, and ICTLEP will continue with its mission. But we gave birth last night to a political action group called 'It's Time, America,' or ITA. ITA could also mean, 'I'm Transgendered, America.' But it's time. It is time!"[50]

While the announcement was generally well received, not everyone on the ICTLEP board was pleased. "Laura Skaer did not want us to become political," recalls Phyllis. "She was a conservative Republican, an oil and gas and mineral attorney, and she thought that we should stay out of politics. She was supportive of ICTLEP and had ordered and purchased the ICTLEP banner and headed the employment law working group, but we did not see eye to eye on political action, and it eventually resulted in me kicking her off the board."[51]

Within a month, ITA began to distribute information about its mission, goals, and tactics. "The mission of It's Time, America!," a document read, "is to educate and influence the Congress, State, and Local Governments, and other transgender and non-transgender political organizations, using direct action where necessary to safeguard and to advance the rights of transgendered people."[52] Goals included monitoring legislation and executive and regulatory actions; building political alliances with other sexual minorities; lobbying for laws, decrees, and regulations; and mobilizing support for selected candidates.

In cross-country travels required by her profession, Xavier also acted as ITA's national field director, handing out materials to interested parties and sowing the seeds for various state and local chapters. While ITA's mission promoted lobbying at all levels, Xavier preferred campaigns targeting local and state politics. "Small is beautiful," she says when recounting this work. "I was a transfeminist focused on small and local efforts. Other organizations went after the attorneys, but I recruited local activists in the shadows—FTMs [female to male], people of color, intersexed—so they could connect with one another and lobby their local politicians. Lobbying for ENDA was important, but it detracted from local efforts. I thought by lobbying at the local and state levels, we could build precedent for a successful campaign at the national level."[53]

With this focus, Xavier founded It's Time, Maryland!, pledging to govern by consensus, a transfeminist method that she thought the entire trans rights movement would do well to adopt. Around this same time, Sarah DePalma founded It's Time, Texas! and It's Time, Houston!, both of which won Phyllis's support even as she kept her eyes on the prize of trans inclusion in ENDA.

In October 1994, Phyllis headed to Portland, Oregon, to present a workshop on transgender law at the Lavender Law Conference. Phyllis took the occasion not only to teach Transgender Law 101 but also to lambaste HRCF and allied politicians for excluding trans people from ENDA. Representative Barney Frank was one of those politicians, and his chief of staff Robert Rabin attended the sessions and approached Phyllis with a request that they discuss the matter further. They met, along with Sharon Stuart, and during their conversation, Rabin confirmed that LCCR and HRCF were behind the exclusion. He also added that HRCF consultant Chai Feldblum in particular had advocated for the exclusion and that Feldblum was attending the annual Lavender Law Conference, which focused on legal issues related to the gay and lesbian community.

Phyllis was furious, and she took Feldblum's name in vain more than a few times when she and Stuart visited the restroom after their discussion with Rabin. They were not alone. Feldblum was also in the restroom, and she casually mentioned that she had heard her name. "You're Chai Feldblum?" Phyllis asked. "You're the one who excluded us from ENDA?"[54]

The three agreed to talk, and in between later sessions, trans activists Melinda Whiteway and JoAnn McNamara joined Phyllis and Stuart as they sat down with Feldblum and a small group of prominent gay lawyers.

"We confronted the group with the news that we were aware of the HRCF-led meetings of the previous year when it was decided to omit transgenders from ENDA," Phyllis remembers.[55]

As the informal meeting dragged on, Stuart felt that Feldblum was "resistant and not well-informed or acquainted with the transgender movement."[56] The meeting ended in a stalemate.

But the conference had more fruitful outcomes as well. Phyllis learned that she'd been elected alternate director on National Lesbian and Gay Law Association's (NLGLA) board. The news came as a pleasant surprise, and she headed to the board meeting to voice her concern about trans exclusion in ENDA and in the wider movement for gay and lesbian rights. Even more pleasing than having that opportunity was sensing that many board members agreed.

At its next board meeting, in January 1995, NLGLA entertained a resolution calling for transgender inclusion in ENDA. As an alternate director, Phyllis was not permitted to vote, but she was allowed to use her voice to argue on behalf of the resolution. "They gave me great deference," she recalls.[57] After the question was called, NLGLA became the first national gay and lesbian organization to support transgender inclusion in ENDA. For Phyllis, it was the perfect way to start the New Year.

Chapter Thirteen

On Capitol Hill

As 1995 began, a number of fresh ideas for transgender mobilization were in the air. Three possibilities in particular stood out to Phyllis: an umbrella organization for trans groups, tentatively called the National Transgender Education and Advocacy Coalition (NTEAC), to focus on education or political action; a transgender march on Washington; and expanded lobbying for trans rights.

With these and other dreams swirling around, Sharon Stuart, NTEAC's acting coordinator, called a meeting for February of 1995 in College Park, Maryland, to strategize about the future of trans politics. About a dozen activists showed up, including movement leaders Riki Wilchins, Karen Kerin, Jessica Xavier, Jane Fee, and Phyllis.

Wilchins had recently attended the Southern Comfort transgender conference at a hotel in Atlanta, and the experience had left her dissatisfied. Although she recognized the benefits of the conference, she said, "what we did was wander around in an upholstered closet for three days ... one we'd bought for the weekend." The conference was full of workshops on passing, makeup, styling hair, and training voices, but "there was nothing on the oppression we as trans people face every day of our waking lives, and therefore none whatsoever about how we might change our lot for the better."[1]

Wilchins wanted more. "It is time we start speaking about real freedom," she wrote. "It is time we begin organizing to leave today's transgendered children a much *better* world than the twin prisons of secrecy and silence we inherited and to which we have lately become so unconsciously and sadly accustomed." Her brief biography at the end of the piece stated that she was "working with Lynn Walker, Leslie Feinberg, Holly Boswell and Dallas Denny to organize the first National Transgender/Transsexual March on Washington for Civil Rights."[2]

Wilchins also publicized the proposed march in her colorful, humorous, and engaging newsletter, *In Your Face: Political Activism against Gender Oppression.* "And no," she wrote, "this isn't a 'march of the gender organizations'; it's for you and me and your mom and my mom and your cousin Fred who wore Mom's panties that Sunday afternoon and the rest of us who are gender oppressed or just plain pissed off at all the fear and violence which haunts the borders of our lives (quick, get me an agent . . .)."[3] Wilchins had received tentative support for her idea from several other activists, and she had even begun to recruit by putting up posters at Southern Comfort. But when she expressed her idea at the February meeting in College Park, she encountered resistance.

Phyllis and others were concerned that the march would not be well-attended, partly because many trans folks simply didn't have the money to travel to DC. A small march, they argued, would give Human Rights Campaign Fund and its allies all the more reason to dismiss the trans community as a minor player unworthy of sustained attention and support. They also recalled that earlier gay and lesbian marches required massive efforts and that the trans community simply lacked the resources to pull off anything similar. Finally, they made the case that a small group of well-organized and trained lobbyists would be far more effective than a march in advancing pro-trans legislation in the halls of Congress.

While Wilchins planned to revisit the possibility of a march at a later point, she was willing to see if lobbying, which she had considered before, could be effective. The very next day, she left behind her Menace T-shirt and joined Phyllis and Trish, Kerin and her partner Mary Aschenberg, and Fee, for a lobbying trip to the Hill.

As the group emerged from the Metro station and trekked up to the House and Senate offices, they carried copies of their suggested amendments to the Employment Non-Discrimination Act (ENDA). Although trans inclusion in ENDA was their primary goal, they also asked to be included in any other proposed legislation that sought to advance gay and lesbian rights, especially health care bills.[4]

By the end of their trip, the activists had met with the staffs of Senators Jim Jeffords (VT), Daniel Patrick Moynihan (NY), Ted Kennedy (MA), Jay Rockefeller (WV), Carol Moseley Braun (IL), Kay Bailey Hutchinson (TX), and Paul Wellstone and Rod Grams (MN), as well as the staffs of Representatives Barney Frank and Gerry Studds (MA), Ken Bentsen and

Gene Green (TX), Lloyd Doggett and Sheila Jackson Lee (TX), Charles Rangel and Jerry Nadler (NY), Bruce Vento and Bill Luther (MN), and Mark Foley (FL), among others.[5] It was a heady experience for all of them, and especially for Wilchins, who described the event as "outrageously successful."[6]

"I found that just sitting in a Congressional office, talking about our issues, about *transgender issues*—hate crimes, job discrimination, insurance exclusion—was incredibly empowering," she later wrote. "In many ways it was the antithesis of what I'd once thought transgender was about—being accepted, passing, blending in. I had a voice. I had opinions. And important people in our nation's capital—our elected leaders—would listen to me, if I talked seriously about the problems we faced."[7]

Wilchins also experienced something personally transforming, a shift in identity that she hadn't expected or predicted. As she puts it, "I think it's the first time since starting my transition almost two decades earlier that I started to feel again like a civilian instead of a combatant in the gender wars. It felt like being a normal person, not some perpetual *gender outlaw* confined to the outskirts of civilized society. I mean, talking with your Congress Member was about as civil and mainstream as you could get."[8]

At the end of the afternoon, the lobbyists were so enthusiastic about their experiences that they began planning a much larger lobbying day in October. At Wilchins's insistence, Phyllis and Kerin agreed to join her in tri-chairing the event. At the very least, a national lobbying day would allow many other trans people to experience that same feeling of pride and power, legitimacy and validation.

At the ICTLEP held that June, Phyllis highlighted the positive receptions they had experienced in Congress. "We didn't get laughed at a single time," she said. "We didn't get snickered at a single time. The reason why this was true . . . is because they're not interested in making enemies. We got taken seriously in very many ways. We will not be laughed at."[9]

To emphasize her point, Phyllis turned to Wilchins and asked her whether they had been treated respectfully. "You don't screw around with Phyllis," Wilchins replied. "Of course she was treated respectfully. When she raised her voice in one session, I damn near wet my pants, and I'm sure the legislative assistant did."[10]

Wilchins also shared an account of their policy conversations with the congressional staffs. "They were really curious," she said. "It was like their own private *Geraldo* show, and they had no idea what was going on. They would say, 'Well, aren't you covered under this gay and lesbian stuff coming through?' And we'd say, 'No.' . . . Then they'd say, 'Well, aren't you covered under the sex discrimination, this stuff for women?' And we'd answer, 'No, that's not been held by the courts to apply to us, either.' And then they'd realize, 'Oh, you're not covered at all.' And we'd go, 'Now you got it.'"[11]

A month after walking through the halls of Congress, Phyllis was back in the streets, protesting another instance of trans exclusion. Her target this time was the Lesbian/Gay Rights Lobby of Texas (LGRL). At the end of 1994, LGRL had begun in earnest to push for a new hate crimes bill that would provide protection based on race, color, disability, religion, national origin, and sexual orientation. Their proposal did not include protections for gender orientation, gender identity, or gender expression.

Phyllis immediately telephoned Houston resident and LGRL executive director Dianne Hardy-Garcia. "I knew her, and I just told her that this legislation has got to be transgender inclusive," Phyllis says. But Hardy-Garcia rebuffed her, offering no rationale for excluding trans people. In response, Phyllis, Sarah DePalma (of It's Time, Texas!), and Tere Frederickson (of It's Time, San Antonio!) began laying plans for a counterprotest at an April march in Austin sponsored by LGRL—The Texas March to Stop the Violence / Stop the Hate. "I told her [Hardy-Garcia] about our plans to protest, and she didn't think it would amount to much," Phyllis recalls.[12]

DePalma and Frederickson issued a press release a week before the march. "We ask that people join with us to demonstrate to the LGRL the 21st century concepts of welcoming human diversity and recognizing human dignity," they wrote. "A hate crime against anyone is a crime against everyone."[13]

The activists also made three demands that LGRL would have to satisfy in order for the counterprotest to be called off: include "gender orientation" in the legislation, add a transgender person to the LGRL board, and allow DePalma to speak at the march. "The truth is we never expected to get much of what we demanded," DePalma said later. "The

LGRL had never negotiated with us in good faith before; there was no reason to think they would suddenly start doing so at this last moment."[14]

But in a surprising move, the LGRL board agreed to form a committee to study the feasibility of including trans people in hate crime legislation. They also invited DePalma to speak at the post-march rally on the steps of the capitol. Nevertheless, the activists kept to their original demands and refused to cancel the protest.

On the night before the march, Phyllis and several others gathered together at an Austin hotel to prepare signs, make banners, and copy flyers. The counterprotesters planned to meet at the staging area for the march, hand out flyers explaining their counterprotest, and then head to the rally area, in front of the capitol, where they would hold their banners and signs in the path of the march, forcing the marchers to walk around them.

The counterprotest turned out to be an exercise in friendliness. As Phyllis recalls it, "We gathered at one of the parks next to the Colorado River—that's where the parade began—and we started handing out flyers saying that the LGRL didn't recognize transgender rights and so we were going to picket the march. As we handed these out, a lot of the people we saw were our friends, and they said, 'Of course you're part of this organization!' And we said, 'No, we're not, and we're going to have to picket you, and don't be mad.'"[15]

"Then, as the march started, we headed downtown to the capitol and unfurled our banner and got out our signs and posters. When the marchers reached us, there was a lot of love, a lot of hugs, and a lot of support for our rights." Not everyone was supportive, of course. "Hardy-Garcia had a shit-fit when she saw us protesting," says Phyllis. "But the friendly response to our counterprotest was very much a turning point in Texas. It felt as if the tide was turning."[16]

Phyllis experienced another turning point in April, this one personal, when she opened the pages of *Esquire* and saw John Taylor's glowing profile of her in his article on "the transgender revolution."[17] The article marked Phyllis's first national coverage in mainstream media since she had appeared on *Donahue*.

In preparation for his article, Taylor had spent the better part of a day with Phyllis as she represented clients in the Harris County Courthouse and made the rounds at two fundraisers for political bigwigs. He was struck by her self-assurance, a quality he featured in his article's lead quotation from Phyllis: "I went to law school to defend myself, to let people know that if they'd fuck with me, I'd fuck them back." Taylor called Phyllis "one of the most visible transgender activists in the country," a reputation she earned, he noted, during the protest of Stonewall 25.[18]

"Phyllis is broad-shouldered and stocky," Taylor wrote. "Her face is pale and soft from years of estrogen pills. At the courthouse that morning, she wore a gunmetal-blue jacket, a matching calf-length skirt, gray tights, and low-heeled shoes. She also had on a kind of Australian bush hat with a jaunty, iridescent feather in the band. It was, she said, her trademark. She had a brisk but affable manner, and as we made our way through the courthouse, she stopped to joke with almost every lawyer, cop, judge, and secretary we passed."[19]

Taylor captured Phyllis's intensity, too, when he observed how she firmly held onto the arm of a Texas legislator she was lobbying at the first fundraiser, and he shared her humor when he quoted her reaction to the men dressed up like cowboys at the second: "They feel sexier when they do it. . . . When you ask them about it, they say they're expressing their personality. But it's as fetishistic as any cross-dressing. We call them transwestites."[20]

What Phyllis appreciated most about the profile was a quote from Judge Jim Barr. "I'd be less than honest if I said you don't hear talk," Barr told Taylor. "You always do. But Phyllis defuses a lot of that by being so open." The criminal court judge then offered his own take on Phyllis's gender expression. "If you think it's not normal, that's true. It's not. But is it deviant? Who gives a shit? I want a lawyer who can handle a case and kick butt. Phyllis can do that, so I give her the harder cases."[21]

Phyllis was so pleased with the article that she distributed copies to courthouse employees, friends in the movement, and anyone who attended one of the many talks she gave around the country. "Back in those days, I thought education was the best way to respond to people who said they didn't like my lifestyle," she says. "They didn't know fuck about my lifestyle, so if something good about me came out in print, I'd make copies of it and hand them out wherever I went. It was another step forward—it was me becoming normal to other people—and it worked. People would start coming up to me and say, 'Why don't you run for judge?' And I'd say, 'Right now I'm running to be a human being.'"[22]

Less than a month after the march on Austin, Phyllis had her first opportunity to testify at a Texas House hearing on transgender rights, and she could not have been more excited. "You can change the law through the appellate method, but I thought that the best way to change the law is to get the lawmakers to change it," she says. "That way you have an opportunity to change a lot more minds, to reach the public, and you have a better chance of the change becoming permanent. That's usually been my goal."[23]

On April 26, Phyllis, DePalma, and Frederickson testified on behalf of a bill, sponsored by Rep. Debra Danburg, that would have given judges the authority to grant changes of gender and name at the same time. "What makes this so exciting is the legal change of gender would take place during transition rather than waiting until after surgery," DePalma explained. "In other words, one would no longer be forced into surgery in order to obtain all the legal documentation needed to work and live in society."[24]

The three trans leaders had worked on the bill in the prior legislative session, but time constraints did not allow them to finalize the language. Now, with the proper language in place, they lobbied hard for the bill's passage. At the end of one of her meetings with a legislator, Phyllis had a brief and friendly exchange on an elevator with a well-dressed man. When he got off the elevator, DePalma told Phyllis that he was the speaker of the house. "Damn!" she said. "If I'd known that, I wouldn't have let him off."[25]

The hearing offered DePalma and Phyllis a shot of confidence about the effectiveness of their efforts. When DePalma suggested during her testimony that the lawmakers were "probably not going to take us very seriously," a legislator stopped her and said, "If we didn't take you seriously, you wouldn't be here."[26]

Like DePalma, Phyllis was nervous—it was their first hearing, after all—but she found the overall experience to be positive and beneficial. "There were other trans people present for the hearing, and I didn't know them, but it must have been empowering for them to see us treated with respect and to see that we could make a difference."[27]

With help from neutral testimony offered by the state agencies that would have been affected, the bill passed out of committee by a vote of 7 to 2. It was Phyllis's (and DePalma's) first political victory on the state level, and they went home feeling on top of the world.

The following month, the Houston Gay and Lesbian Political Caucus debated a proposed amendment that would make its bylaws include bisexual and trans people in the statement of purpose. Phyllis did not play a leading role in the debate—she had left the organization over its failure to include trans people—but she tracked the proceedings from the sidelines.

Caucus member Tim Granger, who had proposed the amendment, argued for including trans people and bisexuals because he saw all parties as oppressed for their sexuality and, more practically, because the caucus was losing numbers and influence. But fellow member David Westerkamp countered that expanding the mission to include "sexual minorities peripheral to homosexuality" would result in a loss of focus and deplete the caucus's already limited resources. "Just what does the term transgender mean anyway?" he asked.[28]

Westerkamp's side won by a vote of 26–16, and DePalma immediately called the vote "transphobic," adding that she and others saw "the refusal to include transgenders in the mission statement as being no different than white country clubs who refused to admit African Americans."[29] For Phyllis, the vote was a blow to her optimism following the march in Austin and her lobbying successes and a reminder of how immovable resistance to the transgender community could seem. Indeed, it would be another four years before GLPC officially changed its mission to include trans people. When Phyllis learned of the unanimous vote, she had a double reaction, calling it "glorious" and "long overdue."[30]

The fourth ICTLEP, held in June, focused heavily on political action. Just after it began, Sarah DePalma learned that Senator Jeffords had just reintroduced the bill, and once again it excluded trans people. DePalma shared the news with Phyllis and others, and Karen Kerin called Senator Jeffords's office and spoke with his staffer, Reg Jones, who confirmed the report. Jones later claimed that the "HRCF approached me in my capacity as an aide to Senator Jeffords to introduce ENDA in the same format as last year's bill that did not address transgender concerns, and the HRCF rejected any amendment to include transgenders."[31]

Jeffords had clearly caved to HRCF. "It had to have been a political calculation," Phyllis says, suggesting that the bill's primary movers, in conversation with HRCF, believed that trans inclusion would have immediately sunk the bill. "Whatever the case, we got fucked. We really did. We got fucked."[32]

Kerin announced the troubling update to a gathering of It's Time,

America! "When she told us we had been excluded again, it was like a bomb had gone off," says Phyllis. "There were a lot of angry, angry people in that meeting. We felt betrayed, we were furious."[33] In Phyllis's view, the moment was historic: "I believe that was the defining and galvanizing moment for the national political and legal movement of the transgender community."[34]

The group's fury was directed not at Jeffords or Jones but rather at the driving force behind the exclusion—HRCF. "Now our goal was to go after HRCF with everything we had," Phyllis says.[35]

Jessica Xavier of Transgender Nation and Riki Wilchins of Transexual Menace were present for the meeting, and their two groups joined ICTLEP in issuing a press release before the conclusion of the conference. The release stated that the groups would work together to protest HRCF at its nationwide fundraising events and that the protests would include leafletting and picketing, with the goal of educating donors about HRCF's discriminatory practice and urging them to halt or reduce their contributions until the organization became transgender-inclusive. The groups also stated that they would halt the protests if HRCF satisfied three demands: (1) immediately stop opposing a trans-inclusive ENDA, (2) issue a press release stating that HRCF would become transgender-inclusive, and (3) distribute another release recognizing transgender inclusion in the wider queer rights movement.[36]

The coalition began their concerted campaign immediately. Wilchins and her Menace leafletted Pride events in Atlanta, Seattle, New York, and Philadelphia, and picketed HRCF meetings and fundraisers across the country. At Houston's Pride, Phyllis used a large sheet to tell people to stop donating to HRCF. Across the country, countless dissenters telephoned, emailed, and wrote letters to HRCF headquarters in Washington, DC. Phyllis also fired up her fax machine and sent a flurry of statements to gay, lesbian, and trans publications across the country, including this one from June 25:

> Today, as before, ICTLEP's position is that the Employment Non-Discrimination Act of 1995 (HR1863 and SB932), if passed, will be bad law because it intentionally omits one-quarter of the lesbian, gay, bisexual AND TRANSGENDER community, and for the following reasons:

1. It violates the spirit of the 1969 rebellion at the Stonewall Inn in New York City wherein transgendered individuals fully participated. . . .

2. It violates the "Action Statement Preamble to the Platform" of the 1993 March on Washington for Lesbian, Gay and Bi Equal Rights and Liberation that specifically includes transgenders in stating that "We must recognize if one of us is oppressed we are all oppressed."

3. It violates the first Demand of the Platform of the 1993 March on Washington for Lesbian, Gay and Bi Equal Rights and Liberation that specifically "demand[s] passage of a Lesbian, Gay, Bisexual, and Transgender civil rights bill."

4. It violates the unanimously passed resolution of the Board of Directors of the National Lesbian and Gay Law Association (NLGLA) in January 1995, which "strongly urges Members of Congress to include the transgendered in the Employment Non-Discrimination Act of 1994 (ENDA) and any successor or amended bills." (NLGLA is the only inclusive-gay legal association affiliated with the American Bar Association.)

5. It violates the spirit of lesbian, gay, bisexual and transgender community inclusion and cooperative effort that is currently working in many cities, states and regions. . . .

6. It creates a false hope for the homosexual drag community that is beneath both the gay umbrella and the transgender umbrella. Once gay liberation is achieved, much upon the fundraising efforts of the homosexual drag community, discrimination will continue against homosexual drags based on gender identification just as it blatantly exists today for heterosexual cross-dressers and for all transsexuals.

ICTLEP urges all transgender political action groups—It's Time America, Transsexual Menace, Transgender Nation, Transgender Caucus and others—and individual national, regional and local transgender activists to consider this information as they decide their collective and individual responses, if any, to the Human Rights Campaign Fund.[37]

On the same day Phyllis sent that fax, Tri-Ess made a historic move, which DePalma explained in a report she later published in *Renaissance*.

"Today is June 25, 1995," she wrote. "Let it burn into your memory. On this day a truly national transgender movement has been born. You will someday be able to tell your friends and family you were a participant in this event." Tri-Ess—which De Palma described as "the world's largest association of mostly heterosexual cross-dressers"—had passed three formal resolutions on transgender-related politics. Taken together, the resolutions condemned intolerance and bigotry, supported hate crimes legislation, and backed the passage of legislation targeting discrimination in the workplace, all while encouraging Tri-Ess members to work against discrimination.[38]

The passage of these resolutions was surprising and monumental because Tri-Ess had long appeared disinterested in the rough-and-tumble of transgender politics. "Wow!" DePalma wrote, adding that on the same day she learned about Tri-Ess, she had also heard that Tere Frederickson had just spoken with HRCF and that the organization was still digging in its heels on ENDA. "Imagine that!" DePalma continued. "On the very day that Tri-Ess Sorority issues one of the most powerful statements in memory, the HRCF slams the door on inclusion."[39]

"Ladies and gentlemen," DePalma added, "meet the issues on which the national transgender movement will be built . . . employment discrimination, employment discrimination, and employment discrimination. All delivered in a nice bow, courtesy of the HRCF."[40] Further, she said, the issue was perfect for bringing the transgender community together. "Is there a transgendered person anywhere that does not understand employment discrimination? . . . Is there an easier message to explain than a tiny minority asking to receive protection versus a giant who wants to discriminate?"[41]

With Tri-Ess now on board, the movement—including ICTLEP, Transexual Menace, Transgender Nation, and It's Time, America!—was coalescing in a way it never had before. "Mark the date in bold red letters . . . we have become a community today," DePalma wrote. "Savor this moment, a movement has just been born."[42]

In their leaflets and postings, trans activists identified Georgetown University law professor Chai Feldblum, an HRCF consultant, as one of the main culprits behind the decision to exclude trans people from ENDA. Feldblum responded in an online statement claiming that the best method for protecting trans folks from employment discrimination was not including them in ENDA—a strategy that would most certainly lead to the bill's death—but "doing everything we can to argue that sex discrimination does include gender identity discrimination under these existing laws [Title VII of the Civil Rights Act of 1964, as well as state laws that sought to enact Title VII principles]."[43] Feldblum thus called for HRCF and trans activists to work together to devise "a long-term legal and political approach for achieving protection against gender identity discrimination under existing laws."[44]

But Phyllis, Wilchins, and other activists weren't buying that argument. They weren't interested in delaying justice by mapping out a long-term strategy, especially while gays and lesbians fought for immediate protection, and they knew that existing laws, except in Minnesota, did not protect transgender people from discrimination in employment. The activists continued to turn up the heat. "HRC[F] became the whipping post, and we whipped hard," Phyllis recalls.[45]

Elizabeth Birch, executive director of HRCF, telephoned Phyllis to ask for a September meeting where the two of them, plus other representatives from their respective groups, could air their concerns and seek resolution. Phyllis agreed, but only when Birch offered to cover all the travel costs incurred by the trans activists—no small matter given the financial stress suffered by those devoted to the movement.

In September, Phyllis, DePalma, Frederickson, Kerin, Stuart, Wilchins, Xavier, and two trans men Phyllis met for the first time—Kitt Kling and Gary Bowen—arrived at the HRCF headquarters in Washington, DC. The HRCF team included Birch, Feldblum, Nancy Buermeyer, Winnie Stachelberg, Daniel Zingale, David Smith, and Gary Roybal. After awkward but cordial introductions, Feldblum headed to the whiteboard and began a formal presentation about ENDA.

"She started explaining to us what the bill was about, but without addressing our exclusion," Phyllis recalls. "So I stopped her and said something like, 'Chai, that's not why we're here. We know what the bill is, and we know all about discrimination. We're here because you excluded us.'"[46]

At that point, Feldblum sat down, and for the next several hours the two sides laid out their positions. The HRCF side argued that trans people weren't included in HRCF's mission, that trans rights would best be achieved by using federal lawsuits appealing to Title VII, and that the inclusion of the trans community in ENDA would result in HRCF's inability to secure the number of votes required for passage. The opposition countered that sex discrimination laws had never been used in the past to protect trans folks, that using the federal court system would take time and money that the trans community could not afford, and that the promise of seeking trans justice after ENDA passed was hollow in light of HRCF's history of excluding trans people. Wilchins also recalls asserting that the issue of trans exclusion was not merely about political strategy but about basic morality. "The *moral* question is not: Why *are we bothering HRC?* The *moral* question is: *Why do we have to!*"[47]

The stalemate dragged on, interminably, Phyllis felt, until the group finally agreed on several points: (1) that if a trans-inclusive ENDA were introduced in Congress, HRCF would not oppose it; (2) that a subgroup of the two parties (including Xavier, Stuart, Feldblum, and Birch) would draft a trans-inclusive amendment; (3) that working on this amendment would not commit HRCF to support its introduction in Congress; (4) that HRCF and the trans community would work together on including trans people in the Federal Hate Crime Statistics Act and other federal hate crime bills; and (5) that the two groups would cooperate in reaching out to women, people of color, and other marginalized groups to build a broad-based coalition.

Following the meeting, HRCF issued a press release: "HRCF has made a commitment to work with representatives of a spectrum of the transgendered community with a specific focus on hate crimes. HRCF has also committed to assist transgender representatives with an amendment strategy in the context of ENDA. The strategy does not include re-introduction of the current ENDA; the language of the current bill remains as is. Both groups will work in good faith to continue dialogue and to build coalition in the context of ending violence and discrimination against this community."[48]

"We all left feeling good," Phyllis recalls. "We felt good because Sharon, who we trusted, and Jessica, who we trusted, would be working on trans-inclusive language, and HRC felt good because they found a way to shut us the fuck up without saying, 'Shut the fuck up.' It was their job to get us to cool off. They couldn't afford to have us leave and trash them again. It was a win for us and a win for them."[49]

Wilchins issued her own statement following the meeting: "For the first time in history, transactivists have coordinated a concerted, sustained, and ultimately successful nationwide demonstration on behalf of our political rights. Our time has come."[50] In consultation with her colleagues, Wilchins suspended Transexual Menace's protests at HRCF fundraising events; other transgender activists stopped theirs too, effecting a truce while Stuart and Xavier made plans to begin crafting language acceptable to all parties.

At one point during the September meeting, HRCF executive director Elizabeth Birch had wondered aloud why trans activists weren't targeting the National Organization for Women (NOW) rather than HRCF. She didn't know that her opposition had already pressured the feminist organization into supporting trans rights. Wilchins had taken the lead on this. In the spring of 1995, she had worked with a group of activists in NOW's New Jersey branch to pass a trans-inclusion resolution at the state level, a move that made it possible for the resolution to be considered at NOW's national convention in July.

Wilchins reached out to other Menacers, including Phyllis, who often wore a Menace T-shirt in her neighborhood and around Houston. Phyllis quickly made plans to join Wilchins, Leslie Feinberg, Menacers, and local trans activists at the national convention, scheduled for July 21–23 in Columbus, Ohio.

Phyllis found most of the conference attendees to be friendly and receptive as she educated them about trans rights and collected signatures for the trans-inclusive resolution. One of her fellow activists, Tony Barreto-Neto, a Florida-based deputy sheriff who had just founded Transgender Officers Protect and Serve (TOPS) for fire and police officers, approached former NOW president Eleanor Smeal early on and secured her signature. About half of the convention's seven hundred attendees joined Smeal in signing on the dotted line.

But the resolution met resistance on the conference floor, and along with many other resolutions, it was tabled when the conference ran out of time. Nevertheless, Smeal promised to work for its passage in the months ahead, and the head of the national membership committee agreed to mail the resolution, as well as trans-friendly information packets, to all of NOW's state chapters.

On the last day of the conference, as NOW activists protested for women's rights in a march to the state capitol, Phyllis, Wilchins, and the other trans activists positioned themselves on the steps of the capitol, stood behind the blue banner Phyllis had brought with her—"TRANS-GENDERED AND PROUD & WE VOTE"—and raised their fists high. Many of the demonstrators erupted in cheers as they marched directly toward the trans contingent, and Phyllis felt much as she had at the Austin protest several months earlier—encouraged and hopeful that coalition-building was beginning to pay off.

After the September meeting at HRCF headquarters, Phyllis began planning in earnest for the First National Gender Lobbying Day. She was not entirely pleased with the official name—the first lobbying day, she said, had taken place at the beginning of the year—but she was excited when she thought of trans men and women climbing Capitol Hill and going to battle for trans rights.

In preparation for the big event, Phyllis sent a letter to the Clinton White House explaining the upcoming lobbying day and requesting a meeting in which she and a few others might lay out the concerns of the trans community. To her surprise, the White House responded positively, calling her at home and inviting her to an official meeting with presidential assistant Marsha Scott, whose job portfolio included acting as a liaison to sexual minorities. Phyllis accepted the invitation without a second thought and then announced her visit to trans media outlets, adding that she hoped to extend the invitation to even more activists.

But her plan did not come to fruition. "I made the dumb-ass mistake of letting people know about the meeting, because when I did that, guess what? They canceled it." Phyllis believes that her pride led to her downfall. "My ego got in the way on that one. I was so proud of myself. I was just elated about the fact that I was going to be the first trans person to be officially invited to the White House. It would have been the first time the White House hosted a trans activist to talk about trans rights—if I had just kept my mouth shut. As soon as I got the call canceling the meeting, I thanked them and then walked around the house kicking myself. I fucked up, and I knew I fucked up. It was no one else's fault. It was my fault."[51]

Although humiliated, Phyllis soon stopped sulking, grabbed her copy of the Capitol directory, and began assembling Lobbying Day information packets for the 535 members of Congress. Each packet had the congress-person's name and contact information on the front cover, and included information about trans concerns (ENDA, hate crimes, health care, federal imprisonment, and military service), as well as copies of a trans-inclusive amendment to ENDA. "At the end of the packets was a tear-off sheet for our folks—who they met with and what the result was," Phyllis adds.[52] "My goal when I got back home was to organize a spreadsheet by issue so we would have clear data about our results."[53] For the Texas contingent, Phyllis also negotiated prices with the Quality Inn in College Park, Maryland, for an affordable hotel with easy access to the Metro, settling on approximately sixty dollars per room.

Wilchins had been working hard, too, spending much of her time traveling to conferences where she promoted Lobbying Day and recruited both the willing and the wary. She also recruited through email and phone calls and by sending announcements and advertisements to trans media outlets. One of her early advertisements read, "**Your Uncle Samantha wants you!** . . . Our past 2-day trip to DC was amazingly successful . . . **What was our biggest hurdle?** Most of them had never met a transperson, never thought of us as constituents, never considered our rights and concerns. We've been invisible as citizens. **Now YOU have the chance to change that, once and for all!**"[54]

Wilchins booked a block of rooms for her own recruits, but she quickly realized she needed to add more. Thanks to her recruiting, along with the efforts of Phyllis, DePalma, Xavier, and others, Lobbying Day drew a grand total of 104 trans lobbyists representing about 35 states. The group created quite the buzz when they gathered in the hotel conference room on the evening before Lobbying Day.

Wilchins began the meeting by standing on a chair and shouting: "It was a JOKE! We were kidding—can't you people take a JOKE!"[55] The chatting turned to laugher as Wilchins welcomed everyone, gave an update on the HRCF meeting, walked the activists through the issues to focus on, and introduced representatives and veteran lobbyists from HRCF and the National Gay and Lesbian Task Force, who offered their insights about what the trans activists should expect to encounter in the halls of Congress.

Phyllis stepped to the microphone, too, and after offering her own welcome, she invited the activists to pick up their lobbying packets at one of the tables and group themselves according to state. In her comments on the handouts, which included a detailed map of House and Senate offices, she emphasized that the activists should dress professionally—and that they should probably refrain from wearing their Transexual Menace shirts during their stay at the hotel. "This was an open motel and we had to go eat elsewhere within blocks of the University of Maryland," she recalled. "I was simply afraid that by Tuesday night the college toughs would figure us out and mug some of us."[56]

Phyllis and Wilchins then asked the recruits to take an hour or so to get to know one another, learn the packets, and resolve outstanding questions of strategy: how to schedule visits, how to divide the labor, whether to begin at the House or the Senate, and who would be the main speaker in each office.

What happened next shook Phyllis's confidence. "There was nothing for me to do for about an hour, and that's when Riki got a hold of me," she remembers. "Riki came up to me and asked to talk, and we went into a separate room. I didn't know what we were going to talk about. I just figured it was an organizational thing."[57]

As Wilchins recalls the incident, she and Phyllis had "a major disagreement about the tone, tenor and schedule. [Phyllis] wanted to lower the boom on people for not being more politically involved. I thought this was just plain nuts for a number of reasons."[58] Wilchins believed that, given the courage and bravery it took for the recruits just to show up for a public event that held so much uncertainty, including the possibility of arrest, it would be far more preferable to "keep people's energy up, applaud their bravery and build *esprit de corps* for whatever is to come. What you don't do is upbraid them for what they're not doing or have failed to do in the *past*."[59]

Phyllis recalls the incident differently. "Riki started talking about me and my ego, how my father and mother must have done this and that to me, how I was in way over my head. She was really taking me apart very skillfully. Then she told me she had brought a lot of people—and she had—and that if I didn't capitulate, she would take them away and kill the whole thing."[60]

Phyllis recalls feeling more hurt than angry. "I was just devastated. I had put all this work into this, and here was someone, who I didn't see as an enemy, who was trying to take it all away. I was almost in tears, but I just said something like, 'I'm not going to fight with you tonight.' So we went back into the meeting, and it was all I could do to keep from crying in front of everybody."[61]

The First National Gender Lobbying Day kicked off the next morning at 7:15 a.m. with a three-block walk to the Metro. "It looked like a Sunday School group with all the business suits and conservative dresses and slacks with sport coats and ties streaming down the road," Phyllis recalls.[62] It was sunny and warm, and the group was in a buoyant mood.

Disembarking from the Metro, the activists made the short walk to the south steps of the Capitol, where Phyllis approached the Capitol Police, told them that the group was a church group from out of town, and asked permission to gather on the steps for a photograph. After almost everyone was in position—a few elected not to have their photo taken—she and a few others unfurled the blue banner, no doubt leaving the police a bit perplexed.

The group then moved to the south lawn of the Capitol for a press conference that Wilchins had arranged. None of the leaders had thought to secure a permit for the event, but the Capitol Police did not appear interested in shutting it down. Wilchins took her place at the podium before an impressive group of media outlets that included CNN, Fox News, Reuters, and ABC. "We are here today to begin the long process of saying a resounding 'NO!' to discrimination and violence based simply on the way one expresses their gender," she said in her introductory remarks.[63]

As Phyllis stood with others awaiting their turn at the microphone—Jamison Green of FTM International; Dawn Wilson, representing trans people of color; Nancy Nangeroni, founder of the Boston-based GenderTalk Radio; and Tony Barreto-Neto of TOPS—she still felt stung by her conversation with Wichins the previous night. "I pretended nothing happened, and it was difficult," Phyllis says.[64]

After Wilchins finished speaking, it was Phyllis's turn. "We are here to destroy stereotypes," she said. "To allow members of Congress to see our faces, and see that we are not caricatures. We are not out for special rights, other than if special means that somebody gets extra sensitivity training on a police force, so they don't automatically think it's fair game on transgenders."[65]

Politely shooed away by the Capitol Police, the activists made their way to the halls of Congress for two days of intense lobbying. Phyllis stationed herself in the cafeteria at the Longworth House Office Building, where she set up an informal command center. Commandeering a couple of tables near the beginning of the food line, she spent the two days fielding questions from her colleagues, strategizing with them over lunch, and engaging in conversations with passersby, including one sympathetic staffer who shared that her transgender nephew had died by suicide several years earlier.

DC lawyer Dana Priesing, who had helped develop the lobbying packets, established another command center at the Rayburn House Office Building. Like Phyllis, she served as a resource for trans lobbyists with questions and concerns about their tasks. Wilchins joined Priesing at points during the day, and the two learned from their colleagues that "there was a lot of sympathy for our cause on the hate crimes issue, but Human Rights Campaign (HRC)'s staunch opposition to including 'gender identity' to ENDA, the big Employment Non-Discrimination Act, was a huge obstacle."[66] Even the staffs of liberal Democrats were telling the lobbyists that trans people did not belong in ENDA.

Back at the hotel after the first day of lobbying, the group gathered in the conference room to debrief, adjust their workloads, and plan for the next day. They also turned on the television to catch themselves on the news, only to discover that reports on the verdict in the O. J. Simpson murder trial had obliterated any coverage of Lobbying Day.

Wilchins used the evening to finalize plans for a Transexual Menace protest the following morning. The demonstration would center on the lack of medical care provided to Tyra Hunter, a twenty-four-year-old trans woman, who had bled to death after an August 7, 1995, car accident at the corner of 50th and C streets in the southeast section of DC. Eyewitness Catherine Poole claimed that when an ambulance medic discovered that Hunter had a penis, he stopped treating her, jumped back, and said, "This bitch ain't no girl. . . . [I]t's a nigger, he's got a dick."[67] Poole also stated that Hunter was left without treatment for two to five minutes while the medic and his partner laughed and joked. Hunter died two hours later at DC General Hospital.

Wilchins, who had spent much of her time drawing attention to violence against trans people, wanted to stage a protest at DC mayor Marion Barry's office. On the morning of their second day in DC, Wilchins and

Tony Barreto-Neto led a group of activists to the mayor's office, where they called for a formal investigation and handed out a thousand protest flyers.

Phyllis was not part of the protest. "I wanted to be there, but a blind [transgender] Utah resident had gotten an appointment with Orrin Hatch for 8:00 a.m. Tuesday morning and needed me there," she recalls. "JoAnn Roberts, Sharon Stuart, and Alison Laing joined us. Although Hatch had left town on something else, we five met with Hatch's senior legislative counsel for thirty-five minutes. It was productive."[68] Following the meeting, Phyllis headed back to her command center for the rest of the day.

At the end of the two-day event, only fifteen lobbying packets remained undelivered. To be sure, not all congressional offices welcomed the lobbyists with open arms. The office of Jesse Helms, the ultra-conservative senator of North Carolina, was one of a handful that refused to free up any staff member to talk with the lobbyists, and staff members of an Oklahoma representative laughed at the visitors and said there were no trans people in their state.

But positive receptions far outnumbered negative ones, and there were some pleasant surprises, too, mostly from many Republicans who privately expressed sympathy for trans concerns. One of the lobbyists even told Phyllis that a conservative Republican senator from a rural state had made a Russian delegation wait while he allowed his meeting with her to extend from ten to thirty-five minutes.

Nancy Nangeroni later observed that Lobbying Day had emboldened and empowered its participants. "Walking down the hallways," Nangeroni wrote, "one of the lobbyists, Jamie Stowell, spoke her mind: 'This is wild. Ten years ago, I could never have imagined being here in Washington, lobbying Congress, [while] wearing a dress.'" Nangeroni also reflected on the historic dimension of Lobbying Day and its effects on the legislators: "For the first time, the many eyes of those who would vote on equal rights for TGs saw a constituency willing to stand up and be counted, a constituency willing to pull its weight, a constituency recognizing the need to earn political respect, and doing something about it. The eyes of those legislators who look down upon 'genderqueers' did not turn friendly overnight. But those eyes did see something new: they saw genderqueers who were not afraid to ask for—and one day, no doubt, demand—their rights."[69]

Wilchins also reflected on the historic nature of the event. "For many this unprecedented and historic event marked the coming-of-age of the transgender movement, the first time activists from across the US have worked openly in unison for national political change," she wrote. "It also signaled a definitive step past the 'conference culture' [*no diss intended—ed.*] which has long been the primary feature of the gender community."[70]

Shortly after returning home, Phyllis wrote a detailed report on Lobbying Day, including a list of thirteen accomplishments:

1. We put twice to three times as many tg people on the HILL as was predicted. Over 100 from 35 states!

2. We destroyed the stereotypes in a very big way.

3. We met face to face with M.C.s and staffers and soberly asked for our rights. 520 of the 535 offices were visited!

4. We trained over 80 (some already knew) on the *how to* of this type of work.

5. We handled the press without incident.

6. We destroyed the fears of arrest and police harassment. Not one single bathroom incident has been reported. Folks went in, did their business and went right back out.

7. We demonstrated to HRCF and NGLTF that we are indeed a force to be respected. I think we may have put more on the HILL than HRCF did last February.

8. We demonstrated to them that we knew what we were doing and we could do it. HRCF praised the organization.

9. We distributed by hand good tg literature that spoke to our needs. HRCF praised the scorecards and the packets.

10. We now know who our friends are and can deliver floor votes in the future. Much will be done with future contacts by tg constituents.

11. We worked in a nonpartisan fashion.

12. We organized many new chapters of It's Time . . . (America).

13. We alerted many about the federal prison system problem. Many M.C.s or staffers were shocked and will send letters.[71]

Phyllis also sent trans publications a thank-you reflection in which she credited Wilchins for working "tirelessly" to making the day a rousing success.[72] In her letter, Phyllis also suggested she would be taking a break from activism. "You probably will not hear much from me for a while. As with Riki and several others, the toll of the past 6½ months has caught up with me in mental strain, physical exhaustion and a loss of income from having to defer clients. I will be around for sure, but I must rest and catch up to some extent." She closed by sharing a dream, a political vision, for the days ahead:

> I dream of you, the transgender community, as having now been baptized under the fire of the Washington Lobbying Establishment and of the Washington Press. . . . I have always known that *you could do it*; now, you know that *you can do it*. To have convinced you of your abilities in this area—that was my special victory, and I do relish it.
>
> I dream of you telling your folks at home just what we did, and either organizing "It's Time" chapters or strengthening the one you already have. . . .
>
> I dream that you will vote in the Primaries next Spring and go to your Party precinct convention (non-cross-dressed is ok) and get elected to your Party County Convention or Party State Senatorial District Convention and . . . push to get elected to your Party State Convention. . . .
>
> I dream that more tg men will get involved and make this into the 50/50 effort that it must be.
>
> I dream that more people of color will get involved and allow us all to build on the strengths of a multicultural experience.
>
> I dream that both Democrats and Republicans will work together and make our freedom train a truly bipartisan effort.
>
> I dream that the remaining homophobes in our community will recognize the wisdom of coalition and the dignity of the homosexual community.
>
> I dream that remaining transphobes in the l/g/b community will melt into transgender inclusion.
>
> I dream of doing as little as I can for the transgender community for at least two weeks. In short, I am beat.[73]

Phyllis intentionally left out of her dream an expressed hope for cooperation among the various trans political activists. But it was clear to all who knew her that she wanted her supporters to back It's Time, America!, rather than what she saw as its main competitor, GenderPAC, which was synonymous with Wilchins.

The history of GenderPAC was indeed closely intertwined with Wilchins's undeniable charisma. In June 1995, before Lobbying Day, Wilchins had attended the "Be All You Can Be" conference in Atlanta, Georgia. While she was there, she brought so much attention to Transexual Menace, primarily through the sheer force of her personality, as well as the striking black Menace shirt she wore everywhere she went, that the organizers invited her to give a talk. An established public speaker, Wilchins accepted the invitation and thrilled the audience with stories about Menace's work across the country. "I launched into a very angry and at times funny speech completely off the cuff about the need to organize, to fight back, and to stop meeting privately in out-of-the-way hotels, however nicely appointed," she recalls.[74]

The audience loved her talk so much that they gave her a standing ovation; some even gave about six hundred dollars in cash and checks to her good friend, Alison Laing, to support the type of political action that Wilchins demanded. When Laing dropped off the cash at Wichins's hotel room, the Menace founder agreed to throw in another four hundred dollars to jump-start a new political action group that would direct and fund national political activism. Wilchins and Laing then pitched the idea to members of the Transgender Alliance for Community, including AEGIS, IFGE, Outreach, Renaissance, and Tri-Ess, and they all agreed to found what they began to call GenderPAC. A steering committee was formed out of the participating groups; at a later point, active members also included representatives from FTM International and TOPS.

GenderPAC was not free of controversy, primarily because its founding was also the concrete expression of dissatisfaction among some trans leaders, especially cofounder JoAnn Roberts, with It's Time, America! Not long after Lobbying Day, Roberts explained her position in the pages of *AEGIS News*: "[T]he leadership of many of our community's organizations are disenchanted and disenfranchised with It's Time America! When ITA! was announced in 1994 there was much thundering fanfare about this new political lobbying organization. But, as Thomas Edison once said, 'Thunder is good. Thunder is impressive. But it's lightning that does the work.'"[75]

Roberts faulted ITA for being unorganized and inept, unable to fulfill even her simple request for copies of its organizing documents and its concrete plans for action. "That was what faced the organizational representatives in June of 1995 at the Be All convention," she wrote. "ITA was not a legal organization. It had no firm basis for actually performing its stated objective." ITA also reminded her of the Gender Activist League (GAL) that trans activists had founded in California in 1991. "GAL's objective was the same as ITA's, political lobbying. GAL does not exist anymore than ITA exists."[76]

Roberts was partly mistaken. By the time she wrote her scorching critique, ITA had indeed been incorporated, although few people knew it. But Roberts was also partly right. ITA had struggled out of the gate and appeared ineffective to skeptics. Complicating matters were internal divisions at ITA, as Xavier conceded in a written reply to Roberts: "Shortly after ITA began, we were in the process of making overtures to the national organizations and leaders (including JoAnne) when ITA became crippled by a series of disagreements among its leadership over the future direction of the organization, which stopped the preparation of bylaws, plans for membership structure, etc. . . . Our leadership problems, more than any other factor, prevented us from moving forward with our mission and goals."[77]

Given the existence of two national political action groups, Xavier proposed a way forward, at least on the issue of lobbying: ITA would focus on the local and state levels, and GenderPAC would be responsible for the national level. The proposed division of labor reflected Xavier's preferred method for political change. As she put it, "ITA's bottom to top, small is beautiful approach, with our focus on winning small, precedent-setting victories at the local and state levels first, may be more successful over the long term than attempting to effect changes at the national level immediately."[78]

But Phyllis wasn't willing to cede national-level work to GenderPAC. She detested the organization, especially as it grew more synonymous with whatever work Wilchins was undertaking. The rift between her and Wilchins had been cemented in her mind at Lobbying Day. For Phyllis, the path forward was to let Wilchins do her own thing and to encourage everyone else to support ICTLEP, ITA, and whatever action Phyllis led or undertook. She never spoke to Wilchins again.

One month after her split from Wilchins, Phyllis attended the Creating Change Conference of the National Gay and Lesbian Task Force in Detroit, Michigan, and went to a trans caucus meeting that discussed the idea of formally cooperating with the bisexual movement. Phyllis supported the idea.

When the two caucuses met during the conference, they agreed that each would include the other in their respective political action. "We decided that we would carry each other's water, and that from then on, the bisexual community would say 'bisexual and transgender' and the transgender community would say 'transgender and bisexual,'" Phyllis recalls.[79]

The highlight of the conference for Phyllis was when she received the "Creator of Change Award." When NGLTF staff director Tracey Conaty presented the award, she praised Phyllis as having transformed the lives of not only trans people but also gays and lesbians. "1995 was the year that the transgender community had stood the lesbian and gay community on its ear," Conatey said.[80] On hearing those words, Phyllis shed a few tears, even while knowing that the battle for trans rights and inclusion was far from over.

PART IV
JUDGMENTS

Chapter Fourteen

Transitions

It had been a watershed year. "Trans people everywhere were empowered—and juiced," Phyllis reflects. "In 1995, the community had learned and internalized that it could successfully act in a political fashion. We now knew who we were, we weren't alone, and we could act politically—and win."[1]

"But I was worn out," she adds. "I was still carrying all that hurt from October, and I was also suffering from sideroblastic anemia, which left me feeling wiped out."[2] She decided to make a few changes in her life. "My plans for 1996 are being trimmed back," she wrote in her annual Christmas letter. She would fulfill her commitments to the Texas T-Party, NGLTF, IFGE, and, of course, ICTLEP, but everything else was "up in the air."[3] While encouraging her supporters to contact her about private concerns, she also urged them not to overload her. "Until ICTLEP gets the financial support of enough monthly pledges to support a real office and a real secretary, that is the way it will have to be. I just cannot handle the load anymore."[4]

Phyllis carved out a bit of relief in February of 1996 when she arranged to move the ICTLEP office from her home to a modest house owned by a friend who was going through a divorce and no longer wished to live there. The rental cost was six hundred dollars per month, plus utilities, and Dee McKellar, who had lost her job as an engineer when she came out as a trans woman, agreed to live there rent-free and serve as ICTLEP secretary on a salary of five hundred dollars per month. The salary was far from a living wage, but McKellar was happy enough with the arrangements to offer her service for the cause.

Phyllis also made another major adjustment: she moved the bulk of her activism online. Inspired by Gwendolyn Ann Smith, the trans activist who had founded the popular Gazebo chat room on AOL in 1994, Phyllis

signed up for an AOL account. "I started picking up email addresses wherever I went, and I developed a list with about three hundred addresses,
some of them list-serves."[5]

She initially signed her messages as "Phyllatollah," a name first recommended by Wilchins as a playful way to express Phyllis's reputation as a
"kick-ass" in the trans community. But the moniker did not go over well
with everyone. "Les Feinberg contacted me one day and suggested I use
another name. [Ze] was concerned that others might see me as racist, and
at first, that pissed me off, but I came to see [ze] was right, so I took the
issue to my online group, and someone, I don't know who, suggested I
call myself 'Phyllabuster.' I loved it."[6]

She also began referring to her emailed messages as "Phyllabusters."
"Almost everything I did from 1996 on was focused on Phyllabusters,"
she says. "I now had a national and international platform for advocating
for trans rights, and I used the internet as a cheap and easy tool to educate
and cajole, and encourage and shame, and to beat up, too, when necessary.
It was another type of activism. I had always been out beating the drum,
trying to communicate with the LGBT community, and now I could do
it online."[7]

Phyllis found that she preferred online activism. "I never miss the
fights," she says. "They were so goddamn stressful. Nobody in their right
mind wants to do the kind of shit I did, but it had to be done. It's not
that I wanted to do it; it's just that I wasn't afraid to do it. That's what
separated me from so many others in those early years." Fighting continued, of course, but now a lot of it was restricted to the constant stream
of messages she shared with her online community of followers. "At first,
it was me preaching," she says of her early work on the Phyllabusters. "It
was my new soapbox."[8]

The fifth ICTLEP took place at the Ramada Astrodome Hotel in
Houston from July 3 to 7, 1996. Phyllis felt it was the best one to date.
While ENDA was still a pressing topic, it did not consume the conference
as it had in 1995, and this allowed participants to devote their attention to
three new workshops: trans law outside the United States, trans people of
color, and trans men. The workshops were groundbreaking in the sense
that their topics were new to ICTLEP—and virtually all other trans
conferences.

The workshop on international issues was moderated by Stephen
Whittle, a trans attorney and law professor at Manchester University,

whose 1991 letter of query about ICTLEP had led Phyllis to add "international" to the name of the conference. Whittle delivered the news of a recent ruling at the European Court of Justice which meant that "now all transsexual people have full employment protection" throughout the European Economic Community.[9] After reporting additional successes in other parts of the world, Whittle critically observed that "much work is still to be done before ICTLEP can truly be said to be an INTERNATIONAL organization."[10]

The panel on trans people of color, moderated by Dana Turner, an African American attorney, sketched a brief history of people of color in the trans movement. Turner warned against thinking that "every minority person is of a lower social economic status or background," and called for the inclusion of people of color, especially women and the poor, to be a priority for the movement.[11] The mostly white audience was evidence enough that Turner's comments were sharply on-target.

Issues of economics, however, were not new in conversations about ICTLEP. In a letter to Phyllis sent in 1993, just after the second ICTLEP, Susan Stryker wrote, "By way of critique, I think there's room for improvement in how you deal with class issues at ICTLEP. Especially in a population that experiences an inordinate amount of economic hardships due to discrimination, I think it's important to do whatever one can to mitigate disparities of income. Classism and segregation make me uncomfortable wherever I see them."[12] Stryker suggested eliminating the luncheons and banquet dinners, but Phyllis refused to do so on practical grounds: payment for the luncheons and dinners made it possible for ICTLEP to secure their conference rooms free of charge.

The Female to Male (FTM) panel, moderated by attorney Spencer Bergstedt, highlighted the marginalization of trans men in the movement and offered basic education about trans men and the issues they faced. "The issues of transmen will sometimes be the same as others in the trans communities, sometimes they will dovetail, and still others will be uniquely ours," said Bergstedt. "Care should be taken that the concerns of transmen are considered and included in discussions regarding the transsexual/transgender community, not as an afterthought, but on equal footing."[13]

Phyllis appreciated all three workshops, but she was especially delighted with the growing presence of trans men at ICTLEP and in the wider movement. "I'd long said that when they came out, that would be another watershed moment in the trans rights movement. Until then, many would just see the rest of us as a bunch of crazy guys in dresses. I thought that when trans men came out, they would wreck all the stereotypes and help the rest of us be taken seriously. And that's what happened."[14]

The most meaningful part of the conference for Phyllis was a candle-light vigil held on July 4 at 10:00 p.m., in an empty lot next to the hotel. With city fireworks exploding in the distance, Sharon Stuart introduced the event: "We know that our progenitors yearned for the same freedom of identity that we seek. We know that they struggled and suffered for the sake of reimagining themselves. . . . And so, in the stead of our transgen-dered ancestors, mindful of the dangers and pitfalls they faced, but uni-formly resolute in purpose and confident of the outcome, we cheerfully take up the cause of justice and liberty to free ourselves and our posterity from the tyranny of gender."[15]

Then Stuart read from "The Declaration of Gender Liberty," which she had penned for the occasion: "By these precepts we propose to tran-scend the bonds of gender oppression and prejudice. We proclaim that our identities are not determined by virtue of our chromosomal sex, our genitalia, our assigned sex as males or females, or our initial gender roles. We cherish and uplift above all else the universal right to define and rede-fine new identities in accord with our own images and self-conceptions and without regard for the limitations and conformations dictated by the tyrant called gender."[16]

"That vigil meant a lot to me," Phyllis says. "Ten years earlier, bookend-ing the July 4th celebration were two Supreme Court decisions—*Bowers v. Hardwick* and *Baker v. Wade*—where the Court basically said, 'Fuck the queers.' That really stuck in my craw, and now, here we were ten years later, standing up and saying, 'We're free, and we're not going to take it anymore!'"[17]

The next day, Phyllis delivered a talk she titled "Freedom from the Have-To of the Scalpel." But before she began her prepared remarks, she took a few minutes to address the Defense of Marriage Act (DOMA) before Congress, which defined marriage as between a man and a woman. Phyllis decried DOMA as an assault against the right of trans adults to enter into marital contracts without regard to gender. She also pointed out how the experiences of trans people in marriages illustrated the absurdity of a Defense of Marriage act based on biological sex:

[What] you have is a legal marriage already if it began with a penised person and a vaginaed person. There is no law that I know of where the state can intervene, where your parents can intervene, where your children can intervene, where the Baptist Church or anybody else can intervene and file a lawsuit to void, nullify and invalidate your legal marriage. The only two people who have standing in a legal marriage to file a divorce are one of the two parties. . . . Once you are legally married, and then you become two people of the same sex, you remain a legal marriage.[18]

Two and a half months after ICTLEP, Congress indeed passed DOMA, setting off a firestorm of criticism from gay, lesbian, bisexual, and trans activists. Phyllis issued a press release making many of the same points she had made in her ICTLEP address: "[The LGBT] community should use transgender, same-sex marriages as both an equal protection argument to obtain same-sex marriage and as an argument against the passage yesterday of the misnamed Defense of Marriage Act (DOMA) by the U.S. Congress," she wrote.[19]

Around this same time, Phyllis also issued a statement on the Senate's recent 50–49 vote against the Employment Non-Discrimination Act. "It is the opinion of ICTLEP, that if ENDA had been transgender inclusive, it would have passed that vote," she wrote.[20] To support her claim, Phyllis pointed to the success of the lobbying days in October 1995:

The meetings with the Members of Congress or their staffs went very well. During the follow-up, I chatted with several paid lobbyists for the gay and lesbian political community. They were surprised at a handful of Senators and number of the Representatives that we got good and supportive messages from. Those lobbyists had been unable to have that same rapport with that handful of Senators and number of the Representatives. So, if ENDA had been transgender inclusive, and if transgenders weren't continuously shut out of the gay and lesbian political game in DC, would ENDA have been passed this week in the US Senate? Absolutely!!! Abso-damn-lutely!!![21]

Elizabeth Birch scheduled another ENDA strategy meeting with trans leaders for the day after the November elections. The group again gathered in the DC offices of the Human Rights Campaign (the HRCF dropped "Fund" from its name before the elections). Tension was once again palpable, especially given the act's recent defeat. Joining Phyllis was a solid representation of the community of trans activists—Alison Laing, Phyllis Dickason, Yosenio Lewis, Gary Bowen, Jon Banks, Stephanie Young, Jamison Green, Janice Galeckas, Shannon Minter, and Melissa Dixon—a group that included people of color, cross-dressers, people from the West Coast, and trans men.

Since the last meeting, HRC had fulfilled its promise to seek the inclusion of trans people in a hate crime bill extending protections based on sexual orientation. In addition, a small working group—Chai Feldblum and Erin Leveton of HRC and trans activists Jessica Xavier, Sharon Stuart, and Dana Priesing—had successfully developed "potential gender identity amendments" to ENDA. But, as Feldblum later put it, "the negative political ramifications of making such an addition had not changed at all."[22] Unlike Phyllis and her colleagues, Feldblum and HRC remained convinced that a transgender-inclusive ENDA would have no chance in Congress.

"The thrust of the meeting was to reposition old stances," Phyllis later reported. "HRC was not going to put us into ENDA. We, on the other hand, were going to settle for nothing less."[23] Phyllis intended to continue lobbying Congress and building coalitions with other gay and lesbian groups. "More and more lesbian, gay and bisexual organizations are coming to see the need for transgender coalition," she had written after ENDA's collapse in September.[24] She noted the Gay, Lesbian, Bisexual Veterans of America; the National Lesbian and Gay Law Association; and the National Gay and Lesbian Task Force (NGLTF) as organizations working toward trans-inclusiveness.

Despite the frustrations of the HRC-hosted meeting, the trip to DC turned out to be worthwhile. NGLTF was holding its annual Creating Change conference across the Potomac River in Arlington, and Phyllis called executive director Kerry Lobel to request a meeting with her and her colleagues. "She was blown away," Phyllis recalls. "We were professionally dressed, mature, poised, diverse, with people of color and from various states, and we were one-half men, and all that really impressed Lobel. She knew we were a force to be reckoned with."[25]

Back home, Phyllis planned for yet another gathering in the nation's capital, this one titled the Third National Transgender Event. She had first publicized the idea at the fifth ICTLEP, saying, "On Sunday, February the 23rd, 1997, I am going to be in Washington, DC. We are not going to lobby because, although ICTLEP can lobby to a certain percentage under its 501(c)(3), I don't want ICTLEP to lobby at this time. I want ICTLEP to educate."[26] Phyllis also used the *ICTLEP Reporter* to explain her emerging plan, as well as her rationale. "One of our main goals is to demonstrate to the Members of Congress and their staffs that the transgender community is more diverse than they might believe:

—it is fully 1/2 FTM;

—it is filled with beautiful and active people of color;

—it is heterosexual cross-dresser, and gay drag as well as transsexual;

—the transsexuals can be finished as either surgical or nonsurgical;

—includes a spectrum of conservative Republican to liberal Democrat;

—includes a spectrum of religious believers;

—includes a spectrum of married, same-sex married and single-parent families; and

—IT IS THE TARGET OF HATE CRIMES AND EMPLOYMENT DISCRIMINATION![27]

The Third National Transgender Event was in part a response to the already-announced Second National Gender Lobbying Day, organized by Riki Wilchins and Dana Priesing at GenderPAC. Phyllis was still stinging from her October 1995 encounter with Wilchins, and some observers noted that Phyllis's call for her supporters to attend what she billed as the *third* national transgender event, with the first having taken place in February 1995 and the second in October 1995, was a muscle-flexing move.

Phyllis did not describe the event in these terms. Recognizing that she would be criticized for her event, and especially for scheduling the DC trip a mere two months before GenderPAC's, she publicly claimed that the two events were complementary:

I feel that in February—when the Human Rights Campaign is beginning its big push, and we have new Members of Congress, and new bills are being introduced—I think that's the best time.

The point is this: the Members of Congress are going to see us two times this spring. Not just one time, but two times. And instead of the May people having to be there and kind of open up doors and have people rethink everything, we will have already been there in February. . . . But at the same time, we won't be able to plant all the seeds that need to be planted in February, because we'll have a time restriction just like they will. So, they'll be able to plant a lot of seeds in May that we couldn't plant in February. I see both events as complementary, and I'm going to operate them that way no matter what.[28]

Phyllis anticipated criticism from Wilchins's supporters, and she received it. JoAnn Roberts of Renaissance in Philadelphia ridiculed Phyllis's claim that hers would be the *third* national transgender event:

Now, I'm all for giving credit where credit is due, but that visit in March 1995 was no more a national event than is a regular meeting of a Renaissance chapter. . . . I am reminded of a puzzle: If you consider the tail as a leg, how many legs does a dog have? A: Four: because no matter what you say, a tail is *not* a leg. So, let's be clear: The *Second National* Transgender Lobby Days sponsored by GPAC will be held May 5–6, 1997. Any other event can call itself anything it likes, but I know a tail from a leg."[29]

GenderPAC was certainly on the move at this point, notching successes in lobbying and testifying before Congress—Dana Priesing, GenderPAC's congressional advocacy coordinator, testified before the House's Subcommittee on Government Programs on July 17, 1996, becoming the first trans person to testify in person before Congress. But GenderPAC was still structurally unsound. At best, it was an informal association of groups hoping to combat discrimination based on gender. In an effort to formalize its structure and work, GenderPAC's supporters gathered together in Philadelphia in November. *Renaissance* reported on the meeting in dramatic fashion: "In what has been called the most important event in the history of the transgender community since the Stonewall Riots, and certainly the defining event of the decade, twelve transgender organizations representing national, regional, and local constituencies signed Articles of Association to form the Gender Public Advocacy Coalition (GPAC), a community-wide association dedicated to working issues of gender, affectional and racial discrimination at a national level."[30]

The list of signatories was impressive. It included the American Educational Gender Information Service, FTM International, the International Foundation for Gender Education, It's Time, America!, Renaissance Education Association, Society for the Second Self, American Boyz, Intersex Society of North America, Transgender Health Action Coalition, Transgender Officers Protect & Serve, Deaf Transgendered Alliance, and Expressing Our Nature Inc. But Phyllis did not attend, focusing instead on her March event, a decision that she thought proved wise two months later when JoAnn Roberts, a GenderPAC board member, reported that the umbrella organization was already "falling apart."[31]

According to Roberts, as of January 1997, only one of the signatories had fulfilled the requirements for official membership in GenderPAC. "As for me personally, I have dissociated myself from GPAC completely," she added. "I believe if you say you agree to a certain set of rules, then you damn well ought to abide by them."[32] Roberts was disgusted by a small group, headed by Wilchins, that had formed an executive committee to make decisions more quickly and expediently than the board could. Roberts argued that GPAC's bylaws vested authority in the board and did not allow for the formation of the committee, and she resigned her role as policy advisor.

Meanwhile, Phyllis headed to Washington for the Third National Transgender Event. Though only twenty people attended, the group was able to meet with the staffs of forty-six senators. "Time and again we were told that if Senator Ted Kennedy and Representative Barney Frank put transgenders into the next ENDA bill, they would support it," Phyllis reported. "Time and time again we were also told that if Kennedy and Frank left us out, they would still support it. It was up to Kennedy and Frank."[33]

So Phyllis decided that she and JoAnna McNamara would visit Frank, no doubt the more resistant of the two politicians:

> We went in there to talk with him about transgender inclusion in the ENDA bill, and from the moment we started talking, he interrupted us and talked the whole time about how he wasn't going to do it, how transgenders weren't part of the community. He really berated us. He'd gotten all of this grief from his associates in Congress, when Clinton was trying to get gays into the military, about gays using bathrooms and showers with straight guys, and he wasn't going to open that can of worms again—not for the trans community. He was a total and complete ass.[34]

After finding Kennedy's staff equally immovable, the group headed to the offices of the Equal Employment Opportunity Commission where they met with Reg Jones, now an EEOC commissioner, and his colleagues. McNamara made the case that EEOC could issue its own ruling that Title VII of the Civil Rights Act of 1964 protected trans people as a class from discrimination in employment. According to Phyllis, the commissioners "understood, but declined, noting that the Republican Congress would retaliate by reducing appropriations for the EEOC in the next budget."[35]

Back home again, Phyllis worked on the sixth ICTLEP, which she marketed as TRANSGEN '97. She had the distinct feeling that the conference had run the good race and was now out of breath, so she publicly announced that unless ICTLEP received an influx of support, the 1997 conference would most likely be the last one.

Though moving the office out of Phyllis's home had helped her mental health, monthly pledges to ICTLEP, totaling fewer than a hundred, were unable to cover the ongoing costs of the office. The lack of a healthy operating budget also made it impossible for Phyllis to implement any of her long-term goals for ICTLEP.

"My dream, if you imagine with me, is that 4,000 folks will consistently contribute at least $10 per month," she explained in her 1996 report to ICTLEP. "Do the math, and you will see that ICTLEP could kick some serious butt."[36] Phyllis dreamed of hiring a larger professional staff, offering legal workshops at judicial conferences (not only LGBT ones), inputting ICTLEP proceedings into scholarly databases, writing amicus briefs for precedent-setting trans law cases, offering grants to attorneys working on those same cases, expanding lobbying at all levels, and employing a part-time lobbyist in Washington, DC. But the funding was not forthcoming.

Phyllis was relieved when the conference was over. There were no published proceedings, and Phyllis wrote about the sixth conference far less than the prior five, even failing to publish her usual report. Phyllabusters following the conference suggest that the highlight for Phyllis was the presence of EEOC commissioner Reg Jones, who praised Phyllis and ICTLEP for their ongoing efforts to ensure that trans people were protected from employment discrimination.

ICTLEP took another major hit in August when Phyllis fired Dee

McKellar from her position as secretary. Phyllis had learned that McKellar had been making anonymous online posts that were sharply critical of her personality and work. "Dee considered herself to be my intellectual superior, and she knew all of my hot buttons and how to get me revved up," Phyllis says. But Phyllis also says that wasn't the reason for Dee's dismissal. "Dee was leaving the office and doing personal things when she was supposed to be working on ICTLEP. I'd called her on this and warned her twice, and the second time I said, 'The next time I catch you doing this, I'm going to fire you.' And that's what happened. One day I showed up at the office and she wasn't there. I could see her walking back from the bus, and when she got back to the house, I fired her on the spot. You don't fuck around with your boss that way."[37]

Phyllis soon discovered that the former secretary had mismanaged ICTLEP's correspondence. "I found letters never opened, checks never opened, credit card monthly commitments never dealt with. That's why ICTLEP funds were going down the toilet. She was having a high-heeled good time. That was really the end of ICTLEP."[38]

Phyllis shut down the office and announced through a Phyllabuster that Sharon Stuart was coming aboard ICTLEP as the new secretary. "Unfortunately in 1995, she was fired from her job for being too 'out' as a cross-dresser," Phyllis wrote about Sharon. "She now has a paying job with ICTLEP and will be giving it her full attention. My experience with Sharon is that she is dedicated and meticulous."[39]

"But," Phyllis continued, "I have some apologies to make to our ICTLEP supporters as well. During the office move, I found many undeposited checks and several unfilled orders."[40] Stressing that there had been no theft or dishonesty, that it was all a matter of mismanagement, Phyllis pleaded for her supporters to send new checks to the trustworthy Stuart.

Three days after Phyllis sent this message, Dee McKellar died of a massive heart attack while volunteering for a neighborhood watch group in Montrose. On the morning after her death, about fifteen people stopped by Phyllis's home to offer words of comfort. "But I didn't give a shit," Phyllis recalls.[41] Still, she relented a bit and offered faint praise in a statement she passed along to the trans community: "Dee was an activist and died while in our service, and we are going to honor her activist spirit."[42]

There was, however, one thing that Phyllis particularly appreciated about McKellar: along with Phyllis, she had won election to the board of the National Lesbian and Gay Law Association (NLGLA), and together, they had worked to make the organization trans-friendly. Just a few days before McKellar died, the NLGLA board had voted to redefine its original bylaws to incorporate bisexual and trans people.[43]

The following month, in September, Phyllis attended the first National Policy Roundtable sponsored by the National Gay and Lesbian Task Force. The meeting's purpose was to forge relationships between national LGBT organizations, creating a space for them to share their concerns about public policy issues and collaborate to advance common goals. Phyllis considered her invitation a monumental event:

> In 1975, I got into this queer rights activism business as I began to lecture at local universities about being transgendered. From the beginning, I embraced the full queer community as part of my community. I had then been told and am still being told repeatedly that if I'd just give up the 'gay rights thing' then my TG self would be accepted more quickly: I'll not do that! And yet, by 1979 I'd been pretty well convinced by many folks who were in the 'gay rights thing' that I, as a transgender, was welcome to invest my time and energy, but that transgenders were not part of their 'gay thing.' Since 1979, everywhere I went to where there was a 'gay rights thing,' I have had to fight, I have had to fight again, and I have had to fight still more to get transgenders reincorporated back into this 'gay rights thing.' ('Reincorporated,' since we TGs were at the Stonewall Riot, rather than 'included,' which implies that we were asking to join for the first time.) Until this fall.[44]

For the first time, Phyllis had not pounded on door after door to gain access to this new inner sanctum. NGLTF recognized her as an important leader in the community they were seeking to build, and Phyllis could not have been more pleased. She was also delighted to realize that she did not have to fight for inclusion during the roundtable meeting. "Since I was part of a group of Executive Directors of which 20 percent was transgendered or intersexed, there was nothing to fight about. Mellow was the order of the weekend for me. So was networking."[45]

In October, Phyllis attended NLGLA's Lavender Law Conference in West Hollywood, California. Though she had once banged on NLGLA's door, now she was inside, a full-fledged member: "Bisexual and transgendered were already in the NLGLA bylaws and mission statement, and with some few remaining screwups, the text of most brochures, membership applications, and such were either inclusive or are getting that way. There was a transgender legal issues cluster of workshops; plus, where appropriate, there was integration of transgender input in other legal issue cluster workshops. Once again, mellow was the order of the weekend for me, and so was networking."

Then came Creating Change in November, and the experience confirmed for Phyllis the victories she had been experiencing since September. In a Phyllabuster about the conference, she listed twenty "wonderful things" that she had experienced there, including learning from Kerry Lobel that the meeting between her and Phyllis's group during the prior Creating Change "was *the* turning point for her on transgender reincorporation"; sharing hugs with Elizabeth Birch of HRC and thanking her for using the word "transgender" twice during a recent speech she gave at a fundraising dinner attended by President Clinton; hearing four keynote speakers call for all gay and lesbian organizations to add "bisexual" and "transgender" to their names; seeing not one but seven transgender workshops and participating on a panel titled "Sexual Orientation Is a Subset of Gender"; speaking with gay and lesbian activists who expressed a desire for trans people to serve on their various boards; and seeing representatives from the National Organization for Women, who had just helped pass a NOW resolution titled "Oppression of Transgendered People."[46] The tide had finally turned.

In her Christmas letter, Phyllis wrote that she had moved into "a 3/4 semi-retirement mode."[47] Her law practice was reputable and solid, with about half focused on criminal defense and the rest on family and probate law, but the reduction was necessary to hold stress at bay, she said.

The professional transition freed up time for her to spend with her son Randy, who had recently moved to Fort Worth, his spouse Estee, and their toddler daughter Megan. "We never knew how much fun grandparenting would be," Phyllis wrote. "They are all coming to our home this year for Christmas. This will be the first Christmas Day for me and Randy to be together since 1971."[48]

The more relaxed schedule also made it possible for Phyllis and Trish to spend more time together. Trish was in her thirty-second year of teaching elementary children, directing school plays, and putting on holiday programs. "She is teaching children of the children she taught long ago," Phyllis wrote proudly.[49]

The long-married couple decided to take some of their extra time to remodel their kitchen and to relax at their lake house, just a few miles north of Cut-N-Shoot, Texas, with their two dogs. "In closing, we invite you to look back with us to twenty years ago and our Christmas of 1977," Phyllis wrote.

> Phyllis had been blackballed from engineering after her transition in the summer of 1976, and we were scrimping along on 1/3 of our prior income. We had all the usual bills and child support, and were terrified of losing the house if we couldn't service the mortgage. Except for Trish's mom, both families had ostracized us completely. Our church, the Metropolitan Community Church of the Resurrection, brought us the canned goods that had been placed under their altar during the previous services; yes, we were the Church's 'needy' family for that Christmas. Since we did not have to buy food for several weeks, we could afford some warm shoes. It was a scary and embittering time twenty years ago. If we could make our way back from that in 1977, then you can make your way back from almost anything in 1997. So take hope! Grab and hold onto all things positive in your life. Build people up, and be more careful to protect and nurture each other's feelings and emotional health.[50]

Chapter Fifteen

Back to Battle

Early in the morning on January 24, 1998, Phyllis's father Donald died. Though she had kept in touch with her mother through occasional letters and phone calls, she had not been in touch with her father since 1976. Phyllis learned of Donald's death from her cousin Margaret, with whom she remained in contact. In fact, back in 1991, when Phyllis was lamenting her disconnection from family, Margaret urged her to write to her aunts, uncles, and cousins, and Phyllis did. "Many remained unforgiving," Phyllis recalls. "But I did get back my Uncle John and Aunt Marion, Uncle Lindsay and Aunt Aileen, and Aunt Gerry," along with six more first cousins.[1]

Phyllis and Trish attended Donald's funeral on January 25. "[My sister] LaNell was in charge," Phyllis remembers. "She was not happy to see me but did not make a stink." During the eulogy, Phyllis learned that she, Randy, and Randy's daughter had not been listed in the obituary. "In effect, I was no longer in the family. . . . It was crushing." Following the service, Phyllis says, she sought to correct the record by purchasing a separate obituary and listing herself, Randy, and her granddaughter among the surviving relatives. "I heard that really pissed off a lot of people."[2]

At the funeral, Phyllis also heard that her brother Donald Jr. was asking a cousin, a former police officer, if he was carrying his pistol. "He wasn't," she remembers. "I can just imagine what my brother would have done if he'd gotten hold of a gun that day."[3]

Following her father's death, Phyllis visited her mother from time to time. As the years passed, it became clear that Alto was showing signs of Alzheimer's, which her mother and siblings had also had. As the disease progressed, LaNell became Alto's primary caregiver and no longer allowed Phyllis to see her. When Alto died in 2009, Phyllis and Trish decided not to attend the funeral since their experience at Donald's service had been so painful.[4]

On January 26, 1998, ICTLEP announced that the board had elected Sharon Stuart as its new executive director and that Phyllis had agreed to continue serving as a board director. The press release announced: "Stuart sees her job as providing a year-long transition from a 'founder-driven' organization (which began in 1991 when its founder was the only, totally out and totally active, TG lawyer in the United States) to one with more structure and a deeper organizational base."[5]

The announcement noted Phyllis's reason for stepping down. "Outgoing ED and founder Phyllis Randolph Frye told her Board three weeks ago that she had had enough. 'Being an activist for over two decades is one thing, but being on the point for all of those two-plus decades is more than enough. And six years as Executive Director of this organization with its six annual conferences and its six annual bound Proceedings was also enough.'"[6]

Phyllis shipped her files to Stuart's home in Cooperstown—and breathed a sigh of relief. "It wasn't tough to let go. Dee [McKellar] had pretty much destroyed it, there was little money, and I was not going to go around and ask people to rebuild the finances. Beyond that, I was tired of working as a vendor for ICTLEP. Everywhere I went I would schlep around T-shirts and mugs and proceedings, and I was tired of all that."[7]

Phyllis conceded that ICTLEP had not taken off as she had hoped. Yet, even though it never scaled up to become a truly national organization with enduring political power in the halls of Congress, she was enormously proud of the work she and others had accomplished through the pioneering organization. "It did what it was supposed to do," she says now, in retrospect.

> [It] got us included in the gay and lesbian political movement, and in the gay and lesbian legal movement. We wanted to be reincorporated into our rightful place—and for me that was in the legal and political movement.
>
> ICTLEP also published all those proceedings with our thinking about various subjects of law at that point in history—what the law was and how we could change it. We were a grassroots movement—in the beginning, trans lawyers were a minority in ICTLEP and we were mostly laypeople—coming up with policies that we

wanted to become law. And what was significant about this is that we trans people were the ones coming up with the policies; we weren't standing by any longer and letting others shape our lives. And these proceedings live on. I've done everything I can to get the proceedings out to law libraries and trans LGBT lawyers and the LGBT community.

ICTLEP was also a training ground for so many people who went on to become leaders in the trans movement. When I looked around at organizations and conferences, I saw people who got their start at ICTLEP.

So I felt pretty good.[8]

Stuart did what she could with limited resources. In April, she organized a nationwide canvas to secure an up-to-date list of trans-friendly attorneys in every state, the District of Columbia, and Puerto Rico. She also began to investigate "the feasibility of mounting an appellate program to support important precedent-setting cases" and the formation of a transgender legal defense fund, a much smaller version of the NAACP Legal Defense Fund.[9]

To make trans law more accessible to the general public, Stuart planned to produce a series of pamphlets on various topics of law based on material from ICTLEP proceedings, not unlike the booklet *Legal Aspects of Transsexualism*, first published by Mary Elizabeth Clark in 1979.[10]

As Stuart sketched her plans for ICTLEP, she also played a leading role, along with Jessica Xavier, Maggie Heineman, Mary Boenke, Nancy Sharp, and others, in successfully lobbying the Parents, Family and Friends of Lesbians and Gays (PFLAG) to become trans-inclusive.

Meanwhile, Phyllis continued her activism primarily through the writing and distribution of the Phyllabusters, and in May 1998, she received a surprise email from reporter John Cloud asking for her opinion on the mainstreaming of transgender politics for an article he was writing for *Time*. Cloud said he had already spoken with Riki Wilchins and Shannon Minter, and that he also wanted to speak with Phyllis.

The mention of Wilchins set Phyllis off, and in her email reply, she wrote: "I want to briefly set you straight on a few items. 1. Riki and GenderPAC are not 'the' transgender political movement. They like to think so, but they are not. They are not the only ones who have done organized TG events in DC, nor did they start the DC ball rolling in 1994."[11]

Phyllis was glad that Cloud had spoken with Minter, whom she described as a good friend and "one of the great men of our community," and she supplied him with contact information for a list of national trans leaders that included her friends Stuart, Karen Kerin, Jessica Xavier, Jamison Green, Gary Bowen, and Dallas Denny. "There are so many more," Phyllis added. "Riki is but a latecomer and self-hornblower to much of this."[12]

Phyllis also questioned just how mainstream the trans movement was becoming. "[Human Rights Campaign] may seem to be coming around on tg inclusion, but it still has a long way to go," she wrote.[13] But Phyllis agreed with Cloud's point that trans issues were being included more often than before in state and local civil rights bills—a development she credited to those who had been active with ICTLEP through the years.

On July 20, *Time* published Cloud's article asserting that trans people and issues were becoming mainstream, drawing examples from entertainment, business, higher education, and city and state governments. "Lawyers with the Transgender Law Conference have helped pass statutes in at least 17 states allowing transsexuals to change the sex designation on their birth certificate, which means their driver's license and passport can reflect reality," Cloud wrote. Cloud also noted that HRC had not fully integrated trans people into its mission and work. "But the Campaign is coming around," he added, using Phyllis's phrasing.[14]

Cloud mentioned Wilchins by name, although he focused primarily on her book *Read My Lips* and her declaration of "the end of gender."[15] Curiously, he did not mention Wilchins's substantial political work at all. After she and Phyllis had gone their separate ways, in effect conducting trains on parallel tracks in the movement, Wilchins, along with Dana Priesing, acted in the name of GenderPAC to carry out a wide variety of political actions, including lobbying Congress, enlisting a dozen members of Congress to sign a letter that denounced trans violence, completing a groundbreaking national survey on violence against transgender persons, and advocating for trans inclusion in hate crime legislation. In addition, they met with the Department of Justice about trans violence, successfully lobbied NOW to become trans-inclusive, attended White House meetings about hate crimes, organized (with the National Center for Lesbian Rights) a "Gender & the Law" meeting with national law groups (including NOW and the ACLU), supported local trans protest campaigns, and focused national attention on the murders of transgender people, among many other things.[16]

Wilchins and Priesing accomplished all this without Phyllis and ICT-LEP. Phyllis recalls that when she saw Priesing at a trans meeting during this period, Priesing told her that GenderPAC didn't need her help—that it could get along just fine without her. "She was as nasty as can be," Phyllis says.[17]

Phyllis continued to form and strengthen relationships with leaders in the gay and lesbian movement. She identified National Lesbian and Gay Law Association (NLGLA) as the heir apparent to ICTLEP and began to build her public case about this in a July 1998 email in which she proudly announced that she and other trans attorneys would be speaking at the upcoming American Bar Association (ABA) meeting. This historic engagement was made possible by Phyllis's work with NLGLA, the only queer law organization affiliated with the ABA, and especially with Mark Agrast, NLGLA's representative to ABA.

"In 1995 NLGLA Board resolved unanimously that transgenders should be included in the Employment Non-Discrimination Act (ENDA) before Congress," Phyllis wrote to her email list. "Last year the NLGLA Board amended its bylaws to be bisexual and transgender inclusive." Moreover, she wrote, NLGLA had slated several workshops on transgender law for its upcoming 1998 Lavender Law Conference. "As a result, the Transgender Law Conference (ICTLEP, which is an NLGLA affiliate), has chosen to forego its 1998 conference and ask its usual attendees to instead support, publicize and go to the Lavender Law Conference."[18]

"Trans inclusion in Lavender Law was and is the continuation of ICTLEP," Phyllis explains now. "NLGLA was the only group that had an annual conference on our issue, on transgender issues, and they were so receptive to us."[19] With NLGLA subsuming ICTLEP's work, ICTLEP faded away.

While NLGLA was Phyllis's favorite national gay and lesbian organization, her least favorite, at least by the end of 1999, was Lambda Legal, with the Human Rights Campaign coming in a close second. HRC was still troublesome on ENDA, but Phyllis conceded that the major gay and lesbian organization had included trans people in their advocacy for hate crimes legislation and had published a guide about transgender workplace issues. By contrast, she said, "Lambda Legal remains at square zero. Lambda Legal has done No—None, Nix, Nay—meaningful work in favor of trans folks."[20] Phyllis encouraged her supporters to blast Lambda with protest letters, faxes, phone calls, and emails, and to boycott and picket Lambda events wherever they occurred. "MY CONCLUSION IS THAT LAMBDA LEGAL DEFENSE AND EDUCATION FUND IS NOW THE #1 TARGET OF OUR LIST OF ENEMIES TO TG-IN-CLUSION AND TO GENDER-VARIANT LGB INCLUSION," she wrote.[21]

Beatrice Duhon of Lambda took issue with Phyllis's characterization, noting that the organization was involved in a number of cases with transgender clients. This response further infuriated Phyllis, who forwarded her reply to Duhon to her Phyllabuster list. "You are the wealthiest legal organization in our community by a long shot, with by far the most extensive docket, the largest number of attorneys, and the greatest ability to take on new cases and new issues," she wrote. "In light of those facts, you and I both know that filing two amicus briefs in two trans-related cases does not reflect a significant commitment to transgendered issues."

Phyllis also criticized Lambda for failing to represent trans clients seeking access to medical care, as well as trans students who were assaulted because of their trans identity. She pledged "to urge those who care about transgendered people to push Lambda to include us on equal and unembarrassed terms by making a real commitment to advocating for trans people in employment, health care, education and other areas, as demonstrated through your docket and public education."[22]

As the new millennium rolled in, Phyllis seemed content. She was seeking a full-time professorship at a law school, rebuilding an Amway distributorship, and continuing to practice law. Her trans advocacy work had taken on a life of its own, branching out in ways she had never predicted. In January, she wrote:

> I derive much hope about the future from standing back and watching so many things that now go on without my help, push or initiation. Except for two national organizations, the TG community is fully reintegrated back into the LGBT political rights movement. TG activists are busy in most cities in EVERY state of the USA, in many other countries in the world. Back in the fall of 1991 when ICTLEP was merely a committee of the Houston GCTC group, there was no nationally focused TG legal or TG

political rights focused movement. There had been some local and some state successes by some very dedicated people, but there was no nationally focused TG legal or TG political rights movement. Now there is MOMENTUM everywhere. People who used to curse me for my activism now apologize and ask how to get involved. I am satisfied and I am filled with hope.[23]

In February, Phyllis participated in the first symposium on transgender law sponsored by a US law school. The event, hosted by William & Mary Law School, offered further evidence that her calls for the study and advancement of transgender law were beginning to take root in the academy. It also provided her with an opportunity to present a paper at a law school symposium that attracted national scholars in the growing field of gender law. Phyllis highlighted her participation in the symposium, as well as the subsequent publication of her paper in the *Journal of Women and the Law*, as she continued to seek a full-time position as a law professor. Not long after this symposium, Albany Law School came calling with another invitation—this one on family law and the political landscape for LGBT people.

Phyllis chose not to take part in the planning of the Millennium March on Washington for Equality, to be held in April. Though she had attended the first three marches for gay and lesbian rights, she participated in the Millennium March only as an online activist. Jonathan Zucker, a Millennium March board member, kept her informed about some of the planning details and sent her a copy of the board's resolution on trans issues and the trans community. Phyllis forwarded the resolution to her list members, requesting that they write the board to demand that they strengthen the resolution.

At the end of March, Phyllis stepped back into the limelight when she agreed to become one of the lead attorneys representing Christie Lee Littleton, a San Antonio–based trans woman who was facing a legal fight for her right to be considered a woman.

Christie Lee had undergone gender confirmation surgery in 1979, a fact she did not hide from her husband-to-be, Jonathon Mark Littleton, when they met in Lexington, Kentucky, where she was recuperating from surgery following a car accident. The couple soon fell in love during her hospital stay and were married. In 1996, Mark became ill and, according to Christie Lee, died as a result of medical malpractice.

Christie Lee filed suit against the doctor, and during the course of an investigation, the doctor's insurance company discovered that she had had gender confirmation surgery. Hoping to avoid a payout, the company argued that because she had male chromosomes, Littleton was a man; that because same-sex marriages were illegal, her marriage to Mark was illegal; and that because her marriage was illegal, she had no legal standing to sue as Mark's surviving spouse.

After losing in trial court, Littleton turned to the Fourth Court of Appeals in San Antonio. Phyllis responded to the case in a Phyllabuster, forcefully arguing against any decision that would adopt a chromosomal standard of legal sex. "If the chromosomal standard is adopted by Texas courts," Phyllis wrote, "transgender activists may do the following: Invite all legally declared, XY neo-vagina possessing males who like women to come to Texas, establish residency and legally marry a legally declared, XX vagina possessing women. The genitals will match, and in everyday society it will look like two women having a wedding, holding hands and kissing in public, but it will be a legal, Court-declared XX-XY opposite sex marriage."[24] She suggested the same for transgender men attracted to men.

The appeals panel ruled 2–1 against Littleton, with Judge Phillip Hardberger writing for the majority that "male chromosomes do not change with either hormonal treatment or sex reassignment surgery. Biologically, Littleton was not a female. We hold, as a matter of law, that Christie Littleton is a male. As a male, Christie cannot be married to another male. Her marriage to Jonathon was invalid, and she cannot bring a cause of action as his surviving spouse."[25]

Following the ruling, Phyllis received a deluge of inquiries from trans people concerned about the legality of the changes they had made to identification documents like birth certificates, driver's licenses, and passports. She encouraged them to wait and see how Littleton's attorneys would respond and, in the meantime, become active in the movement. "If you are in the closet, you just cannot cry and gnash your teeth because other people are not protecting your rights," she said. "If you do not like to fight, well guess what? The bigots just brought the fight to your front door. Grow up! If you do not come out and fight, the bigots are going to bust down your door and do whatever they legally wish in the name of religion, morality and conservatism."[26]

Littleton's lawyers elected not to request a hearing *en banc*—that is, before all the members of the court rather than just the three-judge appeals panel. The decision seemed questionable to Phyllis, especially when she heard that other judges on the court were angered by the decision, but the attorneys hedged their bets and asked the Texas Supreme Court to review the case. When the court refused in March 2000, they stepped away from the case, leaving Littleton in search of a new attorney.

With encouragement from Phyllis's friend Tere Fredrickson, also of San Antonio, Littleton turned to Phyllis, who accepted the invitation to be lead attorney. She immediately asked the court for an extension to file a motion for reconsideration, and the court granted the extension. In an effort to build public support for her client, Phyllis headed to the media. "Every heterosexual involved in a wrongful death suit, a divorce, anything involving communal property, insurance benefits, stands to lose something," she said, adding that she had every intention to take the case beyond Texas. "I have an appellate attorney in Virginia waiting for my call. If need be, we'll take it to the Supreme Court."[27]

Phyllis also called her friend Alyson Dodi Meiselman, a Maryland attorney with extensive experience with the appellate process, to help argue the case. "We'd first met at NLGLA, and we quickly became friends," Phyllis recalls. "We were both lawyers, we were out, and we were advocates."[28] With Phyllis's knowledge of Texas and Meiselman's knowledge of appeals, the team set out to draft and file their motion for rehearing.

In the introduction to their motion, which they submitted in April, they wrote: "The court of appeals developed a simplistic test that focuses solely on the physical appearance of a child's genitals at birth and ignores all other factors deemed relevant by medical experts." The attorneys then cited *Corbett v. Corbett* (1970), in which a United Kingdom court ruled that four factors must be considered when assessing an individual's sexual identity: "These four factors were chromosomal factors, gonadal factors (i.e., the presence or absence of testes or ovaries), genital factors (including internal sex organs), and psychological factors."[29]

On May 18, 2000, the Texas Supreme Court denied the motion for rehearing. When Phyllis broke the news to Littleton, she burst into tears and erupted in anger that she directed to Phyllis. "She had a right to be angry," Phyllis says. "She'd lost her husband. Her marriage had been invalidated by a hateful, homophobic court system. And she felt alone.

She had every right to be hurt." A day later, Littleton sat down and wrote a letter to Phyllis:

> Sorry, for last night's messages, guess I was feeling sorry for myself. Didn't mean any harm, please forgive me. But, I can't stop crying, it's hurt so much, if only, they could feel the pain, the loneliness & discrimination that I feel. No—No—one can put themself in my place, IT HURTS, OH GOD, IT HURTS.
>
> I can't believe this, 40 years ago I came out to my mother, before the word coming-out was heard of, I had to go to hell and back to be who I am. 20 years ago, after I fully became a woman, Paul Tomsons, an S. A. news reporter gave a bad reported about me & two other tg's. We got spit at, rocked, egged, bit-up & almost raped four times, I thought the discrimination was over. Guess I was wrong again.
>
> Today, at 8 p.m., I had a so call friend of 20 years, come to me & said she read the newspapers about me & ask why I never told her. Then she said not to feel bad about the outcome, cause I should know, I never could be a real woman, I WAS MAN-MADE. And she had truly believed I was a woman since day one, a true chance of mind & so-called true friend. Now, I know what's to come in the future.
>
> In 20 years, I hadn't felt so much pain, I hadn't cried so much. What happened?
>
> Mark Littleton, if I could bring you back to life, I would do it tonight, so you could hold me & comfort me, cause oh GOD, I am a woman and a human woman & I hurt & miss my man, my husband. OH, Christie stop, whoever heard of a tg, feeling love & having civil rights, so the LAW says!
>
> Sorry, ladies, guess I'm feeling sorry for myself, please accept, my forgiveness. Please excuse me.
>
> Damn it, fuck it, it's not over yet! since my husband dead, I've never wanted to fuck anyone, but I want to fuck the system now!!!!!!!!!!!!!!!!!!!!!!!!!!!!!! this is not over, if you still want to fight, let's go for it! what do we have to lose now, shame, humiliation, or discrimination, I don't think so, yet & still we have our pride to fight for.
>
> You were looking for fighter, well, you got her, I my story, my life, my fight is here, let's go.
>
> Ladies, I mean ladies, Tere, Phyllis, Please forgive me for last

night's command, s————I'm so—so—sorry, please understand it just hurts to feel all alone.

My eyes hurt so much now from crying, how can I say this without making myself to look like a bad lady, I could use & needed a man's shoulder to cry on now.

What would I give if, my mother-in-law, would let me place some flowers on & let me sit next to my husband's grave, just for one second, GOD only knows.[30]

In consultation with Littleton, Phyllis and Meiselman quickly announced that they would petition the US Supreme Court to grant a *writ of certiorari.* If granted, the *writ* would require the lower courts to turn over all materials related to the case to the US Supreme Court for review. If denied, the lower courts' rulings would stand. "It's just so damned unnecessary," Phyllis wrote. "If it was not so sad for Mrs. Littleton, I could almost laugh!"[31]

In June, Phyllis sought to focus the attention of the Texas State Bar Association on the Littleton case. Even though the case was now moving toward the US Supreme Court, she thought it important to attend an upcoming state bar meeting in order to educate her colleagues about the prior ruling and its potential implications. "I was doing everything I could to draw attention to fucking Hardberger [the judge who wrote the opinion] and this goddamn case," she says. "Across the street from the meeting, there was an organized protest giving Hardberger the blues, and because I was a member of the bar, I could take my protest inside. After a well-attended luncheon, I planted myself at the only convenient exit, and with a smile and a cheery tone, I handed out 450 pink flyers on the case. . . . Littleton became a topic of many workshops the next few days."[32]

Phyllis soon announced that Meiselman would file the *writ of certiorari* petition on July 3. "We do not plan to lose," she said. "We did not work this hard to lose. Even so, win or lose, it is a victory for transgender freedom. Win or lose, the posted Writ for Certiorari . . . is the work product of the best legal minds we could assemble in this cutting-edge area of law. Win or lose, this is the first organized effort by OUT transgender lawyers to stand up and fight all the way to the Supreme Court. And win or lose, this posted Writ will serve as the roadmap for any attorney, any attorney representing transgendered clients, as to the status of transgender law."[33]

In August, the NBC news program *Dateline* featured the case, focusing on Littleton's personal story. Phyllis had been present for the taping, but she did not see the final program until it was broadcast on August 2. "I taped and watched the NBC DATELINE show last night with the segment on Christie Lee Littleton," she wrote in a Phyllabuster. "I watched it over a dozen times, and every time I cried along with my friend, Christie Lee Littleton. I trust that you did too. The Texas courts had made her into a 'thing,' but last night on television, she was treated like a real human being who possessed feelings and dignity."[34]

Phyllis attracted additional publicity to the Littleton case a few weeks later when she sent out a press release about a couple planning to use the decision in order to secure a marriage license. Jessica Wicks, a trans woman, and Robin Wicks, a cis woman, had been together for four years. Robin had already taken Jessica's name, and they wanted to be legally married.

Their first attempt to secure a marriage license failed when the clerk at the Harris County Courthouse told them it was against the law for him to issue licenses to same-sex couples. At that point, they turned to Phyllis, who said, "'You can get married in any county in the state, so let's go to Bexar County [home to San Antonio and the Fourth Court of Appeals] and shove the Littleton case up their fucking ass.' Jessica and Robin thought that was a great idea."[35] Phyllis called Tere Prasse, who was familiar with the dynamics of Bexar County politics, and she contacted Bexar County clerk Gerry Rickhoff, who agreed that state law authorized him to issue the license.

In announcing the upcoming marriage to the media, Phyllis said: "Two women will show up to get a marriage license Sept. 6. Thanks to the 4th Court's recent opinion, legally it will be a male and a female. The main objective is to get Jessica and Robin married. She and Robin are very much in love, which is why they share the last name. . . . But we're also trying to get the Legislature's attention."[36]

On the morning of September 6, Phyllis, Jessica, and Robin arrived in San Antonio with a plan to hold an afternoon press conference and then secure the license. "But I was scared to death that we'd be served a writ and would have to delay, so around 11:00, Robin and Jessica and I went to the clerk's office and got the marriage license," Phyllis remembers. They had to wait a few hours until the scheduled press conference time, and then the three exited the courthouse. "About fifteen feet from the door, I could see people everywhere," Phyllis says. "Goddamn, it was fucking wall-to-wall cameras, and I let out a big 'Yahoo! Look at all those goddamn cameras!'"[37]

The following day, the *Houston Chronicle* published a major story about the event. "A love-struck couple from Houston made history on Wednesday by obtaining the first marriage license issued in Texas to two lesbians—a union that will be legal under current state law because one of them used to be a man," wrote John Gonzalez. The reporter also noted that while Jessica Wicks recognized the historic moment, what really mattered to her was the opportunity to marry the love of her life. "Everybody keeps talking about us making history," she said. "We just want to get married."[38]

Christie Lee Littleton was present for the post-press-conference celebration at a nearby Mexican restaurant. Reporters noted that although she seemed happy for the couple, she also looked as if she was still grieving the loss that had led to the celebratory moment. Phyllis, meanwhile, explained to reporters that the Littleton case was about the right of an individual to choose his or her gender. It was a landmark case, she said, possibly as important as *Roe v. Wade*.

"Jessica and Robin Wicks are legally married!" Phyllis told her email list on September 17.[39] Some recipients publicly expressed their appreciation for her work with the married couple and the Littleton case, but Phyllis also had her fair share of critics in the trans community. She received particularly harsh words from two emailers in Florida, who believed the Littleton case had resulted in their state planning to revoke new identification documents issued to people who had transitioned. One called her a "miserable low-life bitch," and another referred to her as "Mr. Phillip Frye" and a "two-bit castrated male."[40]

Phyllis quickly pointed out that Florida was not planning to revoke identification cards—even as other critics reared their heads with concerns about their own states. The criticisms hurt Phyllis, as did the lack of financial support the Littleton case received from the trans community.

Then, on October 2, 2000, Meiselman phoned Phyllis with the bad news—the US Supreme Court had just denied their petition. Even before she phoned Littleton with the news, she sat down and typed her most blistering Phyllabuster yet. "The Littleton case is now dead!" she wrote. "To those of you who are now scared shitless: you should be. . . . A personal note to all of the post-op transsexuals who have been pissing on me and Alyson for the Littleton and Wicks fights: you just got your wish. I hope you build a very, very, very strong closet and nail it shut with 16 penny nails and adjust to constantly watching over your shoulders for the remainder of your lives, because someday it WILL be your turn, just like it happened to Mrs. Littleton."[41]

After scorching a number of others, including heterosexual cross-dressers, trans men, and trans women who had refused to join the fight, she fired a final slug of indignation: "Alyson and I have worked our legal asses off for six months for less than $3 per hour. Thanks one hell of a lot for the ride. I feel like an old horse who has been ridden into the ground, put up wet and left unfed. NEVER AGAIN!"[42]

Phyllis was still angry when she arrived at the Lavender Law Conference at the end of October, and she and her friend Katrina Rose, along with about five other trans lawyers, decided to protest the absence of trans speakers on the conference schedule. More than any other national gay and lesbian group, NLGLA had opened its doors to trans people and trans issues, but the organization still had not integrated trans concerns as fully as possible.

"We pretty much wrecked that conference," Phyllis says. "We stood up in plenaries and workshops and demanded answers to our questions about why there were no trans speakers. That didn't happen again."[43]

Phyllis then headed to Philadelphia to fulfill her obligation to deliver a plenary address at the International Congress on Cross-Dressing, Sex, and Gender. Around this time, it became clear to her once again that she desperately needed a break. "Even though I appear to be back in the saddle, I am less so than before," she wrote in a Phyllabuster. "But I have spent 25 consecutive years of consistently—the consistently part is what has worn me out—being OUT and on the front line for LGBT rights. I have done my part. . . . I am not going away, but I am taking a significant step back. . . . I want some of the life that most of you were enjoying during those years when you were not involved and I was."[44]

Phyllis shifted her focus back to the Phyllabusters and the online fight against her enemies. A few months earlier, in July of that year, Phyllis had used an email blast to criticize Riki Wilchins as untrustworthy and to announce her support for a new organization called the National Transgender Advocacy Coalition, which was founded as a result of dissatisfaction among some activists who believed that Wilchins had made a pact with HRC to stop protesting the exclusion of trans people in ENDA. Then, at the beginning of 2001, Phyllis reported on the growing dissent over the new directions in which Wilchins was leading GenderPAC.

"Looking at 2001, it looks like GenderPAC is finally being exposed," Phyllis wrote. "I hate to say I told you so, but I told you so, beginning a very, very long time ago!"[45] At the time, GenderPAC had taken on a new mission that, as GenderPAC's own press release put it, "unites all the diverse communities and groups that have a common interest in gender civil rights: people of every gender, gender identity, race, class, age, and sexual orientation."[46]

Critics, including Phyllis, saw the new mission as a betrayal of Gender-PAC's founding purpose, which was to be a political action committee for the trans community, not for all gender and sexual orientation communities. "The transgender community is left with no advocate at the federal level," activist JoAnn Roberts wrote, adding that trans activists should "retaliate in kind" by holding a lobbying day focused on trans issues before GenderPAC held its own lobbying day. Phyllis loved the idea, but she declined when asked to lead it.

Phyllis continued to hammer this point a few months later in a Phyllabuster:

> I've been asked by several folks, who do not know my past relations with GenderPAC and Riki Wilchins, if I will be attending their [lobbying] event in D.C. in May. THE SIMPLE ANSWER IS NO! I do not trust and I do not support GenderPAC or Riki Wilchins. They have scheduled a so-called gender law institute in D.C. in May. Looking at their literature, I do not see a single transgender lawyer listed as a presenter. I have been called by several transgender attorneys who were asked to present. These folks have told me they refused to attend and refused to present because they do not trust and do not support GenderPAC or Riki Wilchins.[47]

Dallas Denny, now editor of *Transgender Tapestry*, lambasted Wilchins in the spring 2001 issue for fueling a split on the GenderPAC board between those who wanted the group to be transgender-specific in its work and membership and those who, like Wilchins, wanted to include all gender expressions. Denny also criticized Wilchins for "high-handed" moves that allegedly included stacking the board with uncritical supporters, distancing

GenderPAC from the trans community, and shifting GenderPAC's focus from national political advocacy to grassroots training.

"In her career as a political activist, Wilchins has run roughshod over many people and any number of organizations, leaving—needlessly—a trail of hurt feelings and bruised egos in her wake," Denny wrote. "She has betrayed colleagues and those who thought they were her friends, reneged on promises, violated solemn agreements, and played person against person and organization against organization in reckless pursuit of her goals."[48] Denny offered specific examples, including the time when Wilchins "heartlessly" grabbed control of Lobbying Day from Phyllis and "managed—some say purposefully—to turn that once well-run and effective event into a confusing, disorganized turmoil with no overall strategy."[49]

When Phyllis read Denny's article, she immediately sent it to the Phyllabuster list. But she soon realized she was weary of granting so much of her attention to Riki Wilchins, and in 2001, she simply stopped writing about her. To this day, Phyllis only reticently agrees to talk about Wilchins. "There's too much hurt there," she says, "and I'd rather not revisit it."[50] For her part, Wilchins aims to be respectful of Phyllis and her legacy. "By being one of the first to see transgender not just as a personal issue but a political, legal, and legislative one, Phyllis helped ignite a new civil rights movement that now literally circles the globe," Wilchins says.[51]

On March 15, 2001, Phyllis received an email from a good friend at the Human Rights Campaign who reported that the organization's board of directors had just voted to amend the mission statement "to reflect our work on transgender and gender identity and expression issues." Phyllis immediately passed the news along to her email list, along with a short commentary. "This is a surprise," she wrote. "Welcome at that! This struggle for TG inclusion began in July 1994 when Karen Kerin & I first learned that HRC led the TG exclusion from ENDA. . . . I am grateful, yet numbed, and cautious of the result. But I am pleased on the face of it. It is champagne time!"[52]

Within two months, Phyllis sent a very different message. "FUCK HRC!" she wrote after receiving an HRC fundraising letter that mentioned gays, lesbians, and bisexuals, but not trans people.[53] By the end of the summer, when she discovered that ENDA once again excluded trans people, she organized a letter-writing campaign against both ENDA and HRC.

She ramped up her action in September 2002 when she joined forces with Sarah DePalma, now president of the Texas Gender Advocacy Information Network, and about a dozen other activists for a street protest outside La Colombe d'Or, a fancy Montrose restaurant where HRC was holding a fundraiser.

Phyllis was dressed in a Transgender Menace (not a Transexual Menace) T-shirt, and she and others held the trusty-dusty blue banner as rush-hour traffic zipped by. Most drivers ignored them, but a good number waved and honked. "We're getting a lot of support," Phyllis told reporter Lisa Gray. "That, or somebody's horny." DePalma, meanwhile, handed out yellow flyers stating, "We are talking life and death. It is just that simple. . . . Please follow your conscience. Make your feelings known by taking your money home."[54]

Phyllis did not see any donors leaving because of their protest, but she did have a direct encounter with HRC's Elizabeth Birch. According to Gray, Birch came outside the restaurant and spoke directly to her longtime opponent. "The Human Rights Campaign is working for the good of everyone, she said. ENDA isn't the be-all and end-all, she said; there were other approaches, other programs. She said she respected the transgender point of view and wanted an open dialogue." As Birch turned to leave, Phyllis said, "Hey, Elizabeth. Are you going to come all the way down here and not hug me?" Phyllis truly liked Birch; it was the HRC board that she detested. According to Gray, "Birch embraced Phyllis like she meant it, then hurried back to the fundraiser."[55]

Then, on June 16, 2003, Elizabeth Birch announced that HRC was now backing a new and inclusive employment nondiscrimination bill. "It took decades to educate the country on gay issues, and we must now educate America about the bias and discrimination facing our transgender brothers and sisters," she wrote. "HRC—working with transgender and community leaders—is opting to work with members of Congress to educate them and to develop a new strategy for a fresh unified bill that will address the discrimination faced by lesbian, gay, bisexual and transgender Americans."[56]

Phyllis sent Birch's announcement to her list that same day. "When I finished reading Elizabeth Birch's words . . . I cried openly," she wrote. "I was crying for HAPPINESS. I have waited nine years to read this."[57] The wait wasn't exactly over yet, but on August 7, 2004, Phyllis's friends Mara

Keisling and Shannon Minter called her to report that they and other trans leaders had just met with the HRC board of governors. The board had finally agreed to inform congressional sponsors of ENDA, especially Kennedy and Frank, that they would not support an ENDA that failed to use language protecting gender identity or expression. Phyllis again passed along the good news, inviting her followers to "feel whole again."[58]

The National Center for Transgender Equality (NCTE), an organization close to Phyllis's heart, then took up the hard work of ensuring that HRC would be true to its word. Founded by Mara Keisling in 2003, the NCTE used the tools of education and advocacy to fight discrimination and violence.

"I first met Mara at the Lavender Law conference in Philadelphia," says Phyllis. "She had done her homework and knew all about me and ICTLEP and GenderPAC and my fights with Riki and Lobbying Day. She came up to me and asked if she could buy me a drink and talk, and I agreed, and she gave me her spiel and put forth her idea about forming a national transgender lobby group that would be on the Hill 24/7. She asked me what I thought, and I essentially, vocally, gave her a kiss. She was going to do what I'd always wanted to do but never had the money and didn't want to move to DC to do it. I told her she had my support 100 percent, and I was glad when she took up the fight against HRC and ENDA."[59]

In the spring of 2004, Phyllis made plans to travel to Washington, DC, for an event honoring the contributions of trans men and women who had served in the US military. Sponsored by the Transgender American Veterans Association (TAVA), the event included gatherings at various war memorials and Arlington National Cemetery.

Phyllis invited her supporters to join her on the pilgrimage. "Too many of us, because of our being TG, have not yet gathered the courage or had the opportunity to remember our 'buds' with a rubbing from the WALL or with a visit to the other monuments, the Tomb of the Unknown Soldier or the Arlington Cemetery," she wrote. "Too many of us, because of our being TG, have not met some of our comrades from our units who, surprise, are also TG. And, while this will be a solemn and respectful event, we will, for the first time, show to the nation that transgenders served, bled and died to protect our and their lifestyle as Americans."[60]

On May 1, Phyllis sat with a diverse group of vets on a chartered bus escorted by a DC police car using its siren and lights. "When you've been outside law and society as long as I have, a police escort is a shocking thing," Phyllis says. "I felt honored."[61]

The group visited the Vietnam War Memorial, and Phyllis saw lots of tears as her colleagues took rubbings of the names of their friends and loved ones. She held one veteran for several minutes as she sobbed after finding the name of her cousin high on the wall. The group also visited the Korean War Memorial and the World War II Memorial, and they talked with visitors who asked about their service, often wondering how many trans people served in the military. Then the group climbed aboard the bus for a trip to the Iwo Jima Memorial and the Tomb of the Unknown Soldier, where they were scheduled to participate in a 3:00 p.m. laying of the wreath ceremony.

But when the vets arrived for the ceremony, there was a problem. "They couldn't find our wreath," Phyllis recalls. "We were so used to being fucked over, I think we just expected that to happen. But when the sergeant major who ran detail for the shift found out, he got angry, and within five minutes, those in his command found the wreath. The attempt to belittle us, if that's what it was, didn't work."[62]

If Phyllis and her colleagues were not surprised when their wreath appeared lost, they were certainly shocked at what happened next, during the ceremony itself. "We all thought our name would be skipped over, but then we heard the sergeant of the guard announce, in a loud and booming voice, 'This wreath is being placed by the *Transgender American Veterans Association!*' There we were, no more closets, all of us out in the open, in our cemetery, and when we heard that, we all just started weeping and crying."[63]

She later wrote about the cemetery experience, comparing it to other moments in the movement. Unlike all those other experiences, this one made her feel that she no longer had to beg and plead for inclusion—that she was finally part of society.

On April 24, 2007, Phyllis forwarded without comment an NCTE news bulletin announcing the introduction of a trans-inclusive ENDA into the US House of Representatives. The announcement characterized the development as "an historic stride forward in protecting the civil rights of transgender people."[64]

Three months later, Rep. Barney Frank announced that he was introducing new legislation that provided protection from employment discrimination on the basis of sexual orientation alone. In response, Phyllis sent out several Phyllabusters imploring her followers to flood Congress with phone calls and letters of protest. At the same time, NCTE undertook some hard lobbying on the Hill. When HRC announced that it would not ask members of Congress to oppose the trans-exclusive ENDA, Phyllis called for street protests against the organization. Despite the lobbying and protests, the bill made it out of committee, and Phyllis wrote numerous emails excoriating HRC for not opposing it publicly and unequivocally.

She continued her campaign against HRC in 2008, advocating for a boycott and more direct-action protests, especially at its major fundraiser in New York City, and along with a few friends, including Josephine Tittsworth and Vanessa Edwards-Foster, she began organizing a small protest to take place at an HRC fundraiser scheduled in Houston on April 12.

Two days before the event, an officer with the Houston Police Department stopped by Phyllis's office to drop off a demonstration guide. During the polite conversation, the officer informed Phyllis that HRC had contacted the department and the hotel where the event was to be held, asking both to keep the demonstrators away from the fundraiser attendees. Phyllis blasted that information in bold font in one of the numerous Phyllabusters she sent in preparation for the local protest.

When the eleven protestors showed up for the demonstration, they were met with police barricades, traffic cones, police officers in riot gear and mounted on horses, and guards posted at the hotel entrances. "It was surreal—all that effort for just little ole, inoffensive us," Phyllis wrote. The group also learned that HRC had changed its mind about keeping them away from the fundraiser. Now permitted to walk through the hotel, Phyllis and two others handed out lapel stickers that read "GLBT & ENDA: United, Not Divided: I Support FULL Transgender Inclusion."[65] The protesters were asked to leave the hotel for handing out the stickers in an undesignated area, but there were no incidents requiring police intervention.

The following day, Phyllis sent numerous Phyllabusters including photographs of the few protesters and the heavy police presence. "By calling the Houston Police, National HRC deliberately set in motion a police over-response," she wrote. "HRC used government and taxpayer monies to intimidate the hell out of TG and Gender Variant people who drove in to participate but were scared away."[66]

"Has National HRC become the BULLY of the previously united LGBT community?" she asked the next day in yet another Phyllabuster. Phyllis pleaded with her followers to stage protests in their own locales and to publicize the protests so their campaign would become truly national.[67] Although the Houston protest was the last anti-HRC event in which Phyllis directly participated, NTCE carried on the legacy and, with the help of many others, eventually forced HRC to support only a trans-inclusive ENDA—a bill that has yet to pass Congress.

Phyllis also regularly used her Phyllabusters to address another topic close to her heart—violence against trans people. With help from Gwendolyn Ann Smith, a trans woman who had founded the Transgender Day of Remembrance in 1999 to memorialize the murder of Rita Hester of Massachusetts, along with all those killed as a result of antitransgender hatred or prejudice, Phyllis passed along information about murders of trans people as they continued to happen, each and every year. She also regularly disseminated news items reporting any violence against trans people—often trans women of color, who were disproportionately targeted.

The Day of Remembrance came to Houston on November 28, 2000, and Phyllis forwarded information from event organizers that listed the eighteen trans-related murders known to have occurred since the first Day of Remembrance the previous year. It had been another bloody year, and the details of the murders—including strangulation, stabbing, torture, drowning, rape, shootings, and throat-slashing—made for awful reading. One particularly gruesome case involved an unnamed intersex infant who had been strangled and died of blunt trauma to the head; an autopsy revealed that the infant also had shards of glass in their esophagus and stomach. Sharing these horrific stories, Phyllis insisted that her readers attend the memorial, which would include reading the names of the victims, lighting and snuffing candles, and ringing a bell. Phyllis agreed to speak after the reading of the names, as did Sarah DePalma, Vanessa Edwards Foster, and Cristan Williams.

Phyllis continued to be involved in the memorial in subsequent years, and in 2003 she sent the *Houston Chronicle* an op-ed criticizing local police and media outlets. "The media's fixation (local television included) and the police's fixation on unseen genitals remains," she wrote. "We transgenders are not dogs! As transgenders are murdered, the media and the police continue to call our transgendered women as being 'men' and 'he.' ... Why are you so callous? Why are you so lazy? Why are you so damned mean?"[68]

During that year's Transgender Day of Remembrance, Phyllis joined other participants in singing lyrics she had written to the tune of the Irish ballad "Danny Boy":

> *Transgender Dead, your spirits are now calling*
> *From coast to coast, in cities o'er the land.*
> *You are like us, but hate has made you fallen.*
> *Yes, you were killed by hate so we must stand,*
> *Stand for you in all the summer's warmness,*
> *Or when the winter's cold and white with snow.*
> *We'll stand for you in sunshine or in shadow,*
> *Transgender Dead, Transgender Dead, we stand for you.*[69]

Chapter Sixteen

From Lawbreaker to Law Enforcer

Protest and politics remained important to Phyllis in the new millennium, but she also relished writing, teaching, and practicing law, and one of her proudest professional accomplishments was joining an openly gay law firm in 2004.

"Two good friends of mine, John Nechman and Jerry Simoneaux, had founded an out and gay law firm," Phyllis remembers. "And shortly after they did that, Jerry and I made a trip to Austin for a state bar meeting. We were talking, and Jerry was telling me about the firm, and I said, 'Gee whiz, I'd love to be part of that.' Well, I discovered later that he'd been hoping I'd say that."[1]

Phyllis was downright gleeful when she moved her practice out of her home—it had been there more than twenty years—and to the offices of Nechman and Simoneaux at 3400 Montrose in Houston. She felt doubly pleased when the firm changed its name to Nechman, Simoneaux, and Frye. "We advertised ourselves as *out*, and to the best of my knowledge, we were the first out law firm with a trans partner west of the Mississippi. We really made a big deal about it."[2]

The environment for LGBT lawyers in Texas in 2004 was far friendlier than it had been when Phyllis graduated from law school. Thanks to her tireless work, as well as that of other LGBT activists, Houston now had its own LGBT law association. Even the State Bar of Texas (SBOT) now had an active and influential LGBT section called "Sexual Orientation and Gender Identification Issues" (SOGI).

SOGI included "gender identification issues" within its purview only because of Phyllis's resistance, in 1997, to a proposed section focusing on sexual orientation alone. "When I found that gay and lesbian lawyers were trying to form a trans-exclusive section, I was so pissed I could spit," she says. "So Dee McKellar and I got the names and contact information for every board member of the State Bar, and we wrote to them, asking them to vote no on the proposal. We were really ticked off."[3]

Phyllis's lobbying paid off when the board voted to deny the petition for the new section. "The vote shocked [the gay and lesbian attorneys]. I hadn't told them what Dee and I had done, but soon after the vote, others told them, 'Don't fuck with Phyllis. She'll make your life miserable.' They were right—I did, and I would."[4]

After the dramatic loss, the gay and lesbian group reached out to Phyllis with the suggestion that all interested LGBT lawyers work together on creating a new section that would be trans-inclusive. Phyllis was pleased to help out, and she eventually garnered about 25 percent of the signatures required to petition the board. This time the group succeeded, and SOGI won provisional and then permanent status within SBOT.

With Phyllis, Charles Spain, and Alyson Meiselman leading the way, the new group soon pushed SBOT to adopt an employment policy that offered protection from discrimination based on sexual orientation and gender identification, and in June 2001, the three activists headed to the annual SBOT meeting in Austin to lobby.

Phyllis had told board chair Dick Miller in advance that if the board did not approve a policy that included gender expression, she and others would blanket the convention with protest flyers. Hoping to avoid the spectacle, Miller replied that he would seek a compromise by ensuring that the minutes stated that the words "sexual orientation" would include "gender identification" as part of their meaning.

True to Phyllis's word, the three activists prepared to stage a loud protest at the convention. Phyllis and Spain donned T-shirts said, "Transgender Lawyers: We think using both sides of our brains—if you don't believe it, check out our briefs!" Meiselman brought pink buttons with an unadorned directive: "Stop Discrimination at the State Bar."[5]

During the meeting, as promised, Dick Miller proposed that the phrase "sexual orientation" include "gender identification" as part of its meaning in the new policy. His compromise succeeded without controversy, and after the motion passed, he lavished praise on Phyllis: "Of course, we understand Phyllis Frye is not exactly satisfied with this because it just says sexual orientation and does not say gender identification. . . . I want to tell you that I have developed a respect for Phyllis for her willingness to stand up for an unpopular cause, be spat upon by others because of her beliefs, but to stay true to her heartfelt beliefs and convictions on this. We all admire Atticus Finch and I think those are the qualities about Atticus Finch that we admire."[6]

Back home, Phyllis shared the news, which she described as a "high point" in her life:

> Usually I return to my home and tell my spouse (28 years on June 23) of how during the event I made some friends, how I dulled some criticism, how I moved things along to another level, or how through education I laid the groundwork for the next time. It is all of those little wins that have kept me going for these decades and kept me from burning out. It is the little flame of knowing that all of these little wins do add up to a lot of progress over the decades. But I have only rarely witnessed a BIG WIN. I did so last Thursday, June 14, 2001, in Austin, Texas, as the Texas Bar Convention.[7]

Phyllis added that after the vote she was in "a bit of a shock" and not quite sure what to wear to the conference's more formal events, like the president's ball, since she had packed only her battle-ready T-shirts. "It was a situation I was totally not prepared for, but certainly a welcome situation, nonetheless."[8] Ever resourceful, she found a dress and heels to her liking and celebrated her new status—fully integrated, with presence and power, into the State Bar of Texas.

Perhaps the biggest development in Phyllis's law career happened nine years later, after her longtime friend and former softball coach, Annise Parker, was elected mayor of Houston, becoming the first openly lesbian mayor of a major US city. With a commitment to strengthening the presence of women in city politics, Parker appointed Barbara Hartle as director and presiding judge for the Municipal Courts Judicial Department. Hartle, in turn, approached Phyllis and requested permission to appoint her as one of the city's municipal judges.

"I told her I was honored, but that I'd have to talk with Trish before giving my answer," Phyllis recalls.[9] Trish expressed reservations about the very public nature of the judgeship, not only because of potential blow-back in her own life, but also because she had seen Phyllis lose friendships and suffer intense personal pain in her earlier exposure in the media.

Phyllis reluctantly declined the offer. Soon afterward, she found herself in the public eye anyway when her law firm took on a case about a trans woman, Nikki Araguz, fighting for her right to claim insurance benefits following the death of her firefighter husband, Thomas Araguz. The case attracted significant media attention because of its relative uniqueness: the ex-wife and mother of Thomas Araguz were using the *Littleton* precedent in an effort to declare the marriage between Nikki and Thomas as illegal, thus making Nikki ineligible to receive insurance benefits.[10]

Phyllis and her colleagues were regularly covered by the media as they argued the case, and soon Barbara Hartle approached Phyllis again about becoming a municipal judge. This time Phyllis said yes on the spot. "I told Barbara that I didn't want a full-time judgeship—that I wanted to keep practicing law—but that I'd be honored to be a part-time associate judge."[11]

Later that day, when Phyllis shared the news with Trish, Trish expressed surprise, saying she thought the matter had been settled. Phyllis conceded the point but added that her handling of the media coverage of the Araguz case should give Trish confidence in her maturing ability to handle public scrutiny. Though she still had reservations, Trish gave her blessing.

Mayor Parker soon nominated Phyllis, along with other candidates, and city council planned to review the nominations in November. Meanwhile, Phyllis did what she could to ensure a successful vote. "I knew that there was a possibility of delay if a member had a fly up his ass about me, so while I told a lot of friends about my nomination and invited them to come support me for the vote, I also asked them to keep the news quiet. I remembered what happened when the White House canceled my visit after I blabbed about it, and I didn't want anything like that to happen again."[12]

On November 17, 2010, city council voted to approve the nomination of Phyllis Randolph Frye for the position of associate municipal judge. "Several members said wonderful things about me during the discussion, but I also learned later on that one of the members had planned to red-flag my nomination, which would have delayed the vote," Phyllis recalls. "I heard Mayor Parker told him that if he red-flagged me, she would see to it that his projects would have a hard time passing. He didn't, and I was confirmed."[13]

During her confirmation hearing, Phyllis recalled that thirty years ago, in the very same room, the city council had repealed the cross-dressing ordinance at her relentless urging. "I almost started crying, because I remembered thirty-one years ago, I was subject to arrest," she explains.[14] Now she was being confirmed as a municipal judge.

Having won confirmation, Phyllis was sworn in before Trish and their friends in the ceremonial room on the third floor of City Hall. She had just become the first openly transgender judge in the United States.

"I didn't know at the time that I was the first out transgender judge, but I was still feeling good," she recalls. "By then I had received lots of honors—the Bayard Rustin Award, the Trinity Award, the Virginia Prince Award—so I wasn't jittery. I just felt really honored—and relieved that no one had flagged me and that none of the other nominees had to put up with bullshit about me."[15]

Phyllis, Trish, and a few others then headed for a low-key celebratory dinner at Katz's Deli in the heart of Montrose. Alyson Meiselman, who had flown in from Maryland, presented Phyllis with a gorgeous gavel and striker she had made from cherry wood.

The *Houston Chronicle* published a front-page story about Phyllis's judgeship the following morning. The story quoted Phyllis seeking to put the significance of her nomination in its proper context: "I don't want to underplay this, because it is very significant," she said. "But I don't want to overplay it, either. I don't want people to think I am anything other than an associate municipal judge."[16] But Kris Banks, president of Houston's LGBT caucus, took a more laudatory tone. "Phyllis Frye is a true icon in our civil rights movement," Banks said. "She is an internationally recognized pioneer, and the mayor is to be congratulated for her choice."[17]

Phyllis's very public move to the bench also gave rise to a chorus of criticism from religious conservatives in the area. David Welch, executive director of the Houston Area Pastor Council, depicted the nomination as morally wrong. "Phyllis Frye is a very well-known radical transgender activist," he said. "We don't think it is consistent with the values of the vast majority of the people. We think it is an anti-family lifestyle and agenda."[18]

Phyllis also recalls that "the religious and conservative nuts" used their radio programs to denounce her as a pawn in Mayor Parker's "gay agenda." "I got calls from several conservative radio hosts who invited me to appear on their shows. I declined, and they said, 'Don't you want to present your side of the story?' And I said, 'I already know my side.'"[19]

The same critics claimed that Phyllis lacked credentials and was appointed only because she was trans. "When my friends told me what they were saying, I said, 'Look—I've been a felony trial lawyer for almost thirty years, and these people are saying that I can't listen to traffic cases?'"[20]

The evolution from law breaker to law shaper to law enforcer required Phyllis to adjust her sense of self:

> It took me a while to get used to people calling me "Judge," especially people I knew. But that changed at the first National Transgender Day of Remembrance that happened right after I'd been sworn in. I was the keynote speaker for the event, and I went to the social, and everyone was coming up to me and saying, "Hello, Judge" or "Hello, Judge Frye." I wasn't handling that well yet, and I would say, "Oh, no. You can still call me 'Phyllis.'" But then [gay activist] Lou Weaver grabbed me and said, in a very stern voice, "Let's go talk." We did, and he stuck his finger in my chest and said something like, "Look—these people need a role model, and you're it, so get over it, Judge!"[21]

"Being a judge was never part of my wildest dreams," she says now. It's a curious comment, even virtually unbelievable, because she had dreamed so many creative, colorful, almost impossible, dreams throughout her earlier life—being like her cousin Margaret, wearing women's clothing without judgmental family members glaring at her, marrying a woman who truly loved her for the woman she was, coming out without fear of arrest, using law school bathrooms without harassment, smashing the Houston ordinance against cross-dressing, excelling at a law career focusing on economically disadvantaged individuals and the LGBTQ+ community, stopping police brutality against trans people, integrating trans people into Houston's gay and lesbian political caucus, making statewide gay and lesbian organizations open their doors to the trans community, fighting for the repeal of state sodomy laws, advocating for gay and lesbian rights before the national Democratic platform committee, creating a transgender law and employment conference, training numerous men and women to become leaders in the trans rights movement, critiquing and shaping transgender law, advancing the idea being trans is not mental illness, reincorporating trans folks into national movements for gay and lesbian rights, using the speaker's platform at numerous marches and rallies to demand trans inclusion, stonewalling the organizers of Stonewall 25, lobbying Congress for transgender rights, honoring transgender veterans and victims of hate crimes, making ENDA and HRC trans-inclusive, encouraging NLGLA to carry on the work of ICTLEP, supporting the creation of NCTE, and founding trans-inclusive law associations in her home city and state, among so many other dreams.

It's not that the thought of becoming a judge had never crossed Phyllis's mind. "When I started having some success at the Harris County court-house, a number of people asked me about running for judge," Phyllis recalls. "But I wouldn't even consider it. First, you have to be out every night of the week if you're going to have a successful campaign, and I didn't want to do that. And second, I knew I'd have to deal with one ques-tion over and over again—where's she going to use the bathroom?—and I certainly did not want to do that."[22] Until Hartle came calling, Phyllis had banished the thought of becoming a judge, and she had done so despite her undeniable gift of dreaming in color.

But the dream of becoming a judge took shape when she agreed to be nominated, and today she remains delighted with her decision to pursue it. She chooses to serve on the bench about a dozen times per year, and when she does, traffic and city property cases usually make up the bulk of her docket. But her favorite part of being a judge is marrying couples—lesbian, gay, bisexual, transgender, queer, intersex, asexual, or cis. And Phyllis no longer worries about which bathroom to use at the Harris County Courthouse or the Houston Municipal Courthouse. Judge Frye alone rules on that personal and political issue.[23]

"It's a real kick," Phyllis says. "Who would have thought? All of the shit that I caught when I transitioned, all of the scary shit that Trish and I went through with our families and neighbors, the tons of shit that I had to go through when I fought for trans rights, when I fought for the repeal of the cross-dressing ordinance, when I fought for trans inclusion in the gay and lesbian movement, when I fought against HRC and so many others—all that crazy shit. *And now I'm a judge?*"[24]

"I love the work," she concludes. "My one and only job as a judge is to dispense justice—not *convictions* but *justice*—and I do my job."[25]

Concluding Interview

We (Michael and Shea) conducted an interview with Phyllis on November 27, 2020, just a few days before submitting the manuscript to the publisher. We've edited and condensed the interview for clarity and length.

Let's talk about your legacy. As you look back on your fight for transgender rights, how would you like to be remembered?

I know that I have predecessors. I know that there are people who could easily be called the grandmother of the movement—people like Christine Jorgensen, Jan Morris, Renee Richards, and Virginia Prince. And I know there were early legal writers and local or statewide fighters, like Sister Mary Elizabeth in California, Martine Rothblatt in Maryland, and others. But, as Shannon wrote so graciously in his foreword, I'm the grandmother of the national legal and political movement, and I think that's how I'm going to be remembered. I don't want to claim to be the grandmother of the community, because I'm not. But on the national scene, from a legal and political perspective, that was me.

What are your most significant accomplishments?

One accomplishment is founding and hosting six ICTLEP conferences. The legacy of ICTLEP is going to live in its proceedings. I still think that publishing the proceedings of five of the six conferences is one of the smartest things I did. I know they've been digitized at Cushing Library at Texas A&M.

Another accomplishment is bringing into being generations of transgender activists and encouraging other transgender people to go to law school or to come out if they are already lawyers. There were very few out-of-the-closet transgender lawyers at the time I started ICTLEP. In fact, only four attended the early conferences, and two of the four used pseudonyms in the first year. There's a lot of people today who decided to go to law school and become lawyers as a result of the ICTLEP conferences. I think I can legitimately say that almost every trans activist or trans attorney that we have today is either a second, third, fourth, or possibly fifth generation of somebody that I influenced with the ICTLEP conferences.

I also demonstrated that regular people can be very accepting of me as an out transgender activist, and of Trish and me as an out lesbian couple. I think it's a big accomplishment that I've served as a role model to others, and that Trish and I, as a couple, have been role models for so many trans people—trans couples, lesbian and gay couples, and straight couples—of what friendship is, and what dedication is, and what being true to marriage vows means. After Trish passed, so many people contacted me and said that because of her, they stayed with their trans spouse or partner. Of course, my best accomplishment is the fact that I kept Trish by my side for forty-eight years.

What are you proudest of?

A lot of things. One of them is not getting arrested from 1976 to 1980, even though I was out almost every day, trying to get a job, going to law school, or lobbying to get the ordinance repealed. I'm also very proud that while I was in law school, I took the so-called Christian Legal Society head on, and that by the time I left school, they were on a campus-wide probation for discrimination. That felt really good. I'm very proud that I created the Phyllabuster list. That was an early form of a blog, and it allowed me to lead the transgender community in its struggle for inclusion in gay and lesbian organizations, especially HRC. I'm also proud of receiving numerous awards from LGBTQ+ organizations, and even more so, from organizations outside the community. Texas A&M has named an annual advocacy award after me, and the southwest chapter of the Anti-Defamation League honored me as a civil rights leader in 2018.

Do you have any regrets or failures you'd like to discuss?

Everybody has regrets, and mine are few, and I really don't want to dwell on them. The biggest failure has been the loss of my blood family. They have their religious beliefs, and I don't fit into their interpretations. They've had over forty years to get over it, and they haven't, so that's just too bad.

I also have regrets related to my relationship with Randy. We did get back together after he contacted me. Trish and I went to his wedding and college graduation, and we visited him and his wife and their firstborn for several years. But then something went wrong that I won't detail here. I was feeling very hurt by my perception of what had happened and wrote a hurtful letter, and we've been estranged since. I have not seen our two grandchildren since the oldest one was three. Over the decades, I have written from time to time with no response. Recently, Randy turned fifty. I wrote to acknowledge his birthday and to ask again that he forgive my harsh words. I received no response. So what can I do except wait, just as I did for my dad, brother, and sister? I hope the rift will end someday.

Let's talk about the present and the future in relation to the trans legal and political movement. What do you think the trans movement should focus on right now?

We have a unique situation right now with regard to trans people and the military. Before Trump's presidency, we had already made in-roads into the military, and those should come back during the Biden-Harris administration. I hope and pray that trans people who were pushed out will reapply. I hope they're not so bitter that they won't reapply, and I hope that youngsters will apply. You know, all of the training I received through ROTC and officer courses had something to do with me being the leader I am and having the backbone that I have. The military offers good leadership training, and military service looks good on job applications. I hope that trans people will flood into the military.

This past June, we had a Supreme Court ruling that protects trans people from employment discrimination, and I hope that any trans person who loses their job, or is not being hired, because they are trans will immediately go to the EEOC and file a complaint. I know they'll be receptive.

It's time for more trans folks to start running for elected or appointed office. Yes, get involved in politics. That's how we make it. Slowly we are seeing more trans folks getting elected or appointed to city or county or statewide offices. As a matter of fact, in December 2020, Jill Quinn will become the country's third out transgender judge.

The last thing is that trans folks need to volunteer for local organizations and local government. We can break down stereotypes that way. Plus, the relationships you build in volunteering might help you become a leader in your community. I point to myself as an example. Annise Parker and I volunteered together and played on the same softball team, and after she became mayor of Houston, she appointed me as municipal judge.

Which long-term goals should the movement target?

Elder care.

I'm concerned about religious bigotry in elder care. I had experience with this in 2001 when I went to the hospital following a mini-stroke. Because I was out, the medical staff knew that I was transgender, and every day someone would find their way onto my floor and into my room, and they'd try to "save" me. I can't tell you how many times I had to push the nurse's button and tell the nurse to get this goddamn religious bigot out of my room.

I'm also concerned about bigotry in nursing homes and hospitals toward elderly trans folks who, like me, have elected not to undergo [total gender confirmation] surgery. Trish and I had planned that she would protect me from all of the microaggressions and slights and ugliness that would come when caregivers noticed that I had only a bilateral orchiectomy. The plan was that she would take care of me at home. Although Trish has passed, I will still not go to a nursing home. I will kill myself first. And I think that's a pretty common thought in the trans community. What horrible torture it would be for elderly trans people to experience bigotry five, six, seven, eight times a day.

So I think there needs to be better training for caregivers. We need to insist they use the right pronouns, and we need to teach them that whatever is under the bedsheets should not negatively affect their caregiving. I think we're going to see a lot more suicides if this doesn't change.

Is there reason for trans people to be hopeful about the present and future?

Yes, yes, yes!

The last four years of Trumpism have demonstrated that transgender folks are solidly supported by center and center-left politicians, groups, and people. And the solidarity of the now-inclusive LGBTQ+ community has survived. So I'm very positive about the present and future.

I'd be very surprised if there aren't openly transgender advisers in the White House in the Biden-Harris administration. I'd be very surprised if there aren't more openly trans staff people working in state and federal politics. It's our time, and we've got at least a four-year window, so I think people can take courage, come out, and get active.

Is there anything that worries you?

Yes—people going back into the damn closet. There are people who will use the resources we've provided, and then, when they are comfortable with their transition, they'll go back into the closet. They're selfish people.

Let me tell you about staying out of the closet. After Trish was diagnosed with a brain tumor, we sold our house and moved into a senior living facility. We knew from our past that the best way to go into a new situation is to be completely out. So we made sure to tell management about who we were, and I made copies of the *New York Times* profile of me and handed them out as we met people in our new place. No matter where you live, people are going to gossip, and I want them to gossip about facts. With the exception of one person—who's really an ass—we've been well received here.

You just need to come out of the closet—and stay out.

And will you please give us an update on your personal life?

I've been dealing with my own cancer, myelodysplastic syndrome [MDS], for a very long time. My hematologist told me that statistically, I should have been dead at least five or more years ago. Trish and I knew that she would be the widow of us, and we planned accordingly. But in September 2019 we found a malignant tumor in her brain.

In February 2020, my MDS almost had me. I was being kept alive mostly through the infusion of two units of whole blood every two weeks. A new drug we'd been waiting on came out, and I responded very well. Trish fought valiantly until she passed on September 28, 2020, and now I'm the widow. Let me tell you that being the widow sucks.

On the positive side, Lisa Gray, a local writer for the *Houston Chronicle*, wrote a feature story about Trish. That's positive because Trish shied away from the spotlight, so few know how important her story is to mine. I could not have done what I did without her help, support, and encouragement. I want people a hundred years from now to know everything she did, and I've already paid for her monument to read, "For 51 years, Trish taught music to thousands of school children, and for 48 years, she was Phyllis's best friend and wife."

What next for me? I'm not sure.

When Trish and I moved here, I knew everybody was old and that in time we would all be dealing with similar things. But what I did not expect—did not even think about—is the fact that almost every one of the residents in our community has survived the passing of a mate. They've gone through what I'm going through, and they've been so helpful to me. They have poured themselves on me like honey on pancakes. So I'm going to stay here.

When the COVID-19 pandemic ends, I plan to get back onto the bench at the city courthouse. I took leave when Trish was diagnosed. I still lecture around the country at law schools and law conferences, and my law firm continues, even though I have not been very active myself since Trish was diagnosed.

I've also picked up my guitars again. I played a lot twenty years ago, then tired of it, but I'm back at it with my Martin dreadnaught and my Larrivée twelve-string. The guitar circle that I was part of twenty years ago continues, and I meet with old friends over Zoom every week.

I have no idea what I'm going to do for the rest of my life, but I'm still young.

Notes

FOREWORD

1. Deborah Sontag, "Once a Pariah, Now a Judge: The Early Transgender Journey of Phyllis Frye," *New York Times,* August 29, 2015.

2. See "International Bill of Gender Rights" in Leslie Feinberg, *Transgender Warriors: Making History from Joan of Arc to Dennis Rodman* (Boston: Beacon Press, 1996), 172.

3. Phyllis Frye, "Freedom from the 'Have-To' of the Scalpel," *Proceedings from the Fifth International Conference on Transgender Law and Employment Policy* (Houston: International Conference on Law and Employment Policy, 1996), 29–38.

4. For a tribute to Trish, see Lisa Gray, "The Legacy of Trish Frye: Finding Love and Fighting for It," *Houston Chronicle*, October 7, 2020.

CHAPTER 1

1. Phyllis Frye, interviewed by Michael G. Long, July 11, 2018. Interview recording and notes are in Long's possession. Quotations from her parents are drawn from Phyllis's recollections of their comments. This interview is the main source for the following account of Frye's childhood and young adult years.

2. See also Deborah Sontag, "Once a Pariah, Now a Judge: The Early Transgender Journey of Phyllis Frye," *New York Times*, August 29, 2015.

3. Frye, Long interview, July 11, 2018.

4. See footnote 330 in Phyllis Randolph Frye, "The International Bill of Gender Rights vs. The Cider House Rules: Transgenders Struggle with the Courts over What Clothing They Are Allowed to Wear on the Job, Which Restroom They Are Allowed to Use on the Job, Their Right to Marry, and the Very Definition of Their Sex," *William & Mary Journal of Women and the Law* 7 (2000), http://scholarship.law.wm.edu.

5. Phyllis Frye, interviewed by Shea Tuttle, July 12, 2019. Interview recording and notes are in Tuttle's possession.

6. Frye, Tuttle interview, July 12, 2019.

7. See Phyllis Randolph Frye, letter to Alto Frye, August 8, 1976, The Phyllis R. Frye Collection, 1948–2016, Cushing Memorial Library and Archives, Texas A&M University, College Station, Texas [PRFC], box 2, folder 2. Coauthor Michael Long used the collection's detailed finding aid, available online, to complete footnotes from

his home in Pennsylvania during the COVID-19 pandemic. If any notes include inexact information, the authors will correct this in a subsequent edition of this book.

8. Frye, Long interview, July 11, 2018. See also Sontag, "Once a Pariah," August 29, 2015.

9. Phyllis Frye, email to Michael G. Long, August 14, 2018. This email is in Long's possession.

10. Frye, Long interview, July 11, 2018. See also Phyllis Frye, interviewed by Mason Funk, "Outwards," unpublished transcript, June 1, 2017. This transcript is in Long's possession.

11. Frye, Long interview, July 11, 2018. See also Phyllis Frye, letter to Heath, August 22, 1977, PRFC box 1, folder 2; Phyllis Randolph Frye, interviewed by David Goldstein, unpublished manuscript, August 22, 2018, Houston Public Library, Houston, Texas (a copy of this manuscript is in Long's possession); Phyllis Randolph Frye, "Being Gay Doesn't Negate Adhering to Scout Law," *Houston Chronicle*, May 21, 2013; Kim Hogstrom, "Swinging for the Fences," *OutSmart* (June 2016): 79; Sontag, "Once a Pariah," August 29, 2015; Frye, Funk interview, June 1, 2017; and Lisa Gray, "The Transgender Menace Next Door," *Houston Press* (June 28–July 4, 2001): 34.

12. Sontag, "Once a Pariah," August 29, 2015.

13. Gerald Sharp, interviewed by Michael G. Long, September 7, 2018. Interview notes are in Long's possession.

14. Phillip Frye, untitled lecture notes, n.d. [1975?], PRFC, box 2, folder 1.

15. Frye, Long interview, July 11, 2018.

16. Frye, Tuttle interview, July 12, 2019.

17. Frye, Long interview, July 11, 2018. See also Phyllis Frye, "Transgenders Must Be Brave While Forging This New Front on Equality," *Georgetown Journal of Gender and the Law* 4 (2003): 767; and Sontag, "Once a Pariah," August 29, 2015.

18. Susan Stryker, *Transgender History: The Roots of Today's Revolution* (New York: Seal Press, 2008), 48–51.

19. This account of Jorgensen draws from Stryker, *Transgender History*, 65–68; Joanne Meyerowitz, *How Sex Changed: A History of Transsexuality in the United States* (Cambridge, MA: Harvard University Press, 2004), 51–106; Patrick Califia, *Sex Changes: Transgender Politics* (San Francisco: Cleis Press, 1997), 15–29; Christine Jorgensen, *Christine Jorgensen: A Personal Autobiography* (New York: Paul Eriksson Inc., 1967); and Richard F. Docter, *Becoming a Woman: A Biography of Christine Jorgensen* (New York: The Haworth Press, 2008).

20. Ben White, "Bronx GI Becomes a Woman!" *New York Daily News*, December 1, 1952.

21. "Bronx 'Boy' Is Now a Girl," Associated Press wire story, *New York Times*, December 2, 1952.

22. Quoted in Stryker, *Transgender History*, 67.

23. "Miss Jorgensen Returns," *New York Times*, February 13, 1953.

24. John T. McQuiston, "Christine Jorgensen, 62, Is Dead," *New York Times*, May 4, 1989.

25. Stryker, *Transgender History*, 68.

26. In this manuscript, we have elected to preserve terms that are no longer preferred when they appear in direct quotations. Outside of quotations, we made decisions about our own use of terms with reference to the GLAAD Media Guide, available at https://www.glaad.org/reference. We know that preferred terms will continue to evolve, and we urge readers to consult the above-listed guide or other reputable sources in their search for the most respectful, inclusive, and correct ways to discuss the LGBTQ+ community and related issues.

27. For an excellent account of Benjamin's work, see Meyerowitz, *How Sex Changed: A History of Transsexuality in the United States*, 2004.

28. "Bars Marriage Permit: Clerk Rejects Proof of Sex of Christine Jorgensen," *New York Times*, April 4, 1959.

29. Stryker, *Transgender History*, 68.

30. Frye, Long interview, July 11, 2018; Sontag, "Once a Pariah," August 29, 2015.

31. Frye, Long interview, July 11, 2018.

32. Frye, Long interview, July 11, 2018.

33. Sandy contacted Phyllis decades later, after reading about her transgender journey, and the two, joined by friends and Phyllis's wife Trish, visited together several times. During their first get-together, Sandy gave Phyllis a rose, saying something like, "I now know that the many school proms where you gave me a corsage, you really wanted these for yourself" (Phyllis Frye, handwritten note to Michael G. Long, April 22, 2019; a copy of this note is in Long's possession).

34. Phyllis Frye, handwritten note to Michael G. Long, April 22, 2019.

35. Phyllis Frye, interviewed by Michael G. Long, July 18, 2018. Interview recording and notes are in Long's possession. This interview serves as the main source for chapter material from here to the end of the chapter.

36. Frye, Tuttle interview, July 12, 2019.

37. Frye, Long interview, July 18, 2018.

38. Frye, Long interview, July 18, 2018. See also Frye, Funk interview, June 1, 2017.

39. Frye, Tuttle interview, July 12, 2019.

40. Frye, Long interview, July 18, 2018.

41. Frye, Tuttle interview, July 12, 2019.

42. Jeanne Frye, interviewed by a US Civil Service Commission (USCC) investigator, USCC, *Report of Investigation*, 1977, PRFC, box 1, folders 15–16. This interview occurred as part of an investigation related to Phyllis's attempts to secure a federal job.

43. Phyllis Frye, untitled lecture, USCC, *Report of Investigation*, 1977, PRFC, box 1, folders 15 and 16. While the USCC was conducting its investigation, one of Phyllis's neighbors provided the investigator with a copy of a sixty-minute cassette recording of one of her lectures. The neighbor had this tape because Phyllis had given it to him or her.

44. Phyllis Frye, untitled lecture with Bobbi Bennett, November 12, 1976, PRFC, box 1, folder 61.

45. Jeanne Frye, USCC interview, 1977.

46. Albert A. Kopp, *Report of Psychiatric Evaluation*, March 9, 1972. This report is included in Norton I. German, letter to Commanding General, March 14, 1972, PRFC, box 2, folder 15.

47. Frye, Long interview, July 18, 2018.

48. See also Frye, Funk interview, June 1, 2017.

49. Frye, Funk interview, June 1, 2017.

50. Frye, Funk interview, June 1, 2017. See also Sontag, "Once a Pariah," August 29, 2015.

CHAPTER 2

1. Phyllis Frye, interviewed by Michael G. Long, August 8, 2018. Interview recording and notes are in Long's possession. This interview serves as the main source for the account of Phyllis's move from Germany, her return to Texas, and her stay in Pittsburgh, up to the point where she visits Slippery Rock State College.

2. Frye, Long interview, August 8, 2018.

3. Frye, Long interview, July 18, 2018.

4. The main sources for the section on Trish are Frye, Long interview, August 8, 2018; and "Q&A: Phyllis Randolph Frye, Houston's 'Grandmother of Transgender Law,'" July 10, 2017, http://www.lovewinsusa.com.

5. See also Frye, Funk interview, June 1, 2017.

6. Thomas Krouskup, interviewed by a USCC investigator, USCC, *Report of Investigation*, 1977, PRFC, box 1, folders 15–16.

7. Sontag, "Once a Pariah," August 29, 2015.

8. Phyllis Randolph Frye, "Out of the Closet for Fifteen Years and Making It in Houston, Texas," *TV/TS Tapestry Journal* 59 (Fall 1991): 65.

9. See also "Q&A: Phyllis Randolph Frye," July 10, 2017.

10. Phyllis Frye, interviewed by Michael G. Long, August 15, 2018. Interview recording and notes are in Long's possession. This interview serves as the main source for the account of Phyllis's trip to Slippery Rock State College.

11. The main sources for the section on Suplee, Erickson, and Benjamin are Stryker, *Transgender History*, 100–105, and Meyerowitz, *How Sex Changed*, 209–16.

12. Harry Benjamin, *The Transsexual Phenomenon* (New York: Julian, 1966).

13. Frye, Long interview, August 15, 2018.

14. Frye, Long interview, August 15, 2018. Less than two years later, Frye sent Walker a tape of one of her public lectures and offered to be of any help to him (Phillip Frye, letter to Paul Walker, August 18, 1975, PRFC, box 1, folder 24). Walker replied: "In listening to your tape, and comparing it to my memory of the frightened 'lady in lavender and white' I met two years ago, I was pleased to think how far you have advanced and progressed" (Paul Walker, letter to Phil Frye, August 27, 1975, PRFC, box 1, folder 24).

15. Frye, Long interview, August 8, 2018.

16. See Wallace Mauer, interviewed by a USCC investigator, USCC, *Report of Investigation*, 1977, PRFC, box 1, folders 15–16; Ralph Miller, interviewed by a USCC

investigator, USCC, *Report of Investigation*, 1977, PRFC, box 1, folders 15–16; Blake Hamilton, interviewed by a USCC investigator, USCC, *Report of Investigation*, 1977, PRFC, box 1, folders 15–16; and unnamed colleagues, interviewed by a USCC investigator, USCC, *Report of Investigation*, 1977, PRFC, box 1, folders 15–16.

17. See Phil Frye, letter to Dr. Jerome Sherman, August 29, 1975, PRFC, box 2, folder 1; Phil Frye (also signed Phyllis), letter to Dr. James McCary, September 16, 1975, PRFC, box 2, folder 1; Sheila Wright, letter to Phil Frye, March 22, 1976, PRFC, box 2, folder 2; and Chad Gordon, letter to Phyllis R. Frye, November 3, 1976, box 2, folder 2.

18. Phillip R. Frye ("Society's Prisoner"), letter to Ann Landers, n.d. [March 1975], PRFC, box 2, folder 1. Phyllis also wrote to Dear Abby. See Phillip Frye, letter to Abby, January 2, 1976, PRFC, box 2, folder 2.

19. Lewis Driggers, "Transgenderist," *Egalitarian: The Student Newspaper of Houston Community College*, August 14, 1985.

20. Frye, Long interview, August 15, 2018.

21. Phyllis Frye, letter to Jose Merla, November 18, 1976, PRFC, box 1, folder 1.

22. Frye, Long interview, August 15, 2018.

23. Frye, Long interview, August 15, 2018.

24. Ray Hill, interviewed by Michael G. Long, September 16, 2018. Interview notes are in Long's possession.

25. Frye, Long interview, August 15, 2018.

26. W. B. Mauer, letter to Equal Employment Opportunity Commission, December 20, 1976, PRFC, box 1, folder 14.

27. Phillip Frye, letter to Dick and Helen, May 26, 1976, PRFC, box 2, folder 2.

28. Frye, Long interview, August 15, 2018.

29. Phyllis Frye, interviewed by Michael G. Long, August 23, 2018. Interview recording and notes are in Long's possession.

30. P. R. (Phyllis) Frye, resume, November 18, 1976, PRFC, box 2, folder 2.

31. Phyllis Frye, email to Michael G. Long, August 19, 2018. This email is in Long's possession. See also Sontag, "Once a Pariah," August 29, 2015.

32. Phillip Frye, letter to Alto Frye, August 5, 1976, PRFC, box 2, folder 2.

33. Phyllis Frye, email to Shea Tuttle and Michael G. Long, December 7, 2020. This email is in the authors' possession.

34. Frye, Long interview, August 15, 2018; and Sontag, "Once a Pariah," August 29, 2015.

35. Phyllis changed her legal name from Phillip Randolph Frye to Phyllis Randolph Frye on May 4, 1977.

36. Frye, Long interview, August 15, 2018. Also helpful for the section on neighbors is Lisa Gray, "The Transgender Menace Next Door," *Houston Press*, June 28–July 4, 2001.

37. Gray, "The Transgender Menace Next Door," 36.

38. Gray, "The Transgender Menace Next Door," 36.

39. Unnamed source, interviewed by a USCC investigator, USCC, *Report of Investigation*, 1977, PRFC, box 1, folders 15–16.

40. Fred Bubeck, interviewed by a USCC investigator, USCC, *Report of Investigation*, 1977, PRFC, box 1, folders 15–16.

41. Unnamed source, interviewed by a USCC investigator, USCC, *Report of Investigation*, 1977, PRFC, box 1, folders 15–16.

42. Frye, Long interview, August 15, 2018.

43. L. R. Dillon Sr., letter to Phillip, November 4, 1977, PRFC, box 2, folder 3.

44. Dillon letter to Phillip, November 4, 1977, PRFC, box 2, folder 3.

CHAPTER 3

1. See Phyllis Frye, letter to Jose Merla, November 18, 1976, in which she wrote: "Did you know that I got response from you—Mex—from Edgar Cook—T. J. H. [Thomas Jefferson High] Black—and Roger Vasquez—T. J. H. Mex—and two whites? Ain't it really weird?" For another example of Phyllis identifying trans people as "one of today's 'niggers,'" see Phyllis Frye, "Rejecting Racism and Sexism," *This Week in Texas* (June 17–June 23, 1994): 37.

2. Mark A. Satterwhite, letter to Phil, October 13, 1976, PRFC, box 1, folder 1.

3. Robert L. Boone, letter to P. R. Frye, March 22, 1977, PRFC, box 1, folder 1. Phyllis reports that when she and Boone met several years later, he had softened his stance and was friendly toward her. When he retired, he also ensured that Phyllis attended his party.

4. See Sylvia Baker, letter to Phil, December 29, 1976, PRFC, box 2, folder 2; Lloyd E. Smith, letter to Phillip, October 21, 1976, PRFC, box 2, folder 2; Ann, letter to Phil, November 5, 1976, box 2, folder 2; Barry L. Moak, letter to Phyllis, March 24, 1977, box 2, folder 3. Phyllis did not let her Christian critics go without response; she took them to task in public talks and private letters. For examples of the latter, see Phyllis Frye, letter to Ed Eitelman, April 3, 1985, PRFC, box 2, folder 6; and Phyllis Frye, letter to the editor, *Houston Post*, March 28, 1985.

5. Phil Frye, letter to Friends, February 6, 1976, PRFC, box 2, folder 2.

6. Phyllis Frye, untitled lecture, USCC, *Report of Investigation*, 1977, PRFC, box 1, folders 15–16.

7. Untitled document, list of student questions, PRFC, box 2, folder 3.

8. Untitled document, list of student questions, PRFC, box 2, folder 3.

9. William Martin, letter to Phyllis, February 18, 1977, PRFC, box 2, folder 3.

10. "SOCIOLOGY—Evaluations of April 27, 1977," PRFC, box 2, folder 3.

11. Phyllis Frye, "My Son," *Proceedings from the First International Conference on Transgender Law and Employment Policy* (Houston: International Conference on Law and Employment Policy, 1992), 12, PRFC, box 5, folder 5.

12. Frye, "My Son," *Proceedings I*, 13.

13. Phyllis Frye, interviewed by Michael G. Long, August 28, 2018. Interview recording and notes are in Long's possession.

14. This rule change did not apply to the FBI, the Foreign Service, or the CIA, each of which had its own employment system, but it did hold for the rest of the federal government.

15. Phyllis Frye, "Personal Qualifications Statement," USCC form, October 28, 1976, PRFC, box 1, folder 14.

16. Thomas P. Sandow, letter to Phyllis Randolph Frye, December 14, 1977, PRFC, box 1, folder 14.

17. Chad Gordon, interviewed by USCC investigator, *Report of Investigation*, April 21, 22, 1977, PRFC, box 1, folder 15.

18. Fenley Ryther, interviewed by USCC investigator, *Report of Investigation*, April 21, 22, 1977, PRFC, box 1, folder 15.

19. Phyllis Frye, letter to Thomas P. Sandlow, December 26, 1977, PRFC, box 1, folder 14.

20. Phyllis replied to NASA's rejection letter by calling it "unacceptable" and charging the agency with discrimination based on her transition (Phyllis Frye, letter to NASA, September 19, 1977, PRFC, box 1, folder 43).

21. Phyllis Frye, interviewed by Michael G. Long, August 15, 2018.

22. Phyllis Frye, "White Christmas," *War Stories*, copy in Long's possession.

CHAPTER 4

1. Frye, Long interview, August 28, 2018.

2. Christopher P. Haight, "Anita Bryant Protest (Houston)," *Handbook of Texas Online*, http://www.tshaonline.org.

3. Katherine Shilcutt, "Forty Years Ago, a Protest against a Former Beauty Queen Changed Houston's Gay Community Forever," *Houstonia* (June 2017), http://www.houstonianmag.com.

4. Ray Hill, Houston Human Rights League press release, n.d., available online at http://ww.houstonlgbthistory.org.

5. R McQ, "Bearing Witness to Our Humanity," *Advocate*, July 27, 1977, available online at http://www.houstonlgbthistory.org.

6. Phyllis Frye, interviewed by Michael G. Long, September 12, 2018. Interview notes and recording are in Long's possession. Unless otherwise indicated, Frye quotes on the Anita Bryant event are drawn from this interview.

7. Andrew Edmondson, "Houston's Stonewall, 40 Years Later: The Night Anita Bryant Came to Texas," *OutSmart* (June 1, 2017), http://www.outsmartmagazine.com.

8. See also Frye, Goldstein interview, August 22, 2008.

9. Frye, Goldstein interview, August 22, 2008.

10. "No Bryant Violence," *Houston Chronicle*, June 17, 1977, available at http://www.houstonlgbt.org.

11. Frye, Long interview, September 12, 2018. All Frye quotations about the visit with Bond are drawn from this interview.

12. Phyllis Frye, interviewed by Michael G. Long, September 5, 2018. All Frye quotations about business school are drawn from this interview.

13. Phyllis Frye, "My Prayers Are Being Answered," PRFC, box 1.

CHAPTER 5

1. Frye, Long interview, August 15, 2018.

2. Phyllis Frye, "Hormones—One Person's Experience," *War Stories*, copy in Long's possession.

3. Frye, Long interview, August 15, 2018.

4. Phyllis Frye, letter to Louis Macey, January 20, 1978, PRFC, box 2, folder 17. See also Phyllis Frye, letter to Frank Mann, January 16, 1978, PRFC, box 2, folder 17; Phyllis Frye, letter to Frank Mancuso, January 17, 1978, PRFC, box 2, folder 17; Phyllis Frye, letter to Messrs. Goyen, Westmoreland, Robinson, January 20, 1978, PRFC, box 2, folder 17; Phyllis Frye, letter to Larry McKaskle, January 20, 1978, PRFC, box 2, folder 17; and Phyllis Frye, letter to Homer Ford, January 20, 1978, PRFC, box 2, folder 17.

5. Phyllis Frye, untitled document, statement to Houston businesses, PRFC, box 1, folder 48.

6. "Farenthold Calls for Ending Discrimination," Associated Press wire story, June 26, 1978.

7. "Town Meeting Resolutions," *Upfront*, July 21, 1978.

8. Phyllis Frye, "Law School," *War Stories*, 2001, copy in Long's possession.

9. John Mixon, *Autobiography of a Law School: Stories, Memories and Interpretations of My Sixty Years at the University of Houston Law Center*, n.d., http://law.uh.edu. See also "Six Alumni Reach Great Heights: Phyllis Frye '81," *Briefcase: University of Houston Law Center* 34, no. 1 (2016): 11.

10. Mixon, *Autobiography of a Law School*.

11. According to Lisa Gray, in a discussion about Phyllis and bathrooms, a classmate in law school defended her by saying, "Maybe you'd be happier if Phyllis just used a trash can and squatted in the hallway" ("The Transgender Menace Next Door," 36).

12. Gray, "The Transgender Menace Next Door," 36.

13. Frye, Long interview, September 5, 2018. Unless otherwise indicated, all Frye quotes in this section on law school and the Christian Legal Society are drawn from this interview.

14. Phyllis Frye, email to Michael G. Long, September 8, 2018. This email is in Long's possession.

15. See also Gray, "The Transgender Menace Next Door," 39.

16. "Transperson," *Upfront*, April 18, 1979.

17. Frye, Long interview, September 5, 2018.

18. Phyllis Frye, letter to Donald Frye, June 9, 1979, PRFC, box 2, folder 4.

19. Alto Frye, letter to Phyllis and Trish Frye, n.d. [August 1979], PRFC, box 2, folder 4.

20. Phyllis Frye, letter to Alto Frye, n.d. [August 1979], PRFC, box 2, folder 4.

CHAPTER 6

1. Lillian Faderman, *Harvey Milk: His Lives and Death* (New Haven: Yale University Press, 2018), 169.

2. "The March Is On!" *Lesbian Tide* (September/October 1979): 12.

3. Frye, Long interview, September 12, 2018. Unless otherwise indicated, Frye quotations about the 1979 march are drawn from this interview.

4. "The March Is On!" *Lesbian Tide*, 12.

5. "The March Is On!" *Lesbian Tide*, 12.

6. "GRS Hosts National Conference," *Upfront*, July 25, 1979.

7. Phyllis Frye, "The Marcher's Songbook," *Upfront*, October 12, 1979.

8. Frye, "The Marcher's Songbook," *Upfront*, October 12, 1979.

9. "The March Goes On—1979," *OutSmart* (April 2000): 49.

10. "The March Goes On—1979," *OutSmart* (April 2000): 49.

11. *National March on Washington for Lesbian and Gay Rights: Official Souvenir Program* (October 14, 1979), 40, available at http://www.cristanwilliams.com.

12. Frye, Long interview, September 5, 2018. Unless otherwise indicated, all Frye quotes about the Christian Legal Society are drawn from this interview.

13. Frye, Long interview, August 28, 2018.

14. Phyllis Frye, "'GIRLS' in 'Real' Life," n.d. [1977], PRFC, box 1, folder 62.

15. Frye, "'GIRLS' in 'Real' Life," n.d. [1977], PRFC, box 1, folder 62.

16. For a copy of the radio advertisement, see Phyllis Frye, "for broadcast 20 Jan 77," n.d., PRFC, box 1, folder 62. GIRL's (and Transpeople's) minutes and attendance figures are also available in the Frye collection.

17. Joan Campbell, untitled document, minutes for Transpeople meeting, April 11, 1977, PRFC, box 1, folder 62.

18. Phyllis Frye, "Law Students, Friends of Gay,★" n.d. [1978], PRFC, box 2, folder 4.

19. Phyllis Frye, email to Michael G. Long, September 16, 2018. This email is in Long's possession. See also Phyllis Frye, "Law Students, Friends of Gay.★"

20. Frye, email to Michael G. Long, September 16, 2018.

21. Frye, "Law School," *War Stories*, copy in Long's possession.

22. Frye, Long interview, September 5, 2018.

23. Phyllis Frye, email to Michael G. Long, September 11, 2018. This email is in Long's possession.

24. Frye, Long interview, September 5, 2018.

25. Frye, Long interview, September 12, 2018.

26. Frye, Long interview, September 5, 2018.

27. Frye, "Law School," *War Stories*.

28. *Doe v. McConn* 489 F. Supp. 76 (S. D. TX, 1980).

29. Frye, Long interview, September 5, 2018.

CHAPTER 7

1. Frye, "Law School," *War Stories*.

2. Frye, Long interview, September 5, 2018.

3. On at least one occasion, Phyllis wrote a substantive and lengthy reply to a critic of her work, stating that she aligned with Amway because she enjoyed the products, found the business profitable, and hoped to encourage other gays and lesbians to profit from the company. See Phyllis Frye, letter to Richard, July 9, 1986, PRFC, box 1, folder 6.

4. Phyllis Frye, interviewed by Michael G. Long, November 15, 2018. Interview recording and notes are in Long's possession.

5. Phyllis Frye and Thatcher Combs, "Transgender People and Texas Classrooms: The '80s and Now," *Houston Chronicle*, November 12, 2015.

6. Frye and Combs, "Transgender People and Texas Classrooms."

7. Frye, Long interview, November 15, 2018. Frye quotations about bathroom use are drawn from this interview.

8. See also Frye, Goldstein interview, August 22, 2008.

9. Frye, Long interview, September 5, 2018.

10. Frye, "Law School," *War Stories*.

11. Frye, "Law School," *War Stories*. Phyllis also learned that some of Sydney Buchanan's colleagues openly criticized him for failing to hold CLS accountable for their discriminatory acts. In later years, he apologized to Phyllis and the two became friendly acquaintances.

12. Frye, Long interview, November 15, 2018.

13. Frye, Long interview, August 15, 2018.

14. Frye, Long interview, November 15, 2018.

15. Frye, Long interview, November 15, 2018.

16. Frye, Long interview, September 12, 2018.

17. Frye, Long interview, September 12, 2018.

18. Phyllis Frye, letter to Brother or Sister of MCCR, August 29, 1982, PRFC, box 1, folder 52.

19. See, for example, Johannes Stahl, "Gay Church Debates Use of 'Sexist Language' in Hymnals," *Montrose Voice*, September 17, 1982.

20. Phyllis Frye, no title, statement to Resurrection MCC, n.d., PRFC, box 1, folder 52.

21. Frye, Long interview, September 12, 2018.

22. Annise Parker, "Don't Be Afraid to Ask for Help," *Proceedings from the Second International Conference on Law and Employment Policy* (Houston: International Conference on Law and Employment Policy, 1993), 25.

23. Frye, Long interview, November 17, 2018. Interview recording and notes are in Long's possession.

24. Parker, "Don't Be Afraid to Ask for Help," 25.

25. Frye, Long interview, November 17, 2018.

26. Parker, "Don't Be Afraid to Ask for Help," 25.

27. Frye, Long interview, November 17, 2018.

28. Parker, "Don't Be Afraid to Ask for Help," 25.

29. Frye, Long interview, November 17, 2018.

30. Parker, "Don't Be Afraid to Ask for Help," 26.

31. Frye, Long interview, November 15, 2018.

32. Frye, Long interview, November 15, 2018.

33. Frye, Long interview, November 15, 2018.

34. "Transperson Before Nat'l Party Hearing," *This Week in Texas* (June 1–7, 1984): 15.

35. "1984 Democratic Party Platform," *The American Presidency Project*, http://www.presidency.ucsb.edu.

36. Robert Reinhold, "AIDS Remark Is at Issue in Houston Vote Today," *New York Times*, November 5, 1985.

37. Frye, Long interview, November 17, 2018.

38. "League of Women Voters Seek AIDS Activists," *Montrose Voice*, December 13, 1985.

39. See, for example, "Monumental AIDS Protest at Capitol," *This Week in Texas* (May 12–18, 1989): 17. Accompanying this article is a photo of Phyllis Frye and Eugene Harrington holding a banner that called attention to four thousand AIDS deaths in Texas.

40. D. Ann Beeler, Article on Frye, *The Battalion*, November 21, 1985, PRFC, box 1, folder 2. The clipping of this article in the Frye Collection does not include its title.

41. Beeler, Article on Frye, *The Battalion*, November 21, 1985, PRFC, box 1, folder 2.

CHAPTER 8

1. Frye, Long interview, November 15, 2018.

2. Fred Biery, interviewed by Michael G. Long, September 3, 2018. Interview notes are in Long's possession.

3. Phyllis Frye, "I Enjoyed a Growing Stream of Wonderful Experiences at My 20th High School Reunion," *This Week in Texas* (August 8–August 14, 1986): 29.

4. Frye, "I Enjoyed a Growing Stream," 29.

5. Frye, "I Enjoyed a Growing Stream," 30.

6. Gerald Sharp, interviewed by Michael G. Long, September 7, 2018.

7. Frye, "I Enjoyed a Growing Stream," 30.

8. Frye, "I Enjoyed a Growing Stream," 30.

9. Sharp, Long interview, September 7, 2018.

10. Biery, Long interview, September 3, 2018.

11. Frye, Long interview, November 15, 2018.

12. Frye, Long interview, November 15, 2018.

13. Frye, "I Enjoyed a Growing Stream," 31. Phyllis also enjoyed a positive experience at her thirtieth reunion. See Phyllis Frye, "My 30-Year High School Reunion,"

Femme Mirror (Summer 1996): 23. For her reflections on her fifteenth-year college reunion, see Phyllis Frye, "Attending My 15th College Reunion . . . As a Transperson . . . at Texas A&M University!" *This Week in Texas* (October 18–October 24, 1985): 28–29.

14. Chuck Patrick, "Phillip Becomes Phyllis—A Decade Later," *This Week in Texas* (June 13–June 19, 1986): 31.

15. Faulkner, letter to the editor, 35.

16. Faulkner, letter to the editor, 35.

17. Phyllis Frye, letter to Ms. Faulkner, *This Week in Texas* (July 4–July 10, 1986): 27.

18. Frye, Long interview, November 17, 2018.

19. Sheri Cohen Darbonne, "Business Guild Accepts President's Resignation," *Montrose Voice*, January 27, 1987.

20. Jerry Nicholson, letter to the editor, *Montrose Voice*, February 13, 1987.

21. Frye, Long interview, November 17, 2018.

22. Frye, Long interview, November 17, 2018.

23. Frye, Long interview, November 17, 2018.

24. Frye, Long interview, November 17, 2018.

25. See also Frye, Goldstein interview, August 22, 2008.

26. Frye, Goldstein interview, August 22, 2008.

27. Frye, Goldstein interview, August 22, 2008.

28. "Excerpts from the Court Opinions on Homosexual Relations," *New York Times*, July 1, 1986.

29. Frye, Long interview, November 17, 2018.

30. Frye, Long interview, November 17, 2018.

31. "Jack Valinski Oral History Interview and Transcript," n.d., http://www.scholarship.rice.edu. This interview is also available in the Houston ARCH (Houston Area Rainbow Collective History) Collection, 1981–2004, MS 569, Woodrow Wilson Research Center, Fondren Library, Rice University, Houston, Texas.

32. "The March Goes On," April 2000, 53.

33. Ray Hill mistakenly told a reporter that Phyllis had arranged for a transgender contingent not only to march but also to protest their exclusion by stopping in the middle of it (Hogstrom, "Swinging for the Fences," *OutSmart* [June 2016]: 79). That did not happen.

34. Lena Williams, "600 in Gay Demonstration Arrested at Supreme Court," *New York Times*, October 14, 1987.

35. Frye, Long interview, November 17, 2018.

36. Frye, Long interview, November 17, 2018.

CHAPTER 9

1. Frye, Long interview, December 5, 2018.

2. Frye, Long interview, December 5, 2018.

3. Frye, Long interview, December 5, 2018.

4. "Disowned by Families," *The Phil Donahue Show*, 1989. Unless otherwise indicated, Frye quotations in this section are drawn from this episode. A compact disk of the episode is in Long's possession.

5. Frye, Long interview, December 5, 2018.

6. "Laying Plans for 1989 March on Austin," *This Week in Texas* (August 19–August 25, 1988): 27.

7. "Goals of the March on Austin for Lesbian/Gay Equal Rights," *This Week in Texas* (April 28–May 4, 1989): 35.

8. "Transsexual Wins $20,000 in Court," *This Week in Texas* (March 9–March 15, 1990): 34.

9. Sheri Cohen Darbonne, "Transsexual Leads Effort to Change Names of HGLPC, GLRL," *Montrose Voice*, March 30, 1990.

10. Darbonne, "Transsexual Leads Effort to Change Names of HGLPC, GLRL."

11. Darbonne, "Transsexual Leads Effort to Change Names of HGLPC, GLRL."

12. "What's in a Name?" *This Week in Texas* (April 27–May 3, 1990): 21.

13. "HGLPC Won't Change Name," *This Week in Texas* (May 11–May 17, 1990): 21.

14. "HGLPC Won't Change Name," *This Week in Texas* (May 11–May 17, 1990): 21.

15. Sheri Cohen Darbonne, "New Montrose Randalls Is Greeted with Controversy," *Montrose Voice*, January 12, 1990.

16. Frye, interview by Michael G. Long, November 28, 2018. Interview recording and notes are in Long's possession.

17. Frye, interview by Michael G. Long, November 28, 2018.

18. Frye, interview by Michael G. Long, November 28, 2018.

19. "Attorney Frye Is Honored," *This Week in Texas* (July 27–August 2, 1990): 28.

20. "Frye Resigns Houston GLPC," *This Week in Texas* (September 21–September 27, 1990): 37.

21. "Montrose Man Not Guilty of Prostitution," *This Week in Texas* (November 30–December 6, 1990): 31.

22. Paul Harasim, "Judging by This, Justice Not Blind," *Houston Post*, November 28, 1990.

23. Phyllis Frye, Long interview, December 5, 2018.

24. Phyllis Frye, letter to the Judges of Harris County, November 29, 1990, PRFC, box 2, folder 7.

25. Frye, Long interview, December 5, 2018.

26. Phyllis Frye, letter to the editor, *This Week in Texas* (December 21–December 27, 1990): 37. Phyllis had also lobbied for repeal during the 1987 Women's Legislative Days in Austin, a largely educational program attended by twenty-seven progressive women's advocacy groups. See "Frye Urges 21.06 Repeal," *This Week in Texas* (February 27–March 5, 1987): 17. Frye cites these lobbying efforts as instructive and influential sources for her later lobbying on behalf of transgender issues.

27. Phyllis Frye, letter to the editor, *This Week in Texas* (January 18–January 24, 1991): 33.

28. Frye, Long interview, November 28, 2018.

CHAPTER 10

1. Frye, Long interview, November 28, 2018.

2. Jane Ellen Fairfax, interviewed by Michael G. Long, January 29, 2019. Interview notes are in Long's possession.

3. Tricia Lynn, interviewed by Michael G. Long, December 13, 2018. Interview notes are in Long's possession.

4. Lynn, Long interview, December 13, 2018.

5. Jackie Thorne, email to Michael G. Long, December 23, 2018. This email is in Long's possession.

6. Frye, Long interview, December 12, 2018. See also Michelle Risher, "She Opened Doors," *OutSmart* (August 2012): 39.

7. Frye, Long interview, November 28, 2018.

8. Frye, Long interview, December 12, 2018.

9. Cynthia Phillips, interviewed by Michael G. Long, December 18, 2018. Interview notes are in Long's possession.

10. Phyllis Frye, "First International Conference on Transgender Law and Employment Policy," brochure, n.d. [1992], available at http://www.cristanwilliams.net.

11. Frye, "First International Conference on Transgender Law and Employment Policy."

12. Frye, "First International Conference on Transgender Law and Employment Policy."

13. Phillips, Long interview, December 18, 2018.

14. Phyllis Frye, "History of the International Conference on Transgender Law and Employment Policy," n.d., available at http://www.digitaltransgenderarchive. net.

15. For a photo of the marquee, see Frye, "History," n.d.

16. Frye, Long interview, November 28, 2018.

17. Phyllis Frye, "Welcome and Opening Remarks," *Proceedings from the First International Conference on Transgender Law and Employment Policy* (Houston: International Conference on Law and Employment Policy, 1992): 3.

18. Phyllis Frye, "My Son," *Proceedings I*, 12–16.

19. Fred Biery, "Beware of the Gradual Erosion of Your Rights," *Proceedings I*, 66.

20. Sharon Stuart, "Military Law Project," *Proceedings I*, 118, 127, 128.

21. Stuart, "Military Law Project," *Proceedings I*, 128–29.

22. Marla Aspen, "Health Law Project," *Proceedings I*, 245, 258. Rothblatt filed this report under the name "Marla Aspen."

23. Marla Aspen, "A Minority Report on the Recommendations of the Health Law Committee," *Proceedings I*, 275. Rothblatt filed this report under the name "Marla Aspen."

24. Dana Cole, *Why Is S/He Doing This to Us?* (Dana Cole Associates, 1992), *Proceedings I*, 226.

25. See, for example, Phyllis Frye, letter to Christine W. G. Burnham, November 19, 1993, PRFC, box 5, folder 11; Phyllis Frye, letter to Lt. Moore, November 22,

1993, PRFC, box 5, folder 11; Phyllis Frye, letter to Jackie Walker, November 22, 1993, PRFC, box 5, folder 11; Phyllis Frye, letter to Mike Andrews, September 26, 1993, PRFC, box 5, folder 10; Phyllis Frye, letter to Craig Washington, September 26, 1993, PRFC, box 5, folder 10; and Phyllis Frye, letter to Gene Green, September 26, 1993, PRFC, box 5, folder 10.

26. Frye, Long interview, November 28, 2018.

27. Martine Rothblatt, interviewed by Michael G. Long, April 18, 2019. Interview notes are in Long's possession.

28. Phyllis Frye, interviewed by Michael G. Long, January 2, 2019. Interview notes and recording are in Long's possession.

CHAPTER 11

1. Frye, Long interview, January 2, 2019.

2. Amin Ghaziani, *The Dividends of Dissent: How Conflict and Culture Work in Lesbian and Gay Marches on Washington* (Chicago: University of Chicago Press, 2008), 157–95.

3. Ghaziani, *The Dividends of Dissent*, 176.

4. Ghaziani, *The Dividends of Dissent*, 184.

5. Davina Anne Gabriel, "'We're Queer Too!': Trans Community Demands Inclusion," *TransSisters: The Journal of Transsexual Feminism* (September/October 1993): 15.

6. Phyllis Frye, email to Michael G. Long, January 4, 2019. This email is in Long's possession.

7. Gabriel, "'We're Queer Too!'" 14.

8. Phyllis Frye, "Transgendered People at the March on Washington," *The March on Washington for Lesbian, Gay, and Bi Equal Rights and Liberation Newsletter* (1993): 13. A copy of this is available at the GLBT Historical Society, San Francisco, California.

9. Jessica Xavier, interviewed by Michael G. Long, December 27, 2018. Interview notes are in Long's possession.

10. Susan Stryker, email to Michael G. Long, January 8, 2019. This email is in Long's possession.

11. Xavier, Long interview, December 27, 2018.

12. Frye, Long interview, January 2, 2019.

13. Stryker, email to Long, January 8, 2019.

14. Stryker, email to Long, January 8, 2019.

15. Xavier, Long interview, December 27, 2018.

16. Xavier, Long interview, December 27, 2018.

17. Gabriel, "'We're Queer Too!'" 16.

18. Frye, Long interview, December 12, 2018.

19. Sharon Stuart, interviewed by Michael G. Long, January 4, 2019. Interview notes and recording are in Long's possession.

20. "Transcript of Speech," *Renaissance News* 7.6 (June 1993): 14–15.

21. Gabriel, "'We're Queer Too!'" 16.

22. Terry M., "*En Femme* at the March on Washington," *Renaissance News* 7, no. 6

(June 1993): 1.

23. Xavier, Long interview, December 27, 2018.

24. Stuart, Long interview, January 4, 2019.

25. Frye, Long interview, December 12, 2018.

26. Gabriel, "'We're Queer Too!'" 17.

27. Stuart, Long interview, January 4, 2019.

28. "The March Goes On," *OutSmart* (April 2000): 53.

29. Gabriel, "'We're Queer Too!'" 17.

30. Frye, Long interview, January 2, 2019.

31. Frye, Long interview, January 2, 2019.

32. Frye, Long interview, January 2, 2019.

33. Phyllis Frye, "Non-Operative TS: Clitoral Hypertrophy," *Proceedings from the Second International Conference on Law and Employment Policy* (Houston: International Conference on Law and Employment Policy, 1993): 107–9.

34. Frye, Long interview, January 2, 2019.

35. rye, Long interview, January 2, 2019.

36. Phyllis Frye, letter to Laura, May 6, 1994, PRFC, box 5, folder 29.

37. Frye, Long interview, January 2, 2019.

38. Frye, Long interview, January 2, 2019.

39. Frye, Long interview, January 2, 2019.

40. Leslie Feinberg, "Our History: As a Transgendered People," *Proceedings II*, 75.

41. Stuart, Long interview, January 4, 2019.

42. Stuart, Long interview, January 4, 2019.

43. Stuart, Long interview, January 4, 2019.

44. Stuart, Long interview, January 4, 2019.

45. Sharon Stuart, "International Bill of Gender Rights." This language is in the final draft adopted by ICTLEP. See "International Bill of Gender Rights" in Leslie Feinberg, *Transgender Warriors: Making History from Joan of Arc to Dennis Rodman* (Boston: Beacon Press, 1996), 171.

46. Stuart, Long interview, January 10, 2019.

47. Stuart, Long interview, January 10, 2019.

48. Stuart, Long interview, January 10, 2019.

49. Martine Rothblatt, "Report for the Health Law Project," *Proceedings II*, 107.

50. Rothblatt, "Report for the Health Law Project," *Proceedings II*, 102.

51. Phyllis Frye, letter to Ms. Christine, November 19, 1993, PRFC, box 5, folder 10.

52. Brenda Thomas, "Revise ICTLEP, Not the HBIGDA Standards of Care," *TransSisters: The Journal of Transsexual Feminism* (Summer 1994): 54. For another critic, see Kymberleigh Richards, "Kymberleigh's Clipboard," *Cross-Talk* 50 (1993): 4.

53. Thomas, "Revise ICTLEP," 54.

54. Thomas, "Revise ICTLEP," 54.

55. Phyllis Frye, letter to Martine Rothblatt, July 9, 1994, PRFC, box 5, folder 30.

56. Frye, letter to Martine Rothblatt, July 9, 1994, PRFC, box 5, folder 30.

57. Phyllis Frye, letter to Brenda Thomas, July 5, 1994, PRFC, box 5, folder 30.

CHAPTER 12

1. Phyllis Frye, "Stonewalled!" *TV/TS Tapestry Journal* (Spring 1994): 30–31. See also Phyllis Frye, letter to the editor, *Marquise* (January 27–February 9, 1994): 4.

2. Laura Masters, letter to the editor, *TV/TS Tapestry Journal* (Fall 1994): 20.

3. Jessica Xavier, "Stonewall 25 Revisited: Queer Politics, Process Queens and Lessons Learned," *TransSisters: The Journal of Transsexual Feminism* (Autumn 1994): 15.

4. Xavier, "Stonewall 25 Revisited," 16. See also Jessica Xavier, "1–15–94 SW 25 Address," PRFC, box 5, folder 38.

5. Xavier, "Stonewall 25 Revisited," 15.

6. For contemporaneous notes, see Jessica Xavier, "Notes from US Steering Committee for SW 25 Meeting, January 14–17, 1994 in Atlanta," PRFC, box 5, folder 38.

7. Phyllis Frye, news release from the International Conference on Transgender Law and Employment Policy, March 5, 1994, PRFC, box 5, folder 37.

8. "Transexual" is correctly spelled in "Transexual Menace."

9. For evidence of Phyllis's support, see Phyllis Frye, letter to Deb Ann Thomson, March 15, 1994, PRFC, box 6, folder 1; Phyllis Frye, letter to Shelia Walsh, April 1, 1994, PRFC, box 6, folder 1; and "Transgender Policy Changed," *Washington Blade*, April 15, 1994.

10. Jessica Xavier, letter to Phyllis Randolph Frye, April 15, 1994, PRFC, box 5, folder 38.

11. Jessica Xavier, untitled speech, n.d. [March 1994], personal papers of Jessica Xavier. A copy of this speech is in Long's possession.

12. Xavier, untitled speech, n.d.

13. Xavier, untitled speech, n.d.

14. Xavier, "Stonewall 25 Revisited," 19.

15. "ICTLEP Plans to Disrupt Stonewall 25," *TransSisters: The Journal of Transsexual Feminism* (Summer 1994): 7.

16. Phyllis Frye, "Guidelines for Nonviolent, Transgender-Led, Civil Disobedience at Non-inclusive Stonewall 25 Event in June in New York City," news release, April 15, 1994, PRFC, box 5, folder 34.

17. Frye, "Guidelines for Nonviolent, Transgender-Led, Civil Disobedience at Non-inclusive Stonewall 25 Event in June in New York City," news release, April 15, 1994, PRFC, box 5, folder 34.

18. Laura Masters, letter to Phyllis Frye, April 19, 1994, PRFC, box 5, folder 29. In her reply, Phyllis wrote: "I am returning your letter: it is not even worthy of my trash. . . . You are obviously racist and anti-Semitic. Keep your Ku Klux Klan/Nazi hate to yourself. Neither has a place in *decent* society" (Phyllis R. Frye, letter to Laura Masters, April 27, 1994, PRFC, box 5, folder 29).

19. Kristine W. Holt, "The Grande Alliance," *TV/TS Tapestry Journal* (Summer 1994): 40.

20. Terry M., "Stonewall 25: Pro," *Renaissance News & Views* 8.5 (May 1994): 6. Critics also faulted Phyllis for targeting friends rather than enemies of the transgender movement.

21. Nancy R. Nangeroni, letter to Phyllis Randolph Frye, May 18, 1994, PRFC, box 5, folder 36. In an earlier letter, Nangeroni also expressed her disagreement with Phyllis's view that transgender people were being left behind as the gay and lesbian rights movement moved forward (Nancy R. Nangeroni, letter to Phyllis Randolph Frye, April 19, 1994, PRFC, box 5, folder 36).

22. Martine Rothblatt, letter to Phyllis, May 15, 1994, PRFC, box 5, folder 36.

23. Frye, Long interview, January 2, 2019.

24. R. Keith Brown, "Transsexual Houstonite Takes Stonewall 25 to Task," *Texas Triangle*, June 22, 1994.

25. Jessica Xavier was also an ardent supporter, but she was unwilling to go to jail for the cause. In a letter explaining her decision, she wrote: "I hope I am not disappointing you by my unwillingness to get arrested with you in New York. I was exposed to an extreme amount of hatred from the SW25 Executive Committee in New York, and it was not very pleasant. I have also faced an enormous amount of criticism for my activism from members of my own organization, TGEA [The Transgender Educational Association of Greater Washington Inc.], which you visited last November. (I am leaving the group in a few months because of this.) I am not into self-aggrandizement, and neither am I especially brave" (Xavier, letter to Frye, April 15, 1994).

26. Frye, Long interview, January 2, 2019.

27. Frye, Long interview, January 2, 2019.

28. Frye, Long interview, January 2, 2019.

29. Frye, Long interview, January 2, 2019.

30. Frye, Long interview, January 2, 2019.

31. Frye, Long interview, January 2, 2019.

32. Phyllis Frye, press release from the International Conference on Law and Employment Policy, June 25, 1994, PRFC, box 5, folder 40. See also "ICTLEP Calls Off Planned Disruption of Stonewall 25," *TransSisters: The Journal of Transsexual Feminism* (Autumn 1994): 11.

33. Terry, "Stonewall 25 Impressions," *Renaissance News & Views* 8.8 (August 1994): 18. See also Yvonne Cook-Riley, "Stonewall 25, the Shows, the Parties, the March and the Tears," *TV/TS Tapestry Journal* (Fall 1994): 60.

34. John Gallagher, "For Transsexuals, 1994 Is 1964," *Advocate*, August 23, 1994.

35. Phyllis Frye, "Transgender Presence at Stonewall," *TV/TS Tapestry Journal* (Fall 1994): 10. See also "Transgender Presence at Stonewall 25: Protest March Cancelled Due to Progress Made," *Marquise* (August 1994): 24.

36. Gallagher, "For Transsexuals, 1994 Is 1964," August 23, 1994.

37. Senator Ted Kennedy quoting Coretta Scott King during ENDA hearing. "Employment Non-Discrimination Act of 1994: Hearing of the Committee on Labor and Human Resources, United States Senate, One Hundred Third Congress,

Second Session, on S. 2238 to Prohibit Employment Discrimination on the Basis of Sexual Orientation," available online at https://babel.hathitrust.org/cgi/pt?id=pst.0 00022827265&view=1up&seq=1.

38. Chai Feldblum, "The Federal Gay Rights Bill: From Bella to ENDA," *Creating Change: Sexuality, Public Policy, and Civil Rights* (New York: St. Martin's Press, 2000), 178.

39. Chai Feldblum, "Gay People, Trans People, Women: Is It All About Gender?" *New York Law School Journal of Human Rights* 17 (2000): 628.

40. Phyllis Frye, letter to Mike Iskowitz, July 22, 1994, PRFC, box 5, folder 29.

41. Phyllis Frye, interviewed by Michael G. Long, February 7, 2019. Interview notes are in Long's possession.

42. Frye, Long interview, February 7, 2019.

43. Karen Ann Kerin and Phyllis Randolph Frye, letter to Transgender Persons Who Worry about Keeping Their Jobs, n.d. [July–August 1994], *Proceedings from the Third International Conference on Law and Employment Policy* (Houston: International Conference on Law and Employment Policy, 1994), A-17.

44. Karen Ann Kerin, "Dealing with Quislings, Coalitions, and Federal Legislation," *Proceedings III*, 34.

45. Kerin, "Dealing with Quislings, Coalitions, and Federal Legislation," *Proceedings III*, 34.

46. Kerin, "Dealing with Quislings, Coalitions, and Federal Legislation," *Proceedings III*, 36.

47. Jessica Xavier, "Goals, Strategies, Funding, and Grassroots Organization and a Tip for Those Who Remain in the Closet," *Proceedings III*, 26.

48. Xavier, "Goals, Strategies, Funding, and Grassroots Organization," *Proceedings III*, 27.

49. Xavier, "Goals, Strategies, Funding, and Grassroots Organization," *Proceedings III*, 27.

50. Phyllis Frye, "A Resolution to Be Presented to the United States Congress by It's Time, America," *Proceedings III*, 137.

51. Phyllis Frye, interviewed by Michael G. Long, n.d. Interview notes are in Long's possession.

52. The document "It's Time, America!"—which includes a statement of mission and goals—is part of Sarah DePalma, letter to unnamed, August 31, 1994, East Coast FTM Organizational Records, Sexual Minorities Archives, Holyoke, Massachusetts, available at http://www.digitaltransgenderarchives.net.

53. Jessica Xavier, interviewed by Michael G. Long, February 8, 2019. Interview notes are in Long's possession.

54. Frye, Long interview, February 7, 2019.

55. Frye, "Facing Discrimination," 562.

56. Sharon Stuart, email to Michael G. Long, February 5, 2019. This email is in Long's possession.

57. Frye, Long interview, February 7, 2019.

CHAPTER 13

1. Riki Ann Wilchins, "Closets Are Still for Clothes, Not for Transpeople," *The Transgenderist* (March 1995): 8.

2. Wilchins, "Closets Are Still for Clothes, Not for Transpeople," 8.

3. Riki Wilchins, "March on Washington," *In Your Face: Political Activism against Gender Oppression* (Spring 1995): 2.

4. Sue Fox, "Transgenders Fight for Inclusion," *Washington Blade*, March 17, 1995. Frye, according to Fox, had a double approach: to ask ENDA supporters to withhold support until trans people were included and to solicit uncommitted members to support a trans-inclusive ENDA.

5. Riki Anne Wilchins, "Uncle Samantha Wants You!" *TV/TS Tapestry Journal* (Summer 1995): 78.

6. Riki Wilchins, "Late Breaking News," *In Your Face* (Summer 1995): 1.

7. Riki Wilchins, *TRANS/gressive: How Transgender Activists Took on Gay Rights, Feminism, the Media & Congress . . . and Won!* (Riverdale, NY: Riverdale Avenue Books, 2017), 121.

8. Wilchins, *TRANS/gressive*, 121.

9. "Round Table Discussion on Transgender Activism," *Proceedings from the Fourth International Conference on Law and Employment Policy* (Houston: The International Conference on Law and Employment Policy, 1995), 68.

10. "Round Table Discussion on Transgender Activism," *Proceedings IV*, 68.

11. "Round Table Discussion on Transgender Activism," *Proceedings IV*, 68. Wilchins later made a similar point in Kristina Campbell, "Transgender Lobbyists Meet with Hill Staffers," *Washington Blade*, October 6, 1995.

12. Frye, Long interview, November 28, 2018.

13. Sarah DePalma and Tere Frederickson, "Transgender Protest and Demonstration at the April 2, 1995, March on Austin, Sponsored by the Lesbian/Gay Rights Lobby of Texas," press release, March 27, 1995. A copy of this release is in Long's possession.

14. Sarah DePalma, "TG Alamo in Texas," *Renaissance News & Views* (June 1995): 17.

15. Frye, Long interview, November 28, 2018.

16. Frye, Long interview, November 28, 2018. Coverage of the dissident marchers appeared in "Thousands Converge on Austin for March and Lobbying," *This Week in Texas* (April 7–April 13, 1995): 75–76.

17. John Taylor, "The Third Sex," *Esquire* (April 1995): 102–10.

18. John Taylor, "The Third Sex," *Esquire* (April 1995): 109.

19. John Taylor, "The Third Sex," *Esquire* (April 1995): 109.

20. John Taylor, "The Third Sex," *Esquire* (April 1995): 110.

21. John Taylor, "The Third Sex," *Esquire* (April 1995): 110.

22. Frye, Long interview, February 12, 2019.

23. Frye, Long interview, February 12, 2019.

24. DePalma, "TG Alamo in Texas," 17.

25. Sarah DePalma, quoted in a discussion following Jane Fee, "Bridge Building with the Gay and Lesbian Communities," *Proceedings IV*, 69.

26. Sarah DePalma, *Proceedings IV*, 50.

27. Frye, Long interview, February 12, 2019.

28. David Westerkamp, "Caucus Should Remain Focused," *HGLPC News* (May 1995): 6.

29. "HGLPC Votes against the Inclusion of Transgendered People," *OutSmart*, June 15, 1995.

30. Kay Y. Dayus, "Caucus Votes to Include Transgendered in Mission Statement," *Houston Voice*, July 16, 1999. This move came five years after a similar one made by the San Antonio Lesbian and Gay Political Caucus. When the San Antonio caucus changed its name to be trans-inclusive, Phyllis wondered whether Houston's caucus would ever do the same. See Phyllis Frye, letter to the editor, *This Week in Texas* (September 30–October 6, 1994): 53.

31. "Another HRCF Protest Planned," *Renaissance News & Views* (September 1995): 24.

32. Frye, Long interview, February 12, 2019.

33. Frye, Long interview, February 12, 2019.

34. Frye, "Facing Discrimination," 464.

35. Frye, Long interview, February 12.

36. "Another HRCF Protest Planned," *Renaissance News & Views*, 24.

37. Phyllis Frye, "Employment Non-Discrimination Act of 1995 Is a Bad Bill: It Intentionally Omits One-Quarter of the Lesbian, Gay, Bisexual and Transgender Community," press release, June 25, 1995, PRFC, box 6, folder 9.

38. Sarah DePalma, "A Community Is Born," *Renaissance News & Views* (August 1995): 1.

39. DePalma, "A Community Is Born," 1.

40. DePalma, "A Community Is Born," 1, 6.

41. DePalma, "A Community Is Born," 6.

42. DePalma, "A Community Is Born," 6.

43. Chai Feldblum, "Statement of Chai Feldblum Re: ENDA and Discrimination against Transgendered People," in "Gay People, Trans People, Women," 665.

44. Feldblum, "Statement of Chai Feldblum," 666.

45. Frye, "Facing Discrimination," 464.

46. Frye, Long interview, February 12, 2019.

47. Wilchins, *TRANS/gressive*, 153.

48. Quoted in Riki Wilchins, "HRCF & TG Activists Agree to Work Together," *In Your Face* (Fall 1995): 5. See also "Cross-Talk Newswire," *Cross-Talk: The Transgender Community News & Information Monthly* (November 1995): 12.

49. Frye, Long interview, February 12, 2019.

50. Wilchins, "HRCF & TG Activists Agree to Work Together," 5.

51. Frye, Long interview, February 12, 2019. See also "Phyllis Frye Invited to the White House," *Renaissance News & Views* (October 1995): 16.

52. Examples of the "scorecards" can be found in PRFC, box 6, folder 21.

53. Frye, Long interview, February 12, 2019.

54. Riki Wilchins, "Your Uncle Samantha Wants You," *In Your Face* (Spring 1995): 4.

55. Wilchins, *TRANS/gressive*, 124.

56. Phyllis Frye, "ICTLEP Report: Gender Lobby Days in DC," *The Transgenderist* (November 1995): 4.

57. Frye, Long interview, February 12, 2019.

58. Wilchins, *TRANS/gressive*, 125.

59. Wilchins, *TRANS/gressive*, 126.

60. Frye, Long interview, February 12, 2019.

61. Frye, Long interview, February 12, 2019.

62. Frye, "ICTLEP Report," 5.

63. Nancy R. Nangeroni, "America, We're Here! The First National Gender Lobby Day," *Transgender Tapestry* (Winter 1995): 26.

64. Frye, Long interview, February 12, 2019.

65. Nangeroni, "America, We're Here!" 26.

66. Wilchins, *TRANS/gressive*, 129.

67. Scott Bowles, "A Death Robbed of Dignity Mobilizes a Community," *Washington Post*, December 10, 1995.

68. Frye, "ICTLEP Report," 5.

69. Nangeroni, "America, We're Here!" 44.

70. Riki Wilchins, "National Gender Lobbying Day Takes Off," *In Your Face* (Fall 1995): 1. The *"no diss intended"* was written by Wilchins.

71. Frye, "ICTLEP Report," 5.

72. Phyllis Frye, "Thank You for the DC Experience," *Renaissance News & Views* (November 1995): 1.

73. Frye, "Thank You for the DC Experience," 6.

74. Wilchins, *TRANS/gressive*, 115.

75. JoAnn Roberts, letter to the editor, *AEGIS News* (September 1996): 7.

76. Roberts, letter to the editor, 7.

77. Jessica Xavier, "Jessica Xavier's Reply to Joann Roberts' Letter," *AEGIS News* (September 1996): 8.

78. Xavier, "Jessica Xavier's Reply to Joann Roberts' Letter," 8.

79. Frye, Long interview, December 8, 2018.

80. Frye, "Facing Discrimination," 464.

CHAPTER 14

1. Phyllis Frye, interviewed by Michael G. Long, March 2, 2019. Interview notes are in Long's possession.

2. Frye, Long interview, March 2, 2019.

3. Phyllis Frye, "The Frye Holiday Letter, 1995," *The Transgenderist* (February 1996): 7.

4. Frye, "The Frye Holiday Letter, 1995," 7.

5. Frye, Long interview, March 2, 2019.

6. Frye, Long interview, March 2, 2019.

7. Frye, interviewed by Michael G. Long, March 3, 2019. Interview notes are in Long's possession.

8. Frye, Long interview, March 3, 2019.

9. Stephen Whittle, "Report from the Workshop, International Issues," *Proceedings from the Fifth International Conference on Law and Employment Policy* (Houston: The International Conference on Law and Employment Policy, 1996), 40.

10. Whittle, "Report from the Workshop, International Issues," 43.

11. Dana Turner, "Report from the Workshop: TG People of Color," *Proceedings V*, 67–68.

12. Susan Stryker, letter to Phyllis R. Frye, September 25, 1993, PRFC, box 5, folder 10.

13. Spencer Bergstedt, "Report from the Workshop, Female to Male (FTM) Issues," *Proceedings V*, 61.

14. Frye, Long interview, March 3, 2019.

15. Sharon Stuart, "Declaration of Gender Liberty," *Proceedings V*, 3.

16. Stuart, "Declaration of Gender Liberty," 3.

17. Frye, interviewed by Michael G. Long, March 6, 2009. Interview notes are in Long's possession.

18. Phyllis Frye, "Freedom from the 'Have-To' of the Scalpel," *Proceedings V*, 33–34.

19. Phyllis Frye, "ICTLEP Considers DOMA Impact on Same-Sex TG Marriages," *The ICTLEP Reporter* (June–August 1996): 3.

20. Phyllis Frye, "If ENDA Had Been TG Inclusive, It Would Have Passed the US Senate," September 12, 1996, *Proceedings V*, 17.

21. Frye, "If ENDA Had Been TG Inclusive," *Proceedings V*, 18.

22. Feldblum, "Gay People, Trans People, Women," 632.

23. Frye, "Facing Discrimination," 464.

24. Frye, "If ENDA Had Been TG Inclusive," 17.

25. Frye, Long interview, March 2, 2019.

26. Frye, "Freedom from the 'Have-To' of the Scalpel," 29.

27. Phyllis Frye, "3rd National TG Event in Washington, DC," *ICTLEP Reporter* (June–August 1996): 1.

28. Frye, "Freedom from the 'Have-To' of the Scalpel," 30.

29. JoAnn Roberts, "Hot Buzz," *Renaissance News & Views* (November 1996): 12.

30. "Community Organizations Support GPAC," *Renaissance News & Views* (December 1996): 6.

31. JoAnn Roberts, "Hot Buzz," *Renaissance News & Views* (February 1997): 12.

32. Roberts, "Hot Buzz," 12.

33. Frye, "Facing Discrimination," 465–66.

34. Frye, Long interview, December 19, 2018.

35. Frye, "Facing Discrimination," 466.

36. Frye, "Financial Report to the Community," June–August 1996.

37. Frye, Long interview, March 2, 2019.

38. Frye, Long interview, March 2, 2019.

39. Phyllis Frye, email to Phyllabuster list, September 3, 1997. Copies of all Phyllabuster emails cited in this book are in Long's possession.

40. Frye, email to Phyllabuster list, September 3, 1997.

41. Frye, Long interview, March 2, 2019.

42. "Noted Transgender Activist Dee McKellar Dies," *This Week in Texas* (September 12–September 18. 1997): 61.

43. Phyllis Frye, email to Phyllabuster list, August 6, 1997.

44. Phyllis Frye, email to Phyllabuster list, November 21, 1997.

45. Frye, email to Phyllabuster list, November 21, 1997.

46. Frye, email to Phyllabuster list, November 21, 1997.

47. Phyllis Frye, email to Phyllabuster list, December 13, 1997.

48. Frye, email to Phyllabuster list, December 13, 1997. Phyllis and her son became estranged a few years after this letter. She rarely talks about him in interviews, and major profiles, like Sontag's ("Once a Pariah") and Gray's ("The Transgender Menace Next Door"), have no helpful information on their relationship. See the concluding interview for more information.

49. Frye, email to Phyllabuster list, December 13, 1997.

50. Frye, email to Phyllabuster list, December 13, 1997.

CHAPTER 15

1. Phyllis Frye, email to Shea Tuttle and Michael G. Long, December 7, 2020. This email is in the authors' possession.

2. Frye, email to Tuttle and Long, December 7, 2020.

3. Frye, email to Tuttle and Long, December 7, 2020.

4. Frye, email to Tuttle and Long, December 7, 2020.

5. "ICTLEP Elects New E.D.," *AEGIS News* (April 1998): 18. This article is an ICTLEP news release dated January 26, 1998.

6. "ICTLEP Elects New E.D.," *AEGIS News* (April 1998): 18.

7. Phyllis Frye, interviewed by Michael G. Long, March 6, 2019. Interview notes are in Long's possession.

8. Frye, Long interview, March 6, 2019.

9. Sharon Stuart, "Plans for Expanded Lawyer Referral Service Taking Shape," news release, April 28, 1988, included in Phyllis Frye, email to Phyllabuster list, April 28, 1998.

10. Phyllis Frye, email to Phyllabuster list, July 21, 1998.

11. Phyllis Frye, email to John Cloud, May 5, 1998. A copy of this email is in Long's possession.

12. Frye, email to John Cloud, May 5, 1998.

13. Frye, email to John Cloud, May 5, 1998.

14. John Cloud, "Trans across America," *Time*, July 20, 1998, available at http://www.time.com.

15. Riki Wilchins, *Read My Lips: Sexual Subversion and the End of Gender* (Riverdale, NY: Magnus Books/Riverdale Avenue Books, 1997).

16. See Wilchins's *TRANS/gressive* for a colorful history of Transexual Menace, GenderPAC, and her successful and historic work in gender politics.

17. Frye, Long interview, March 6, 2019.

18. Phyllis Frye, email to Phyllabuster list, July 21, 1998.

19. Frye, Long interview, March 6, 2019. See also Risher, "She Opened Doors," 41.

20. Phyllis Frye, email to Phyllabuster list, October 29, 1999.

21. Frye, email to Phyllabuster list, October 29, 1999.

22. Phyllis Frye, email to Phyllabuster list, February 21, 2000.

23. Phyllis Frye, email to Phyllabuster list, January 6, 2000.

24. Phyllis Frye, email to Phyllabuster list, September 26, 1999.

25. *Littleton v. Prange*, 9.S.W.3rd 223 (1999).

26. Phyllis Frye, email to Phyllabuster list, November 4, 1999.

27. Adolfo Pesquera, "Lawyer Ponders Effects of Transsexual's Case," *San Antonio Express-News*, April 8, 2000.

28. Phyllis Frye, interviewed by Michael G. Long, March 8, 2019.

29. Phyllis Frye, email to Phyllabuster list, April 18, 2000.

30. Christie Lee Littleton, letter to Phyllis Frye, May 23, 2000, included in Phyllis Frye, email to Phyllabuster list, May 23, 2000.

31. Phyllis Frye, email to Phyllabuster list, May 19, 2000.

32. Frye, Long interview, March 8, 2019.

33. Phyllis Frye, email to Phyllabuster list, June 28, 2019.

34. Phyllis Frye, email to Phyllabuster list, August 3, 2000.

35. Frye, email to Phyllabuster list, August 3, 2000.

36. David McLemore, "Same-Sex Pair Expect Wedding License," *Dallas Morning News*, August 26, 2000.

37. Frye, Long interview, March 8, 2019.

38. John Gonzales, "Lesbian Couple All Set for Big Day," *Houston Chronicle*, September 7, 2000.

39. Phyllis Frye, email to Phyllabuster list, September 17, 2000.

40. Phyllis Frye, email to Phyllabuster list, September 25, 2000.

41. Phyllis Frye, email to Phyllabuster list, October 2, 2000.

42. Frye, email to Phyllabuster list, October 2, 2000.

43. Frye, Long interview, March 2, 2019.

44. Phyllis Frye, email to Phyllabuster list, October 7, 2000.

45. Phyllis Frye, email to Phyllabuster list, January 9, 2001.

46. JoAnn Roberts, "GenderPAC Disenfranchises Transgender Community," January 8, 2001, http://www.tgforum.com., included in Frye, email to Phyllabuster list, January 9, 2001.

47. Phyllis Frye, email to Phyllabuster list, March 27, 2001.

48. Dallas Denny, "We're from GenderPAC—We're Here to Help You," *Transgender Tapestry* (Spring 2000): 13–14.

49. Denny, "We're from GenderPAC," 14.

50. Frye, Long interview, March 6, 2019.

51. Riki Wilchins, interviewed by Michael G. Long, April 9, 2019. Interview notes are in Long's possession.

52. Phyllis Frye, email to Phyllabuster list, March 15, 2001.

53. Phyllis Frye, email to Phyllabuster list, May 9, 2001.

54. Gray, "The Transgender Menace Next Door," 44.

55. Gray, "The Transgender Menace Next Door," 44.

56. Elizabeth Birch, "The Transgender Community and ENDA," news release, June 16, 2003, included in Frye, email to Phyllabuster list, June 16, 2003.

57. Phyllis Frye, email to Phyllabuster list, June 16, 2003.

58. Phyllis Frye, email to Phyllabuster list, August 8, 2004.

59. Frye, Long interview, March 8, 2019.

60. Phyllis Frye, email to Phyllabuster list, January 20, 2004.

61. Frye, Long interview, March 8, 2019.

62. Frye, Long interview, March 8, 2019.

63. Frye, Long interview, March 8, 2019.

64. National Center for Transgender Equality, "ENDA Introduced," news release, April 24, 2007, included in Phyllis Frye, email to Phyllabuster list, April 24, 2007.

65. Phyllis Frye, email to Phyllabuster list, April 12, 2008.

66. Frye, email to Phyllabuster list, April 12, 2008.

67. Phyllis Frye, email to Phyllabuster list, April 13, 2008.

68. Phyllis Frye, letter to the *Houston Chronicle*, August 21, 2003, included in Phyllis Frye, email to Phyllabuster list, August 28, 2003.

69. Phyllis Frye, email to Phyllabuster list, November 20, 2003.

CHAPTER 16

1. Frye, Long interview, March 8, 2019.

2. Frye, Long interview, March 8, 2019.

3. Frye, Long interview, March 8, 2019.

4. Frye, Long interview, March 8, 2019.

5. See photo in Mary Alice Robbins, "Board Votes for Clause Prohibiting Sexual Orientation Discrimination," *Texas Lawyer*, June 25, 2001.

6. "Verbatim Transcription of Selected Reports of the Board of Directors Meeting," June 14, 2001, Austin Convention Center, Austin, Texas. A copy of this transcript, provided by Phyllis Frye, is in Long's possession.

7. Phyllis Frye, email to Phyllabuster list, June 17, 2001.

8. Frye, email to Phyllabuster list, June 17, 2001.

9. Frye, Long interview, March 8, 2019.

10. Deborah Moncrief Bell, "Nikki Araguz, Her Story," *Montrose Gem*, August 13, 2010.

11. Frye, Long interview, March 8, 2019.

12. Frye, Long interview, March 8, 2019.

13. Frye, Long interview, March 8, 2019.

14. Brian Rogers, "Storied Career Takes Transgender Attorney to Judgeship," *Houston Chronicle*, November 18, 2010.

15. Frye, Long interview, March 8, 2019.

16. Rogers, "Storied Career," November 18, 2010. See also Phyllis Frye, "Phyllis Frye Becomes Texas' 1st Trans Judge," *Dallas Voice*, November 17, 2010.

17. Frye, "Phyllis Frye Becomes Texas' 1st Trans Judge."

18. Frye, "Phyllis Frye Becomes Texas' 1st Trans Judge."

19. Frye, Long interview, March 8, 2019.

20. Frye, Long interview, March 8, 2019.

21. Frye, Long interview, March 8, 2019. See also "Six Alumni Reach Great Heights: Phyllis Frye '81," 11.

22. Frye, Long interview, March 8, 2019.

23. For her more recent assessment of the bathroom issue, see Phyllis Frye, "The Real Bathroom Laws," *Houston Chronicle*, May 11, 2016.

24. Frye, Long interview, March 8, 2019.

25. Frye, Long interview, March 8, 2019.

Index